# NICHOLSON

# LONDON
# NightLife

GW00715865

The essential guide to
entertainment all through
the night

## Nicholson

*An Imprint of Bartholomew*
*A Division of* HarperCollins*Publishers*

A Nicholson Guide

First published 1977
Seventh edition 1993

© Nicholson 1993

Illustrations by Julian Mosedale

Photographs by Oliver Hewitt
additional photographs on pp46, 144, 150-2 by Nick Daly

Nicholson
HarperCollins*Publishers*
77-85 Fulham Palace Road
Hammersmith
London W6 8JB

Great care has been taken throughout this book to be accurate, but
the publishers cannot accept responsibility for any errors which
appear, or their consequences.

Printed in Hong Kong

**ISBN  07028 2127 6**   77/7/110   CNM   E/J 6115

# INTRODUCTION

The only comprehensive guide to the capital at night, the London Nightlife Guide is invaluable both to Londoners and first-time visitors to the city.

Whether you're looking for a night at the opera or a Mexican meal, this guide is packed with practical information on how to make your night out a success.

Find out where to hear trad jazz or Latin sounds, where to go for a quiet pint in a traditional English pub or tapas in a trendy bar. There is a comprehensive listing of comedy venues, theatres and cinemas, plus the low-down on the fashionable, fast-moving nightclub circuit. For something a little different, visit the haunts of ghosts and robbers on a night walk, or do a bit of sightseeing after dark from the top of a double-decker bus. Go late-night shopping, or even floodlit skiing! And if you're still awake at dawn, go bargain-hunting at the markets or sample an English breakfast. Plus information on where to cash a cheque after hours, how to hire a babysitter or book a hotel room at the last minute.

Whether you want to dance till dawn or eat and drink through the night, this guide tells you how to get the best out of London's nightlife from dusk till dawn.

# CONTENTS

**SYMBOLS AND ABBREVIATIONS**

Credit cards:
A  - Access/MasterCard
Ax - American Express
Dc - Diners Club
V  - Visa/Barclaycard

Average cost of a three-course meal for one inclusive of VAT and service but without wine:
**£**    - £10.00 or under
**££**   - £10.00-£20.00
**£££**  - £20.00-£30.00
**£££**+ - £30.00 and over

*Open to* . . . - Last orders
*(Reserve)*    - Advisable to reserve in advance

**M**  - Membership required

# USEFUL INFORMATION

The best nights out may be spontaneous but, if you want to be sure of a hassle-free evening, it's a good idea to plan ahead. The following information may come in handy before you set out.

## MONEY AFTER HOURS

Normal banking hours are *Mon-Fri 09.30-15.30*, though selected branches are *open on Saturdays*. Cash cards can be used to obtain money from dispensing machines *24 hours a day*. There are many bureaux de change around the West End and a number of the large shopping complexes, and some stores, have exchange facilities. Rates vary considerably and places open outside normal banking hours usually charge higher rates of commission. The following are open later than usual and offer fair exchange rates:

**American Express**      **4 E3**
6 Haymarket SW1. 071-930 4411. *Open Mon-Fri to 17.00, to 12.00 Sat.*
**Chequepoint Services**
Also cash cheques with a cheque card. All Chequepoint branches in

*Bureau de change*

central London are *open until at least 23.00*, the following are *open 24 hrs:*

| | |
|---|---|
| 220 Earl's Court Rd SW5. 071-373 9515. | **6 B2** |
| 71 Gloucester Rd SW7. 071-373 9685. | **6 C2** |
| Marble Arch W1. 071-723 1005. | **4 A2** |
| 58 Queensway W2. 071-727 1399. | **3 C2** |
| 78 Strand WC2. 071-836 5292. | **4 F3** |
| **Thomas Cook** | **7 B2** |

Victoria Station SW1. 071-828 4442. *Open Mon-Sun to 22.00.*

**London Gatwick Airport**
**South Terminal** Travelex Bureau de Change, 0293 567744, *open 24 hrs;* **North Terminal** Thomas Cook, 0293 502783, *open 24 hrs.*

**London Heathrow Airport**
**Terminal 1** Thomas Cook, 081-897 3501, *open 24 hrs;* **Terminal 2** International Currency Exchange, 081-564 7396, *open to 23.00;* **Terminal 3** Travelex, 081-897 3501, *open 24 hrs;* **Terminal 4** Travelex, 081-759 4449, *open 24 hrs.*

## ACCOMMODATION

If you're thinking of making a night of it and staying in a hotel, it would be wiser to book your accommodation in advance, especially as very few hotel booking agents stay open late.

**Accommodation Service of the London Tourist**   **7 B2**
**Board Tourist Information Centre**
Victoria Station Forecourt SW1. Also at Heathrow Central Underground Station. No telephone enquiries. Information and bookings. *Open Mon-Sun to 20.30, to 22.00 Jul & Aug.* Charge.
**Concordia Travel Hotel Reservations**   **7 B2**
Telephone booking service. 071-828 4646. *Open Mon-Sun to 23.00.* Charge.
**Expotel**
Telephone booking service. 071-734 5050. *Open Mon-Fri to 18.00.* Free.
**Hot Line Hotel Reservations**   **6 B3**
89 Harcourt Terrace SW10. 071-373 9531. *Open Mon-Fri to 17.00.* Free.
**Hotel Booking Service**   **4 D3**
4 New Burlington Place W1. 071-437 5052. Excellent and knowledgeable service for business travellers and general public. All types of hotel reservations in London, the rest of the UK and worldwide. *Open Mon-Fri to 17.30.* Free.
**Hotel Finders**
20 Bell Lane, Hendon NW4. 081-202 7000. All kinds of hotels. *Open Mon-Fri to 17.30, to 13.00 Sat.* Free.
**Hotel Guide**
The Coach House, 235 Upper Richmond Rd, Putney SW15. 081-780 1066. *Open Mon-Fri to 17.00.* Free.
**Hotel Reservations Centre**   **4 C6**
10 Buckingham Palace Rd SW1. 071-828 2425. Hotel bookings all over Britain. *Open Mon-Fri to 18.00.* Free.

**Room Centre**
Kingsgate House, Kingsgate Place, West Hampstead NW6. 071-328 1790. Worldwide hotel and conference booking service. *Open Mon-Fri to 17.30*. Free.

The following hotel companies maintain a central reservation system enabling you to book rooms at any of the hotels in each group. This service is free of charge.
**Imperial London Hotels** 071-278 7871. *Open to 20.00*.
**Inter Hotels** 0834 812304. *Open to 16.00*.
**Small Luxury Hotels** 0800 282124. *Open to 17.30*.
**Trust House Forte Hotels** 0345 404040. *Open to 21.00*.

## INFORMATION SERVICES

**Celebrity Service**     **4 D3**
93-97 Regent St W1. 071-439 9840. Issues a twice-weekly bulletin with essential information about celebrities and their whereabouts. Expensive monthly subscription.
**City of London Information Centre**     **5 D2**
St Paul's Churchyard EC4. 071-606 3030. Information and advice with specific reference to the 'Square Mile'. Free literature including the monthly *City of London Diary of Events* which lists a wide choice of free entertainment in the City. *Open Mon-Fri to 17.00*.
**London Tourist Board Information Centre**     **7 B2**
Victoria Station Forecourt SW1. 071-730 3488. Travel and tourist information for London and England. Most languages spoken. Hotel reservations, theatre and tour bookings, guide books and maps. *Open Mon-Sun to 20.00, Apr-Nov; Mon-Sat to 19.00, to 17.00 Sun, Dec-Mar*. Telephone service *Mon-Fri to 18.00 all year*.
**Other London Tourist Board Information centres at:**
Harrods, Knightsbridge SW1.     **3 G6**
Heathrow Central Underground Station.
Selfridges, 400 Oxford St W1.     **4 B2**
Tower of London, West Gate E1.     **5 G3**
**London Transport Travel Information Centres**
For enquiries on travel (underground and buses) phone 071- 222 1234. *24-hr service*. Also free maps in several languages. Offices at:
Euston Station.     **1 F4**
*Open Mon-Sun to 18.00 (to 19.30 Fri)*.
Heathrow Central Underground Station.
*Open Mon-Sun to 18.30 (to 19.30 Fri)*.
King's Cross Underground Station     **2 A4**
*Open Mon-Sun to 18.00 (to 19.30 Fri)*.
Oxford Circus Underground Station     **4 D2**
*Open Mon-Sat to 18.00. Closed Sun*.
Piccadilly Circus Underground Station     **4 E3**
*Open Mon-Sun to 18.00*.
Victoria Station.     **7 B2**
*Open Mon-Sun to 21.00*.

## TELEPHONE SERVICES

For emergency services, see *Emergency Information and Services*.
**Artsline** 071-388 2227. A free advice and information line for disabled people on access to arts and entertainment.
**Direct Dining** 071-287 3287. Free restaurant advisory service. *Open Mon-Fri to 18.00*.
**Restaurant Services** 081-888 8080. Gives free advice and information on eating out and will also make reservations. *Open Mon-Sat to 20.00*.
**Teledata** 081-200 0200. For information on what's on, shops, services, garages, businesses, etc. *24-hr service*.
**Time Check** dial 123 for the speaking clock. *24-hr service*.
**Wake up Calls** dial 100 and book an alarm call through your operator.
**Weather Line** (Met. Office). Greater London 0898 500401; SE England 0898 500480. *24-hr service*.

## MAGAZINES AND NEWSPAPERS

For a weekly guide to events, cinemas and theatre programmes, the following are available from newsagents or bookstalls: *Time Out, City Limits, What's On & Where to Go in London*. London's daily evening newspaper the *Evening Standard (Mon-Fri)* has very good entertainment information, as do *The Times* and *The Independent*.

## TIPPING

There are no hard and fast rules for tipping in London; it should be an expression of pleasure for services rendered, never a duty. Most hotels and some restaurants automatically add a service charge to the bill, so beware of inadvertently tipping twice. This will give you some idea as to who to tip and how much to give.

### Cloakroom Attendants
30p-50p when you collect your coat and/or accessories.
### Commissionaires
For getting a taxi, up to £1.00, depending on the effort expended.
### Hairdressers
15% to the hairdresser, 5% to the shampooer.
### Hotels
Tip individuals for special service otherwise 15% where service is not included.
### Porterage
Depends on the size of your luggage and the distance carried, but about £1.00 a case.
### Pubs and bars
Never tip at the bar, but buy the barman a drink if you wish. For waiter service in the lounge, from 20p a drink.
### Restaurants
12½% is the norm, more if you are pleased with the service.

**Taxis**
10%-15%.
**Washroom Service**
20p-50p if clean towels are provided and individual attention is given.

# BABYSITTERS

A number of professional and highly reliable agencies exist. Some have an annual registration fee, though temporary registration is usually available. Charges are on an hourly rate which sometimes varies according to the time and distance involved. Additional fees will include fares, and taxis late at night.

**Babysitters Unlimited**
2 Napoleon Rd, Twickenham, Middx. 081-892 8888. Their staff are

carefully selected with good references. Office *open Mon-Fri 10.00-17.00, to 12.00 Sat.*

**Childminders**                                                      **4 B1**
9 Paddington St W1. 071-935 9763/2049. Babysitters (mostly trained nurses) supplied to the home, and to hotels in central London and most suburban areas. Office *open Mon-Fri 08.50-17.20, Sat 09.00-16.30.*

**Cinderella Agency**
323 Kirkdale, Sydenham SE26. 081-659 1689/7175. All manner of household staff provided. Annual membership required. Office *open Mon-Fri 09.00-17.30.*

**South of the River Nannies**
128c Northcote Rd, Battersea SW11. 071-228 5086. Reputable and well-established company dealing solely with south London, offering every service a household may require. Office *open Mon-Fri 09.00-17.00, Sat 10.00-14.00.*

**Universal Aunts**
PO Box 304, Clapham SW4. 071-738 8937. A well-known agency that will provide all kinds of domestic help, including babysitting. Office *open Mon-Fri 09.30-17.00.*

# GETTING AROUND

It is very easy to get around in London up to midnight. There is a comprehensive network of bus routes and an underground system, more commonly known as 'the tube', which is one of the most extensive in the world. Maps and diagrams of bus and train routes appear in the map sections of this book, and are also available free from London Transport Travel Information Centres – see *Useful Information*. All tubes stop running at around midnight, as do most buses, but there is an excellent all-night bus service on many routes and it is usually possible to hail a black cab in London, even in the early hours of the morning.

## TAXIS

The famous London black taxi cabs (which can now be any colour, even white!) can be hailed in the street; they are available for hire if the yellow light above the windscreen is lit. Cab drivers are obliged to take you anywhere within a six mile radius; longer distances are at their discretion. All cabs have meters which must be used on journeys within the Metropolitan Police District (most of Greater London and out to Heathrow Airport). For longer journeys the price should be negotiated with the driver beforehand. There is also a minimum payable charge which is shown on the meter when you hire the cab. Expect to pay extra for large luggage, journeys between *24.00-06.00, at weekends and on Bank hols.* There are over 500

ranks throughout London, including all major hotels and British Rail stations. The following numbers can be used to book a taxi in advance, but this can be more expensive than hailing a cab in the street:
**Computer Cab:** 071-286 0286. *24 hrs.*
**Dial-a-Cab:** 071-253 5000. *24 hrs.*
**Radio Taxicabs:** 071-272 0272. *24 hrs.*
**Lady Cabs:** 071-254 3501. For women, driven by women. *Mon-Thur to 00.30, to 01.00 Fri, to 02.00 Sat, to 24.00 Sun.*

## MINICABS

These cannot be hailed in the street, and in any case are indistinguishable from private cars. Unlike the black taxi cabs they are not licensed and neither the drivers nor their cars are subject to the same stringent tests, but they are cheaper on longer journeys and less likely to refuse to take you to out-of-town destinations. Negotiate the price with the company when you phone, or with the driver, *before* you start your journey. Your nearest mini-cab office is listed in the *Yellow Pages*. The following firms are *open 24 hrs*:
**Abbey Car Hire** W2. 071-727 2637.
**Bartley Cars** N5. 071-226 7555.
**Clover Cars** W6. 081-741 1244.
**Greater London Hire** N2. 081-340 2450.
**Hogarth** SW5. 071-370 2020.
**Smart Cars** E14. 071-987 1888.

## PUBLIC TRANSPORT

If you are planning a late night out in town the Night Bus system is very effective; consult *Buses for Night Owls*, available from London Transport Information Centres, tube stations, bus garages and main British Rail stations. For full details of late-night travel by bus, tube and train, phone London Transport on 071-222 1234 at any time.

*Night bus*

## BUSES

Buses normally run *Mon-Sat 06.00-24.00, Sun 07.30-23.30*. Most central bus stops have timetables giving first and last departures. All-night buses serve London every night (see the map in this book) with a greatly extended service to the suburbs as well. Night buses have the letter 'N' before their number and all major night bus routes pass through Trafalgar Square. They run about once an hour on most routes. But bear in mind that one-day bus passes and travelcards are not valid for travel on night bus routes, so keep some money for your fare home!

## UNDERGROUND

All tube stations have notices giving the times of first and last departures. For journeys starting from central London, tubes run *Mon-Sat 05.30-00.15, Sun 07.30-23.30*. If you miss the last tube, you cannot (as on British Rail mainline stations) sit on the platform to await the first one next day, as the stations are locked.

## BRITISH RAIL

Trains generally run *Mon-Sat 06.00-24.00, Sun 07.00-23.30*, but there are exceptions. From Victoria, trains run hourly all night to Gatwick Airport. Other major London railway stations also operate late-night services. Always check with your local station to make sure there's a return train if you plan to travel home in the early hours.

# PARKING IN TOWN

Generally, you park in London at your own risk. Most parking meters and single yellow lines along London streets cease to be enforced as from *18.30 Mon-Fri, 13.00 Sat* and *all day Sun*; but do read the signs on the meters, or affixed to nearby lamp posts, which give the times of operation. Parking on double yellow lines, on the pavement and double-banked parking is forbidden *at all times*, and you may emerge to find your car has been towed away or clamped. The clamping teams operate from *09.00-17.00 Mon-Sat* and in certain areas until *22.00*. If you are unfortunate enough to have your car clamped you will find a notice on the vehicle telling you where to go to pay the hefty fine to get it unclamped. Once the payment has been made the car should be declamped within 24 hours. See *Wheelclamped* in *Emergency and Information Services*.

## 24-HOUR CAR PARKS

The following NCP car parks are *open 24 hrs Mon-Sun* unless otherwise stated. Notice boards at the entrance give details of times and changes.

Abington St SW1. 071-222 8621.  **7 E1**
Arlington St SW1. 071-499 3312.  **4 D4**

| | |
|---|---|
| Audley Sq W1. 071-499 3312. | **4 B4** |
| Brewer St W1. 071-734 9497. | **4 D3** |
| Cadogan Place SW1. 071-235 5106. | **6 F1** |
| Denman St W1. 071-734 5760. | **4 E3** |
| Dolphin Sq W1. 071-834 1077. | **7 C3** |
| Motor Park, Cambridge Circus WC2. 071-434 1896. | **4 E2** |
| Park Lane W1. 071-262 1814. | **4 B4** |
| Park Tower Hotel SW1. 071-235 0733. | **3 G5** |
| Pavilion Rd SW1. 071-589 0401. | **6 F1** |
| Royal Garden Hotel, 2-24 Kensington High St W8. 071-937 8000. | **3 B6** |
| Semley Place SW1. 071-730 7905. | **7 B2** |
| Upper St Martin's Lane WC2. 071-836 7451. | **4 F3** |
| Young St W8. 071-937 7420. | **3 C5** |

## SELF-DRIVE CAR HIRE

**Avis Rent-a-Car**　　　　　　　　　　　　　　**4 B5**
10 Montrose Place SW1. 071-245 9862. For bookings anywhere in
the UK. *Open Mon-Sat 07.30-19.30, Sun 09.00-18.00.*
**Budget Rent-a-Car**
071-935 3518 for your nearest branch in London. *Open Mon-Fri
07.30-19.30, to 15.30 Sat & Sun.*
**J. Davy**
606 High Rd, Wembley, Middx. 081-902 7771. *Open Mon-Fri
08.00-18.00, to 14.00 Sat, to 12.00 Sun.*
**Godfrey Davis (Europcar)**　　　　　　　　　**7 C2**
Davis House, 129 Wilton Rd SW1. 071-834 8484. *Open Mon-Fri
08.00-19.00, to 16.00 Sat & Sun.*
**Hertz Rent-a-Car**　　　　　　　　　　　　　**3 E1**
35 Edgware Rd W2. 071-402 4242. *Open Mon-Sun 08.00-20.00.*
**Kenning Group**　　　　　　　　　　　　　　**3 A4**
84-90 Holland Park Ave W11. 071-727 0123. *Open Mon-Fri 08.00-
18.00, to 13.00 Sat & Sun.*
**Sportshire**　　　　　　　　　　　　　　　　**6 D2**
Reece Mews SW7. 071-589 8309. All sports cars for hire. *Open
Mon-Fri 09.30-18.30.*
**Swan National**
1 National House, 3 Warwick St, Uxbridge, Middx. (0895) 256565.
Phone here for your nearest branch. *Open Mon-Fri 08.00-18.15, to
14.00 Sat.*
**Travelwise Car Hire**
South Lambeth Place, Vauxhall SW8. 071-582 1769. *Open Mon-Fri
08.00-18.00, to 13.00 Sat.*

## CHAUFFEUR-DRIVEN CARS

**Camelot Barthropp**　　　　　　　　　　　　**4 B4**
Headfort Garage, Headfort Place SW1. 071-235 0234. A fleet of 70
vehicles including Rolls Royce Phantom 6, Spirit, Spur and Bentley.

Experienced chauffeurs. *Open Mon-Fri 07.00-23.00, Sat & Sun 11.00-19.00.*

**R & I Tours**
823 Western Rd, Park Royal NW10. 081-965 5333. Chauffeur-driven saloons and 12-passenger minibuses. Also 17-20 seaters. *Open Mon-Fri 07.00-19.30, to 13.00 Sat. 24-hr telephone service.*

## ALL-NIGHT GARAGES

The following is a selection of *24 hour* garages:

**Cavendish Motors**
Cavendish Rd, Kilburn NW6. 081-459 0046.

**Chiswick Flyover Service Station**
1 Great West Rd, Chiswick W4. 081-994 1119.

**City Petroleum**                                                    2 D2
316 Essex Rd N1. 071-226 5991.

**Fountain Garage**                                                   4 B4
83 Park Lane W1. 071-629 4151.

**Kennington Filling Station** 7 G2
212 Kennington Rd SE11. 071-735 2191.
**Star Group Texaco**
63 Fortune Green Rd, West Hampstead NW6. 071-435 2211.
**Vauxhall Bridge Road Filling Station** 7 C2
148 Vauxhall Bridge Rd SW1. 071-828 1371.

## MOTORING: NIGHT SERVICES

Both the AA and the RAC operate a 24-hr emergency service for motorists. If you are a member they will help in practically any motoring emergency.
**AA**
FreeFone 0800 887766.
**RAC**
FreeFone 0800 828282

The following give a *24-hr* breakdown, repair, vehicle-recovery and road-side service. All makes of vehicles.
**Cavendish Motors**, Cavendish Rd, Kilburn NW6. 081-459 0046.
**Trident Recovery**, 55 Star Rd, Hillingdon, Middx. 081-573 7241.

# GETTING READY

Getting ready can be just as much fun as going out! Read on for all you'll need to pamper, preen and prepare.

## BEAUTY TREATMENTS

**Beauchamp Beauty Clinic** 3 G6
42 Beauchamp Place SW3. 071-589 1853. Extensive range of beauty treatments plus make-up lessons for everyday and special occasions. *Open Mon & Thur 10.00-20.00, to 18.00 Tue, Wed & Fri, to 14.00 Sat.* A.Ax.V.
**Cosmetics à la Carte** 6 G1
19b Motcomb St SW1. 071-235 0596. Make-up lessons and re-styled make-up. Beauty workshop. All own-brand products, free from known allergens and not animal tested. *Open Mon-Sat 10.00-17.30.* A.Ax.V.
**Delia Collins** 3 F6
19 Beauchamp Place SW3. 071-581 1810. Well-known and long-established beauty specialists. Also sell their own preparations. *Open Mon-Fri 09.00-18.00, to 13.00 Sat.* No credit cards.
**House of Colour** 3 B6
19 Abingdon Rd W8. 071-938 1982. Personal colour, style and

design analysis. Make-up consultations and personal shopping expeditions. *Open Mon-Sat 09.30-17.30.* No credit cards.

**Joan Price's Face Place**                                                  **6 F2**
33 Cadogan St SW3. 071-589 9062. Body and facial massages, pedicure and manicure. Also make-up lessons using different products from various ranges. *Open Mon, Tue & Fri 10.00-18.00, to 20.00 Wed & Thur, to 17.00 Sat.* A.Ax.V.

**Knightsbridge Nails**                                                      **3 G5**
7 Park Close SW7. 071-225 3695. Sculptured fingernail specialists. Completely natural-looking finish. *Open Mon-Fri 09.00-19.00, to 16.00 Sat.* A.V.

**Molton Brown**                                                             **4 C2**
58 South Molton St W1. 071-629 1872. Make-up lessons and special make-up for evening and daytime looks. Full range of products available. *Open Mon-Fri 10.00-17.30 (to 18.30 Thur), Sat 09.00-16.30.* A.V.

**Ray Cochrane**                                                             **4 A1**
118 Baker St W1. 071-486 6291. Facials, manicures and pedicures as well as aromatherapy and beauty and figure advice. *Open Mon 13.30-17.00 & Thur 09.30-17.00.* A.V.

**The Sanctuary**                                                            **4 F3**
11 Floral St WC2. 071-240 9635. One of the most comprehensive ranges of beauty treatments to be found under one roof in London. *Open Sat-Tue 10.00-18.00, to 22.00 Wed-Fri.* A.Ax.V.

**Steiner**                                                                  **4 A5**
25a Lowndes St SW1. 071-235 3154. A range of treatments including electrolysis, eye care, facials, manicure and pedicure, under the dedicated eye of top beauty therapist Arsho Grimwood. *Open Mon-Fri 09.30-17.30.* A.Ax.Dc.V.

**Stephen Glass at Face Facts**                                             **4 B2**
73 Wigmore St W1. 071-486 8287. Facials and treatments given as well as make-up lessons. *Open Tue-Sat 10.00-17.30.* A.Dc.V.

**Tao Clinic**                                                               **4 A5**
5 Sloane St SW1. 071-235 9333. Electrolysis and waxing specialists who also deal with body peeling, make-up, manicure, pedicure, Slendertone, eye care, facials and ear-piercing. *Open Mon & Fri 10.00-18.00, to 19.00 Tue, Wed & Thur, to 16.00 Sat.* A.V.

**Yves Rocher Beauty Salon**                                                **4 B2**
7 Gees Court, off St Christopher's Place W1. 071-409 2975. The salon adjoins a shop selling all their products, some of which are exclusive. Facials, waxing, body treatments, manicures and pedicures. Advice on make-up application. Emphasis on natural beauty. *Open Mon-Wed & Fri 10.00-18.30, Thur 11.30-19.00, Sat 10.00-18.00.* A.V.

## MEN'S SALONS

**Daniel Rouah**                                                             **1 B5**
7a Station Approach NW1. 071-935 4362. Aromatherapy, electrolysis, facials, laser treatments, shaving, waxing, plus advice on skin problems and hair care. Shaving classes held every *Mon 18.30-19.30. Open Mon-Sat 09.00-18.00 (to 19.00 Thur).* No credit cards.

**Eggison Daniel** 4 C4
Lansdowne House, 23 Berkeley St W1. 071-495 7777. A traditional barbershop environment with copies of the *Financial Times* always on hand and classical background music. Manicures and colouring. *Open Mon-Sat 08.30-18.30.* A.V.

For the quick-change artist, or those in a rush, the following railway stations have superloos with facilities for baths and showers, as well as changing rooms. You can then leave your everyday clothes at the left luggage office or lockers.
**Euston Station** NW1. 1 E4
**Paddington Station** (Platform 1) W2. 3 E2
**Victoria Station** (Platforms 2 & 15) SW1. 7 B2

## CLOTHES HIRE

**The Contemporary Wardrobe** 2 A5
The Horse Hospital, Colonnade WC1. 071-713 7370. 50s style ballgowns, cocktail dresses, casualwear and rock and pop fashion. Also film costume and couture evening wear. *Open Mon-Fri 10.00-18.00 (to 19.00 Thur), Sat 11.00-17.00.* A.Ax.V.
**Kritz** 1 B5
19 Melcombe St NW1. 071-935 0304. Men's formal wear. *Open Mon-Fri 09.00-17.30, to 13.00 Sat.* A.Ax.V.
**Moss Bros** 4 F3
27-29 King St WC2. 071-240 4567. Men's ceremonial and formal wear. Other branches. *Open Mon-Sat 09.00-17.30 (to 18.30 Thur).* A.Ax.Dc.V.
**One Night Stand** 7 A3
44 Pimlico Rd SW1. 071-730 8708. Elegant dresses from leading designers for sale and hire. *By appointment only. Open Mon-Fri 09.30-18.30, Sat 10.00-17.00.* A.Ax.V.
**Pandora** 3 F6
16-22 Cheval Place SW7. 071-589 5289. Well-established dress agency catering for all tastes and budgets. *Open Mon-Sat 10.00-18.00.*
**Putting on the Glitz** 4 F1
Galen Place, Pied Bull Court, off Bloomsbury Sq WC1. 071-404 5067. Also at Hay's Galleria, Tooley St SE1 (**5 F4**). 071-403 8107. Large selection of ballgowns, cocktail dresses, party dresses and accessories. *Open Mon-Fri 10.00-17.30, to 17.00 Sat.* A.Ax.Dc.V.
**Young's Formal Wear** 4 D2
19-20 Hanover St W1. 071-493 9153. Full range of formal wear morning suits, dinner suits, lounge suits and daywear. *Open Mon-Sat 09.30-17.30 (to 19.30 Thur).* A.V.

## FANCY DRESS AND JEWELLERY HIRE

For a ball or fancy dress party you can hire an enormous variety of costumes and accessories from the following firms. Expect to pay a deposit and book in advance.

### Angels
4 E2
119 Shaftesbury Ave WC2. 071-836 5678. Hundreds of costumes with everything from Tillers to gorillas! *Open Mon-Fri 09.00-17.00.* A.Ax.V.

### Carnival Fancy Dress Shop
4 C1
57 Weymouth St W1. 071-486 6361. Over 300 exotic costumes. *Open Mon-Fri 10.00-18.00, Sat 11.00-15.00.* No credit cards.

### Costume Studio
2 C3
6 Penton Grove N1. 071-837 6576. Theatrical costumier and stockist of 3000 fancy dress outfits. Also hires out wigs and costume jewellery. *Open Mon-Fri 09.30-18.00, Sat 10.00-17.00.* A.Ax.V.

### Escapade
1 D2
150 Camden High St NW1. 071-485 7384. A vast and colourful array of masks, hats, jokes and novelties. Also wigs, make-up and costumes. *Open Mon-Fri 10.00-19.00, to 18.00 Sat.* A.V.

### Preposterous Presents
2 C3
262 Upper St N1. 071-226 4166. Animal, historical and contemporary costumes. Also lots of masks. *Open Mon-Sat 10.00-18.00.* A.Ax.Dc.V.

### Theatre Zoo
4 F2
21 Earlham St W2. 071-836 3150. Hires animal costumes, heads, masks and wigs. Also sells make-up, wigs, masks, hats and costume jewellery. *Open Mon-Fri 09.00-17.30.* A.V.

# HAIRDRESSERS

**Antenna**   **3 B4**
27a Kensington Church St W8. 071-938 1866. Synonymous with hair extensions – also cut, colour and perm. *Open Mon-Fri 11.00-20.00, to 18.00 Sat.* A.V.

**Daniel Field**   **4 D2**
8-12 Broadwick St W1. 071-439 8223. Organic and mineral hairdressing – the natural alternative. *Open Mon & Wed 09.00-17.30, Tue 10.00-20.00, Thur & Fri 10.00-18.30, Sat 09.00-16.30.* A.V.

**Daniel Oliver**   **7 C3**
7 The Arcade, Dolphin Sq SW1. 071-834 4595. Small up-market salon. Specialises in long hair, traditional styles and high fashion work. Tiaras and head-dresses arranged. *Open Mon-Wed 09.00-18.00, Thur & Fri 08.00-19.00, Sat 08.00-14.00.* No credit cards.

**Edward's Hair & Beauty**   **4 B3**
Grosvenor House Hotel, Park Lane W1. 071-491 7875. General hair and beauty salon. Specialities include evening styles and hair braiding. *Open Mon-Sat 09.00-18.00 (to 19.00 Fri).* A.Ax.Dc.V.

**Essanelle**   **4 D2**
Dickins & Jones, Regent St W1. 071-734 7070. Busy in-store salon specialising in long hair. *Open Mon-Fri 09.30-18.00 (to 20.00 Thur), to 18.30 Sat.* A.Ax.Dc.V.

**Hugh at 161**   **7 B2**
161 Ebury St SW1. 071-730 2196. Unisex hairdressing. Specialises in dressing of long hair for parties etc. *Open Mon-Fri 09.00-17.00.* No credit cards.

**Molton Brown**   **4 C2**
55 South Molton St W1. 071-629 1872. Creative cutting on long and short hair – specialises in hand-drying techniques for added volume and style. Barbershop for men. *Open Mon-Fri 10.00-17.30 (to 18.30 Thur), Sat 09.00-16.30.* A.V.

**Panache Hairdressing**   **4 D3**
Meridien Hotel, Piccadilly W1. 071-437 1096. The place to get an incredible six-minute perm. *Open Mon-Sat 09.00-18.00.* A.Ax.V.

**Toni & Guy**   **6 G2**
49 Sloane Sq SW1. 071-730 8113/4313. All aspects of the craft of hairdressing carried out to a high standard at this renowned and busy chain of salons. Stylists well trained in the latest trends in hair fashion. *Open Mon-Fri 10.00-18.00 (to 18.30 Thur), Sat 09.00-16.30.* A.Ax.Dc.V.

**Trevor Sorbie**   **4 F3**
10 Russell St WC2. 071-379 6901. Well known for innovative and excellent cutting. *Open Mon-Wed 09.00-19.30, to 20.30 Thur & Fri, to 17.30 Sat.* A.V.

**Vidal Sassoon**   **4 C2**
60 South Molton St W1. 071-491 8848. Chic and innovative cuts. *Open Mon-Wed 08.30-17.45, to 19.15 Thur, to 18.30 Fri, Sat 08.45-17.00.* A.V.

**Vidal Sassoon School**   **4 C3**
56 Davies Mews W1. 071-629 4635. Very cheap cuts by Vidal Sassoon trainees. *Open Mon-Fri 10.00-15.00.* A.V.

# MEETING PEOPLE

## PLACES TO MEET

With over six million inhabitants and a surface area of more than 600 square miles, London is not a place where you're ever likely to bump into your friends. Always having to plan in advance is one of the pitfalls of living in a big city, but this is more than compensated for in London by the huge number of varied and interesting places to meet. There's a rendezvous to suit every occasion. Here are some suggestions.

### RELAXED
The sheer number of pubs in London means there will always be one close to hand. Many have upstairs bars which are often less crowded than at street level and more geared to audible conversation! Others have free live entertainment – always a good ice-breaker – and, on a warm summer's evening, you can't go wrong meeting at a pub with outdoor tables, terraces or a beer garden. Beware, however, of pubs with the same name – more than one evening has been ruined by one person turning up at the Coach & Horses in Greek Street and another waiting at its namesake just a few minutes' walk away in Great Marlborough Street!

### STYLISH
Brasseries, bars and wine bars offer a Continental style; an alternative to the clamorous atmosphere of most West End pubs, and where the chances of finding seats are a lot greater. A range of snacks or light meals are generally available in the evenings and the choice of wines can be extremely good. Bars tend to be pricier than pubs, but the 'Happy Hour' which many of them have (when drinks are offered at reduced prices) can get any evening off to a good start without burning too large a hole in your wallet.

### ENTERTAINING
If you're a committed crowd-watcher, the foyers of theatres can provide endless entertainment in the half-hour preceding the performance (curtain-up time for most is 19.30-20.00). The lower end of Shaftesbury Avenue is alive and bustling as theatre-goers flock through the foyers of the Apollo, Lyric, Queen's and neighbouring theatres. Another good venue is the foyer of the National Theatre on the South Bank. It is light and airy, and you can usually find live entertainment of an arty kind. There is also a bookshop and quite often an exhibition of modern paintings, jewellery or photographs. The Barbican Centre offers similar facilities, but make sure you allow time for orientation on your first visit! At the Institute of Contemporary Arts on The Mall, you can pass a whole evening waiting for friends to arrive – drink coffee, wine or beer, eat a meal, listen to music, see a film or play, or just wander around an exhibition.

### AL FRESCO

Meeting outdoors has definite seasonal limitations, but on a warm evening there are hundreds of parks and squares to choose from. Why not doze in the evening sun to the accompaniment of brass bands or orchestral music in the delightful Victoria Embankment Gardens, or meet up in the bowers of the Rose Garden in the Inner Circle of Regent's Park? And meeting on the bridge over the milling swans, pelicans, geese and ducks in St James's Park is the stuff romantic films are made of. But do remember that some parks close at dusk. Public monuments are another option; the statue of Eros on Piccadilly Circus is probably one of the most famous meeting places in the world and Nelson's Column in Trafalgar Square is a safe bet except on New Year's Eve or if you're allergic to pigeons!

### UNUSUAL

For a healthy alternative to the pub, why not arrange to meet in a gym or a Turkish bath? Working out and toning up is a good way to meet people and there is probably no more relaxing way to begin an evening with friends after a long day at work. Turkish baths and some health clubs are restricted to members of the same sex. See *Health clubs, saunas & Turkish baths* for opening times.

### DISCREET

If you want to be sure of not bumping into anyone you know, the bars of West End hotels are a safe bet. The prices of drinks can range from high to outrageous but, unless you're a film star, the chances of being recognised are extremely slim.

### FUNCTIONAL

If you can't agree on anywhere else, tube stations are perfectly adequate places to meet up, though completely devoid of romantic aura. Many have more than one exit so choosing a central spot is

*Charing Cross tube station*

essential. The area around the main ticket office is a good bet. Meeting under the departure boards of railway stations is another possibility, or at the entrance to a particular platform.

# MEETING NEW PEOPLE

If it is a problem for friends to decide where to meet, it is an even bigger problem working out where to meet new people and make new friends. The generalisation that the English are reserved has its roots in the capital which, like any big city, is not exactly the friendliest place in the world. There are quite a few organisations, however, specifically devoted to helping you meet people, by attending parties, theatre evenings or sporting events, learning new skills or acquiring new interests. Most of these advertise in the weekly events magazines (see *Useful Information*). All the clubs listed below have membership fees.

## SINGLES CLUBS

**Breakaway**
57 Garrick Close, Hanger Lane, Ealing W5. 081-991 2169. Caters for business and professional people aged 23-43.

**Inter-Varsity Club**    **4 F3**
4 Covent Garden Piazza WC2. 071-240 2525. Mainly an activities club for students, graduates and professional people aged 18-35. Organises at least 10 events in London every year. Monthly magazine.

**Kaleidoscope**
57 Garrick Close, Hanger Lane, Ealing W5. 081-997 8684. For unattached professional people over 37.

**London Village**
071-586 7455. Long established and one of the largest contact clubs in London with 3000 members aged 20-45. Monthly magazine and 160 organised events per month. Introductory meetings at the Grosvenor Hotel by Victoria Station SW1 *Tue 18.30 or 20.00* and the Charing Cross Hotel by Charing Cross Station WC2 *Fri 18.30 or 20.00*.

## COMPUTER DATING

If your requirements for a friend or lover can be transferred to software contact:

**Dateline**    **3 B6**
23-25 Abingdon Rd W8. 071-938 1011.

## GAY

See *Gay Nightlife* section, or consult:

**Lesbian & Gay Switchboard**
071-837 7324. Telephone information on all gay clubs, activities and meetings. *24-hr service.*

**Lesbian Line**
071-251 6911. Telephone information on meeting places. *Open Mon-Thur 19.00-22.00, Fri 14.00-22.00.*

**London Friend**
071-837 3337. *24-hr telephone service* giving information on accommodation, activities and entertainment for lesbians and gays.

---

### ESCORT AGENCIES

There are many and varied agencies, too numerous to list. Check magazines for lists of these facilities in London.

---

### LONELY HEARTS

The back pages of *Time Out* and *City Limits* abound with small ads for loving, sharing, warm and friendly people waiting to meet Mr or Ms Right, so if it's a blind date you're after, look to these publications.

---

# NIGHTLIFE

---

### NIGHTCLUBS

Whether you're after soulful tunes, Seventies disco classics or hardcore rave sounds, London has a club, or club night, devoted to you. Younger or more energetic clubbers will be pleased to know that the days when all nightclubs closed at *03.00* are long gone and now it's possible to stay out and dance from *23.00* on a Friday to *05.00* on a Monday without going home – if your feet and your wallet can take the strain! For those with more mature, conservative tastes, the smarter West End haunts of the Eighties jet-setters are still going strong.

Here we've listed a selection of clubs to suit every age and taste. The more established one-nighters (often more famous than the venues that house them!) are mentioned, but it's worth checking *Time Out* or *City Limits* for the latest place to be seen, as fashions change frequently. For a roundup of club nights phone the *Evening Standard* Nightclub Line on (0891) 555196.

Strict dress codes are generally a thing of the past, but check with the club beforehand if you're unsure of their door policy. You should expect to pay entry fees of around £5 during the week and £10 at weekends.

**Annabel's**                                                4 C3
44 Berkeley Sq W1. 071-629 2350. Legendary haunt of the rich and famous. Members include royals, millionaires and showbiz stars. There's a long waiting list for membership, but you can get a temporary three-week membership if proposed by an existing member. *Open to 03.00. Closed Sun.* A.Ax.

**Astoria** 4 E2

157 Charing Cross Rd WC2. 071-434 0403. A semi-converted theatre with 600 seats upstairs, four bars and a huge dancefloor. *Sat* is rave night, live music during the week. *Open from 22.00 Sat to 11.00 Sun*. Other times vary according to the night. Phone for details. No credit cards.

**Bar Tiempo** 2 B3

96-98 Pentonville Rd N1. 071-837 5387. Latin American club above the popular Finca tapas bar and restaurant. Spanish/Latin music and live salsa – great fun. *Open Thur-Sat to 02.30, to 00.30 Sun*. A.Ax.V.

**Bass Clef** 2 G4

35 Coronet St, off Hoxton Sq N1. 071-729 2476. Cool, atmospheric basement club where you can get down to Latin, African, rare groove and soul. Live bands at weekends. Good restaurant. *Open to 02.00*. No credit cards.

**Borderline** 4 E2

Below Break For The Border, Manette St, off Charing Cross Rd W1. 071-734 2095. Tex-Mex-style club with live bands and one-nighters ranging from mainstream dance to industrial rock. *Open to 03.00. Closed Sun*. A.V.

**The Brain** 4 E3

11 Wardour St W1. 071-437 7301. Hyper-trendy club hosting a variety of specialist one-nighters. Friendly and relaxed, with plenty of tables and some particularly wild interior design. Free entry to the bar *Mon-Fri 19.00-22.00*. Club *open to 03.00, to 06.00 Fri & Sat. Closed Sun*. A.V.

**Camden Palace** 1 E3

1a Camden High St NW1. 071-387 0428. A huge multi-storey former music hall, home to 'Feet First', the popular indie one-nighter, on *Tue*, and 'Twist & Shout' for Sixties freaks on *Wed*. A rave crowd at weekends. *Open to 02.00, to 02.30 Fri & Sat*. A.Ax.V.

**Crazy Larry's** 6 C5

533 King's Rd SW10. 071-376 5555. Luxurious and comfortable club with a good restaurant. The crowd here is fairly mixed, you'll probably spot the odd Sloane. *Open to 02.30. Closed Sun*. A.Ax.V.

**The Dome**

178 Junction Rd, Tufnell Park N19. 071-281 2195. Spacious venue on two levels, popular with students getting down to indie, garage and house sounds. *Sun* is 50s night. *Open to 01.30 Thur, to 02.30 Fri & Sat, to 24.00 Sun*. No credit cards.

**Electric Ballroom** 1 D2

184 Camden High St NW1. 071-485 9006. This established no-frills venue has a capacity for 1100. Two clubs in one, offering anything from acid jazz to classic rock. Cafeteria serving snacks, burgers and breakfast. *Open to 02.00, to 03.00 Fri & Sat. Closed Sun*. No credit cards.

**Equinox** 4 E3

Leicester Sq WC2. 071-437 1446. Huge, luxurious, recently revamped venue hosting a variety of one-nighters. Also home to the

*Equinox*

notorious monthly transvestite ball 'Kinky Gerlinky' a must for exhibitionists! *Open to 03.30, to 04.00 Fri & Sat. Closed Sun*. A.Ax.V.

## The Fridge

Town Hall Parade, Brixton Hill SW2. 071-326 5100. Huge, perennially hip dance venue. Frighteningly cool people rub shoulders with plenty of ordinary Joes out for a good time and a boogie. If you're choosing one club to go to in London, this ought to be on your short list. *Open to 03.00. Closed Sun*. No credit cards.

## Gardening Club                 4 F3

4 The Piazza WC2. 071-497 3154. Small, atmospheric underground club, popular with a seriously funky crowd. Intimate and relaxed. *Open to 03.00, to 06.00 Fri & Sat*. No credit cards.

*The Hippodrome*

**Gossips**     **4 E2**
69 Dean St W1. 071-434 4480. A dimly-lit Soho basement, plain and easy-going. It hosts the longest-running one-night clubs in London, 'Gaz's Rockin' Blues' on *Thur* and 'Alice in Wonderland' on *Mon* – psychedelia, garage, rock and punk. *Open to 03.30. Closed Sun.* No credit cards.

**Hippodrome**     **4 E3**
Hippodrome Corner WC2. 071-437 4311. One of London's landmarks, but not a club many Londoners frequent. A black cave of brass and chrome illuminated by an amazing light system. Popular with young European tourists. Six bars, restaurant. *Open to 03.30. Closed Sun.* A.Ax.Dc.V.

**Hombre de Bahia**     **4 D2**
78 Wells St W1. 071-580 2881. Disco, fast food, three bars and a pool room. Mainstream dance music for an older, smart/casual clientele. *Open to 03.30. Closed Sun.* A.V.

**Legends**     **4 D3**
29 Old Burlington St W1. 071-437 9933. Sleek with lots of chrome, tasteful colours and cool, modern design. Attracts a generally cool, smart crowd and some big names from the music business. *Open to 02.00, to 03.00 Fri & Sat. Closed Sun.* A.Ax.Dc.V.

**Limelight**     **4 E3**
136 Shaftesbury Ave W1. 071-434 0572. Uniquely housed in a converted church, this club is a maze of wood-panelled passages and

*Limelight*

stairs leading to three levels. One-nighters range from rock to dance and reggae. *Open to 03.00. Closed Sun*. A.Ax.Dc.V.

### Maximus                                                    4 E3
14 Leicester Sq WC2. 071-734 4111. A packed dancefloor and alcoved seating areas, attracting a hedonistic weekend crowd eager to party until dawn and beyond. *Open to 03.00, to 06.00 Fri & Sat*. No credit cards.

### The Milk Bar                                               4 E2
12 Sutton Row W1. 071-439 4655. Popular with a glamorous party crowd. It's small, so arrive early to be sure of getting in. *Open to 02.00, to 03.00 Fri & Sat. Closed Sun*. No credit cards.

### Ministry of Sound                                          5 D6
103 Gaunt St SE1. 071-378 6528. Huge New York-style venue offering the biggest sound system in Britain, big-name DJs, a cinema, the most expensive entry fees in town – and no booze! *Open from midnight Fri to 08.00 Sat & from midnight Sat to 10.00 Sun*. No credit cards.

### Le Palais
24 Shepherd's Bush Rd, Hammersmith W6. 081-748 2812. Mainstream disco with glitzy, fake art deco furnishing, a restaurant and a spectacular laser show. *Open Wed & Thur to 02.00, to 03.00 Fri & Sat. Closed Sun*. A.Ax.Dc.V.

### The Park                                                   3 C5
38 Kensington High St W8. 071-937 7994. Ultra-modern disco for a sophisticated clientele. *Open Mon & Thur-Sat to 03.00. Closed Tue, Wed & Sun*. A.Ax.V.

### The Rocket
166-220 Holloway Rd, Islington N7. 071-700 2421. Lively   north London club with ever-changing one-nighters. Popular with students and local clubbers. *Open to 02.00, to 06.00 Fri & Sat*. No credit cards.

### Samantha's                                                 4 D3
3 New Burlington St W1. 071-734 6249. Glitzy club with a smart-dress-only door policy. Quirky features include a split-level dancefloor and ornamental water pools. Four bars. *Open to 03.00. Closed Sun*. No credit cards.

### Stringfellows                                              4 F3
16 Upper St Martin's Lane WC2. 071-240 5534. Most celebrities have been photographed flashing their teeth and jewellery here, but the rich and famous tend to keep themselves to themselves. A la carte restaurant. *Open to 03.30. Closed Sun*. A.Ax.Dc.V.

### Subterrania                                                3 A1
12 Acklam Rd W10. 081-960 4590. A trendy and friendly venue under the Westway flyover. Stylish interior with regular live music, and you'll often rub shoulders with a pop star or two on the dancefloor. *Open to 01.30, to 02.30 Fri & Sat. Closed Sun*. A.V.

### Tokyo Joe's                                                4 D3
85 Piccadilly W1. 071-409 1832. This plush nightclub attracts a prestigious clientele. A la carte restaurant. Membership required – phone first for details. *Open to 03.30. Closed Sun*. A.Ax.Dc.V.

### Underworld                                                 1 D2
174 Camden High St NW1. 071-482 2045. Fashionably seedy, this is

a good place to see London's youth cults in action. *Open to 02.00, to 03.00 Fri & Sat. Closed Sun*. No credit cards.

**Wag Club**     **4 E3**
35 Wardour St W1. 071-437 5534. Once the trendiest club in town, the Wag still attracts an exuberant, young clientele. Weekend nights are very popular, and you may have difficulty gaining entry. *Open to 03.30, to 06.00 Fri & Sat. Closed Sun*. No credit cards.

**Woody's**     **3 A1**
41-43 Woodfield Rd W9. 071-286 5574. Situated in two converted Victorian terraces, this is probably the best house party you'll ever go to! *Wed* is indie night, soul and house at weekends. *Open to 03.00, to 02.00 Sun*. No credit cards.

**Xenon**     **4 D3**
196 Piccadilly W1. 071-734 9344. Up-market but unpretentious club with an impressive light show and cabaret-style entertainment. Cock-tail bar. *Open to 03.00, to 06.00 Fri & Sat. Closed Sun*. A.Ax.Dc.V.

## MEMBERS-ONLY CLUBS

To join an exclusive clientele in a relaxed and well-tended setting, choose one of London's traditional members-only clubs or casinos where you will find restaurants, entertainment and good wine. These clubs cater, in most cases, for expense-account businessmen or the young set out for a night on the town. Most clubs employ hostesses whose job it is to boost the sales of drinks, but you will have to pay for the pleasure of their company, and most of them have an expensive taste in champagne. Most clubs will require you to be a member, although short-term membership is often available for visitors. Application to join can be made personally and immediate membership can often be arranged.

**The Clubman's Club**     **4 D3**
5 Albemarle St W1. 071-493 4292. An annual subscription fee gives free membership or benefits to several hundred night clubs all over Britain and worldwide. Also discounts for car hire and hotels.

**£**=inexpensive   **££**=medium priced   **£££**=top priced

## CLUBS

**Director's Lodge**     **4 B2**
13 Mason's Yard, Duke St SW1. 071-839 6109. Wine, dine and dance to a resident band and guest singers. Attractive hostesses. Lounge bar. Seats 50. **M** and entrance fee for guests. *Open Mon-Fri to 03.00*. A.Ax.Dc.V. **£££**

**Miranda**     **4 D3**
9 Kingly St W1. 071-437 6695. Spacious basement club with red velvet decor. Comfortably seats about 100 people. Lounge bar, à la carte menu and dancing to a four-piece band. Strip-tease cabaret and hostesses in the evening. **M** (proposal needed). *Open Mon-Fri to 03.00*. A.Ax.Dc.V. **££**

### Morton's 4 C3
28 Berkeley Sq W1. 071-408 2483. Renowned piano bar-cum-club in 1930s style. English cuisine in the delightfully decorated upstairs restaurant. Pianist and jazz band. **M**. *Open Mon-Sat to 03.00.* A.Ax.Dc.V. **££**

### New Georgian Club 4 D3
4 Mill St W1. 071-629 2042. Club with cabaret every half hour. Lounge bar and hostesses. Gourmet restaurant with an international menu; escalope à la Georgian, shish kebab à la Turque, special châteaubriand. **M**. *Open Mon-Fri to 03.00.* Cabaret *23.00 & 00.30.* A.Ax.Dc.V. **£££**

### Pinstripe 4 D3
21 Beak St W1. 071-437 5143. Victorian-style decor. A club much frequented by businessmen attracted by the topless waitresses. Restaurant and bar. **M** or entrance fee. *Open Mon-Fri to 03.00.* A.Ax.Dc.V. **££**

### Le Rififi 4 C3
15a Hay Hill W1. 071-493 8329. Dancing to a trio and cabaret. Seats 40. **M** and entrance fee *after 23.00. Open Mon-Sat to 03.00.* Ax.Dc.V. **£**

### Stock's Town Club 6 E3
107 King's Rd SW3. 071-351 3461. Smart country-house theme with numerous prints of hunting scenes and green wood panelling. Steak and lobster (flown in from the USA) are the specialities in the grill restaurant where the roof rolls back in the summer. Smart disco and resident DJ, as well as a nightly pianist. **M** (proposal needed). *Open Mon-Sat to 03.00.* A.Ax.Dc.V. **£££**

---

## CASINOS

Gaming, in licensed gaming houses, is legal in the UK and several such institutions are to be found throughout central London. Their activities are strictly controlled by legislation operated by the Gaming Board and the following general information may be of interest to any potential punter.

You can only enter a gaming house as a member or the guest of a member. Generally speaking, in order to become a member, you simply fill in a form and pay an annual fee, which can range from a few pounds to several hundred depending on the establishment; an average fee is around £20. However, some clubs may insist on UK residents being proposed by an existing member. This is likely to be waived in the case of a foreign national. The important thing to remember is that, by law, when you join a gambling club you will not be admitted until you have filled in a declaration of your intention to gamble and 48 hours has elapsed from the time you signed this declaration. This requirement is designed to protect the public from any rash or impetuous action (resulting perhaps from alcoholic over-indulgence!) and is applied to UK and foreign nationals alike. The number **48** after a club's name in the entries below means that this rule applies. Gaming as a general rule begins at *14.00* (though some suburban clubs do not open until *16.00* on Sundays).

*Charlie Chester Casino*

Gambling clubs generally close at *04.00*, except on Saturdays when they close at *03.00*. Most gambling clubs have bars and restaurants and the food served is often first class. Drinks are not usually served at the gaming tables because of the risk of spillages. In addition, it is worth noting that although the restaurants are not cheap they are to an extent subsidised by the club and therefore you can often obtain an excellent meal at a far lower price than in a normal restaurant.

Also remember that most casinos serve free breakfast after midnight. Alcoholic drinks can be obtained in the bars until *23.00*, and in the restaurants, with a meal, until *midnight*.

**Charlie Chester Casino (48)**                                    **4 E3**
12 Archer St W1. 071-734 0255. Modern night club and casino. **M**. *Open Mon-Sun to 04.00*. No credit cards. **£**

**Clermont Club (48)**                                             **4 C3**
44 Berkeley Sq W1. 071-493 5587. An 18thC town house, opulent and comfortable. Select and very expensive to join. Excellent à la carte restaurant with Arab cuisine; good wine list. **M**. *Open Mon-Sun to 04.00*. A.Ax.Dc.V. **£££**

**Golden Horseshoe (48)**                                          **3 C3**
79-81 Queensway W2. 071-221 8788. Casino on two floors with a bar and a small restaurant serving set meals. **M**. *Open Mon-Sun to 04.00*. A.Ax.Dc.V. **£**

## DINNER AND ENTERTAINMENT

To gratify more than just your taste buds, why not try a restaurant where music, dancing and cabaret complement the cuisine? From a traditional sophisticated dinner dance at one of London's top hotels to fiery Middle Eastern fare and belly dancing, the choice is yours. Also see the *Entertainment* chapter for music and cabaret venues where food is available.

The price guide in this section includes the cost of entertainment, plus wine and beer where indicated.

**Anemos**                                                        **4 D1**
32 Charlotte St W1. 071-636 2289. Conjuring, Greek dancing and copious plate smashing are the norm at this lively disco restaurant. Not recommended for a quiet evening for two! *(Reserve) open Mon-Sat to 23.45*. Entertainment *to 01.00*. A.Ax.Dc.V. **££**

**Barbarella I**                                                  **6 B5**
428 Fulham Rd SW6. 071-385 9434. Stylish and sophisticated Anglo-Italian restaurant where you can dance to the early hours. *(Reserve) open Mon-Sat to 03.00*. A.Ax.Dc.V. **££**

**Beefeater**                                                     **5 G4**
Ivory House, St Katharine's Dock E1. 071-408 1001. Situated near the Tower of London, Henry VIII and his court provide dancing and rowdy entertainment. But take care to hold onto your head! Cutlery provided if you wish, otherwise enjoy the five-course dinner in true medieval manner and use your fingers. Unlimited wine and beer flow. *(Reserve) open Mon-Sat to 23.30*. A.Ax.Dc.V. **£££+**

**Brick Lane Music Hall**                                         **5 G1**
152 Brick Lane E1. 071-377 8787. Music hall entertainment for the 1990s in the Old Bull and Bush style. Traditional three-course English dinner – boiled beef or baked trout. Bookings essential. *Open Wed-Sat to 23.00*. A.Dc.V. **£££**

**Le Château**                                                    **4 C4**
Mayfair Hotel, Stratton St W1. 071-629 7777. English and interna-

tional cuisine complemented by popular melodies from the resident pianist, who is happy to play any old favourites. *(Reserve) open Mon-Sun to 23.00.* A.Ax.Dc.V. **£££**

**Cleopatra Taverna**                                      **3 B4**
148-150 Notting Hill Gate W11. 071-727 4046. Spacious, lively spot with plenty of traditional Greek entertainment: plate smashing, belly dancers and a five-piece bouzouki band. Customers are invited to join in the fun, and after one or two glasses of ouzo need very little encouragement! Specialities include peasant mezze, keftedes, afelia (pork simmered in wine) and stifado (beef in red wine with garlic). *Open Mon-Sun to 02.30.* A.Ax.Dc.V. **££**

**Cockney Cabaret**                                         **4 C2**
6 Hanover St W1. 071-408 1001. Music hall entertainment in traditional East End style. Dancing, production numbers and comic acts. Honky tonk piano greets you at the whisky and gin reception. Cockney 'nosh' to follow – roast beef and Yorkshire pudding. Free flowing wine and beer. *(Reserve) open Mon-Sat to 23.30.* A.Ax.Dc.V. **£££+**

**Concordia Notte**                                         **3 E2**
29-31 Craven Rd W2. 071-723 3725. Sophisticated dining room attracting la crème de la crème of society. Patronised by stars and sometimes royalty. Haute cuisine Italian menu: caviar, El Marinaro (shellfish mixed with veal, ham and beef in white wine, garlic and tomatoes). Excellent sweet trolley. Latin American cabaret and dancing to a band with Italian, English and Greek singers. Very spacious, good service. *(Reserve) open Mon-Sat to 01.00, dancing to 02.00.* A.Ax.Dc.V. **£££+**

**Costa Dorada**                                            **4 E2**
47-55 Hanway St W1. 071-631 5117. Daytime reservations: 081-674 7705. A place to hit after midnight when the flamenco dancers appear. The food is Spanish and very good value. Try octopus Galician-style or gambas rebosadas (breaded prawns). Vegetarian dishes and party menus available. *(Reserve) open Mon-Sat to 03.00, to 24.00 Sun. Cabaret at 21.30 & 22.30 Mon-Thur, 21.30 & 00.30 Fri & Sat, 22.30 Sun.* A.Dc.V. **£££**

**Down Mexico Way**                                         **4 D3**
25 Swallow St, off Regent St W1. 071-437 9895. Traditional Mexican food in an authentic Spanish setting – the tiles here were sent over by the King of Spain. Latin American music *on Mon, Fri & Sat. (Reserve) open to 24.00, bar open to 02.30.* A.Ax.Dc.V. **££**

**Elephant On The River**                                   **7 C4**
129 Grosvenor Rd SW1. 071-834 1621. An elegant restaurant right on the river, with an impressive entrance walkway. Inside is opulent marble. Mainly Italian menu and pleasant resident dance band. *Open Tue-Sat to 02.45, to 01.45 Sun.* A.Ax.Dc.V. **£££+**

**Elysée**                                                  **4 E1**
13 Percy St W1. 071-636 4804. Greek, English and French dishes in a taverna-like atmosphere where plate smashing is actively encouraged. Carefree dancing to a four-piece band and bouzouki music. Roof garden open in the summer. *(Reserve) open Mon-Sat to 03.00. Cabaret 23.00 & 01.00.* A.Ax.Dc.V. **££**

**Entrecôte**                                               **2 A6**
124 Southampton Row WC1. 071-405 1466. A spacious restaurant,

yet with a romantic candlelit atmosphere, serving international cuisine with a French influence. The service is first class. Live music *Fri & Sat*. The dancefloor is intimate and well patronised. A split menu is available for those wishing to start their meal before the theatre and return afterwards. Also a set party menu. *(Reserve) open Mon-Sat to 01.00, to 23.30 Sun*. A.Ax.Dc.V. **££**

**Finca**                                                                    **2 C3**
96-98 Pentonville Rd N1. 071-837 5387. Sample traditional Spanish tapas to the tunes of live guitarists and a rumba flamenco band at this well-frequented restaurant and bar. Latin American nightclub upstairs. *(Reserve) open Sun-Thur to 24.00, to 02.00 Fri & Sat*. A.Ax.V. **£**

**Flanagan's**                                                               **4 B1**
100 Baker St W1. 071-935 0287. Victorian fantasy in phoney 19thC dining rooms, with sawdust for spitting on and plenty of cockney songs – a colourful extravaganza. Elegantly costumed waiters and singing serving girls. The pianist slams his music at you, so don't expect an intimate conversation. Tripe, jellied eels, game pie, enormous plates of fish and chips and hearty golden syrup pudding. *(Reserve) open Mon-Sat to 22.30, to 22.00 Sun*. A.Ax.Dc.V. **££**

**Gracelands Palace**
881-883 Old Kent Rd, Southwark SE15. 071-639 3961. Rock 'n' roll fans will be driven wild by Paul Chan, London's only Chinese Elvis impersonator, who'll shake you with all the classics, after which you can be a star yourself with karaoke. *(Reserve) open Mon-Sun to 24.00. Show Fri & Sat 23.30, on request on weekdays*. A.Ax.Dc.V. **££**

**L'Hirondelle**                                                             **4 D3**
199 Swallow St W1.071-734 1511. Comfortable and pleasant with air-conditioning, this theatre restaurant has live music and two floor shows nightly which are well staged and flamboyant. International menu. Suprême de volaille princesse, escalope de veau Hirondelle. A really spectacular night out. *(Reserve) open Mon-Sat to 03.00. Floor shows 23.00 & 01.00*. A.Ax.Dc.V. **£££+**

**Kerzenstüberl**                                                            **4 B2**
9 St Christopher's Place, off Marylebone Lane W1. 071-486 3196. Dinner-dancing. Plenty of 'gute Stimmung' here to warm the heart. An informal atmosphere and excellent Austrian cooking: Leberknödel soup, pork chop, Tafelspitz and Sacher Torte. Follow with Apfelstrudel. Jolly, rhythmic accordion music nightly. *(Reserve) open Mon-Sat to 23.00. Music to 01.00*. A.Ax.Dc.V. **££**

**The Palm Court**                                                           **4 D4**
The Ritz, Piccadilly W1. 071-493 8181. Extravagant Twenties-style decor with dance bands to match. Dress up for the occasion. *(Reserve) Fri & Sat 22.00-01.00*. A.Ax.Dc.V. **£££+**

**Rheingold Club Mayfair**                                                   **4 B2**
361 Oxford St W1. 071-629 5343. Friendly German inn with a spacious dancefloor and live music. Also quiet lounge bar. Good German beer and cooking. *(Reserve) open Mon-Thur & Sun to 02.00, to 02.30 Fri & Sat*. A.Ax.Dc.V. **££**

**Rio**                                                                      **3 B2**
103 Westbourne Grove W2. 071-792 0312. South American, Greek and international cuisine washed down with anything from a

*The Savoy Hotel*

Brazilian carnival show to a lambada extravaganza. *(Reserve) open Mon-Sat to 00.30.* A.Ax.Dc.V. **£££**

**Royal Garden Hotel, Royal Roof Restaurant**　　　　　**3 B6**
2-24 Kensington High St W8. 071-937 8000. An Anglo-French restaurant with dinner-dancing on Saturday evening. Good menu and wine list and excellent views over Kensington Gardens, Kensington Palace and Hyde Park. *(Reserve) open to 22.30, to 23.00 Sat. Closed Sun.* A.Ax.Dc.V. **£££+**

**The Savoy Restaurant**　　　　　**4 G3**
The Savoy Hotel, Strand WC2. 071-836 4343. Elegant and formal with a garden theme. Resident quartet and dancing all contribute to the 'grand hotel' manner. World-famous, well-deserved reputation for classic cooking and near-perfect service. After theatre suppers. *(Reserve) open Mon-Sat to 23.30,* band stops *24.00.* A.Ax.Dc.V. **£££+**

**Talk of London**　　　　　**4 F2**
Drury Lane WC2. 071-408 1001. This purpose-built restaurant with ample seating and contemporary styling features some of London's most popular cabaret acts. Internationally-known singers and performers appear regularly, as do speciality entertainers. A four-course set meal is provided with a good choice of French and international dishes. *(Reserve) open Mon-Sun to 23.00.* Cabaret *approx 21.30 & 22.30.* A.Ax.Dc.V. **£££+**

**Terrace Restaurant**　　　　　**4 B4**
Dorchester Hotel, Park Lane W1. 071-629 8888. Stately and gracious for elegant dinner dances. Waiters in evening dress serve quality French food. Cuisine naturelle – sweetbreads, grouse, salade de foie gras and sole Dorchester. *(Reserve) open Tue-Sat to 23.30.* Music *to 01.00.* A.Ax.Dc.V. **£££**

**Terrazza Est**　　　　　**5 B2**
109 Fleet St EC4. 071-353 2680. Large but cosy basement

restaurant with superb opera singing. Italian cuisine with set and à la carte menus, salads and pasta dishes. Lively atmosphere and lots of fun. *(Reserve) open Mon-Fri to 22.45.* A.Ax.Dc.V. **££**

**Triñanes**
298 Kentish Town Rd, Kentish Town NW5. 071-482 3616. Traditional Spanish cuisine, live South American music and flamenco dancing at this lively and friendly north London restaurant. *(Reserve) open Mon-Sat to 02.00, to 01.00 Sun.* No credit cards. **££**

**Vecchiomondo**                                                            **6 B2**
118 Cromwell Rd SW7. 071-373 7756. Lively atmosphere with dancing and occasional informal cabaret. Authentic Italian cuisine. There is also a smaller, quieter restaurant upstairs. *Open Mon-Sun to 01.00.* A.Ax.Dc.V. **££**

**Villa dei Cesari**                                                        **7 C4**
135 Grosvenor Rd SW1. 071-828 7453. Converted riverside warehouse with a fine view over the Thames. The Roman empire lives on here, with waiters in tunics. Classic decor throughout and Latinised menu. The restaurant is spacious and a resident band plays nightly for dancing. *(Reserve) open Tue-Sun to 02.00.* Ax.Dc.V. **£££+**

**Windows On The World**                                                    **4 B4**
Hilton Hotel, Park Lane W1. 071-493 8000. The name is not an exaggeration! Diners are afforded intoxicating views over the city from 28 floors up. Sophisticated French cooking. Dancefloor, two bands. *(Reserve) open Mon-Sat to 02.00, to 01.00 Sun.* A.Ax.Dc.V. **£££+**

# SEX, SLEAZE AND STRIP CLUBS

Soho, once the red-light area of London, now flashes its neon only at unsuspecting tourists. The number of establishments permitted to show naked flesh is severely limited, and naive punters tempted by billboards promising live bed shows, hostess bars and peep shows will invariably lose large sums of money and see very little. The hostess bars are not even licensed to serve alcohol so you may pay dear for a fizzy drink and light conversation with one of the female inmates.

A relatively new arrival on the West End scene are strip shows for women in the form of male dance troupes such as The Chippendales who will strip down to the tiniest G-string! Such shows are always packed and are good for a laugh, if nothing else. Check the theatre listings in the *Evening Standard* or *Time Out* for details.

## STRIP CLUBS

**Carnival Revue Club**                                                     **4 E2**
12 Old Compton St W1. 071-437 8337. Continuous performances *12.00-23.00.*

**Raymond Revue Bar**                                                       **4 D3**
Walker's Court, Brewer St W1. 071-734 1593. Two shows a night at *20.00 & 22.00.*

**Sunset Strip**                                                            **4 E2**
30 Dean St W1. 071-437 7229. Continuous performances *12.30-23.00.*

# GAY NIGHTLIFE

London's gay and lesbian scene is one of Europe's biggest and best. The capital boasts an eclectic mix of bars and clubs, as well as various social and political groups which get away from the commercialised scene. The best way to get to know about what's going on is to pick up a copy of one of the free newspapers such as *Capital Gay* or *The Pink Paper* at one of the bars listed below. *Time Out* and *City Limits* also have comprehensive weekly gay listings. Some clubs and bars are restricted to gay men or lesbians, others are open to both, and some attract a lot of straights, enjoying the scene's convivial, violence-free atmosphere. Several venues have stringent dress codes, and many have a gay- or lesbian- only night once a week. Bear in mind that the scene changes fast and often, so keep your eye on the magazine listings. And don't be put off going out midweek thinking you'll be on your own – some of the best clubs are on *Tuesday* and *Wednesday*.

A good and reliable source of information on all gay clubs, activities and meeting places is **Gay Switchboard**. They run a *24-hr service*. For details phone 071-837 7324.

Club membership rules vary, so don't be deterred by the **M** sign at the end of an entry. Temporary **M** for visitors is usually available.

### London Lesbian & Gay Centre — 2 D6
67-69 Cowcross St EC1. 071-608 1471. The meeting place for various groups, plus discos, bars, a cafe and a gym (*open to 22.00*). *Open Mon, Tue & Wed to 23.00, to 24.00 Thur & Sun, to 03.00 Fri & Sat*. Also home to **The Orchid**, a stylish and comfortable women-only bar. *Open to 23.00 Fri, to 24.00 Sat*.

### CLUBS

**Aurora** (at Zatopek's) — 7 C6
Linford Film Studios, Linford St SW8. 071-498 1771. Wild gay and lesbian extravaganza with three discos and a swimming pool – take your towel! Also a post-club coach to and from the West End. *Open Fri to 03.00*. No credit cards.

**The Backstreet**
Wentworth Mews, Mile End E3. 081-980 8557. A popular venue for men only, where the dress code is strictly rubber or leather. *Open Thur-Sat to 02.30, to 01.00 Sun*. No credit cards.

**The Bell** — 2 B3
259 Pentonville Rd N1. 071-837 5617. Spacious pub with an easy-going crowd and an alternative disco every night. Women-only on Tue. *Open to 02.00, to 24.00 Sun*. No credit cards.

**'Ciao Baby!'** (at The Fridge)
Town Hall Parade, Brixton Hill SW2. 071-326 5100. Wildly popular glitzy gay/mixed one-nighter with live entertainment and fabulous atmosphere. Don't miss it! *Open Tue to 03.00*. No credit cards.

**Club Copa** — 6 A1
180 Earl's Court Rd SW5. 071-373 3407. Always full of life, fun, noise and gay men from all over town. One of London's most popular venues. *Open to 02.00. Closed Sun*. No credit cards.

### Club Industria
4 D2

9 Hanover St W1. 071-493 0689. Video screens, a funky mixed gay crowd and one-nighters with names like 'Eat My Shorts' – you can't fail to have a good time! *Open Tue-Thur to 03.30, to 06.00 Fri & Sat, to 01.00 Sun (women only). Closed Mon.* No credit cards.

**ff** (at Turnmills)
2 C5

63 Clerkenwell Rd EC1. 071-250 3409. Go-go boys, happy hours and a steamy party crowd at this weekly mixed/gay night run by *ff Magazine. Open Sun/Mon to 05.00.* A.Ax.Dc.V.

### The Haywood Rooms

153 Lee High Rd, Lewisham SE13. 081-463 9255. Women-only membership club with smart but relaxed bar, restaurant and disco. *Open Mon-Thur & Sun to 23.00, to 24.00 Fri & Sat.* No credit cards.

### Heaven
4 F4

Under The Arches, Villiers St WC2. 071-839 3852. Britain's most famous gay club has a vast dancefloor, stylish and relaxed upstairs bars, a sexy crowd and a stage for the odd cabaret performance. Amazing light show. Men-only *Sat. Open to 05.00, to 03.30 Wed.* No credit cards.

### Kinky Gerlinky (at Equinox)
4 E3

Leicester Sq WC2. 071-437 1446. Outrageous monthly drag and costume ball – without doubt the best theme party in London. Prizes for the best costumes – come and compete, if you can! *Check magazine listings for dates and opening times.* A.V.

### London Apprentice
2 G4

333 Old St EC1. 071-739 5949. LA's, as it's known, caters for a macho gay crowd with two bars and two dancefloors. Busy, and packed at weekends. Men-only. *Open to 03.00, to 24.00 Sun.* No credit cards.

### Madame Jo Jo
4 D3

8-10 Brewer St W1. 071-734 2473. Camp, comfortable and fun

*Madame Jo Jo*

transvestite club with outrageous drag artists guaranteeing an unusual but enjoyable night for everyone. Waiter service. Tables can be reserved in advance. *Open Mon-Sat to 03.00. Closed Sun.* A.Ax.V.

**Trade** (at Turnmills) **2 C5**
63 Clerkenwell Rd EC1. 071-250 3409. Serious party atmosphere at this late club created for those who want to carry on dancing after everyone else has gone home. Breakfast served from *06.00. Open from 03.00 Sat to 12.00 Sun.* A.Ax.Dc.V.

**Venus Rising** (at The Fridge)
Town Hall Parade, Brixton Hill SW2. 071-326 5100. The largest women-only night in Europe, held on the first *Wed* of every month. Women may bring one male guest; no unaccompanied men are admitted. Dance music, live entertainment and an exciting atmosphere. *Open to 03.00.* No credit cards.

## PUBS AND BARS

Pubs and bars listed in this section are *open normal pub hours (Mon-Sat to 23.00, to 22.30 Sun)* except where indicated.

**Angel** **2 D3**
65 Graham St N1. Plush, comfortable decor and a varied clientele at this revamped pub that used to be The Fallen Angel. *Open Mon-Sat to 24.00, to 23.30 Sun.*

**The Black Cap** **1 D2**
171 Camden High St NW1. 071-485 1742. Recently refurbished, popular drag pub with dancefloor and entertainment six nights a week. Quieter bar upstairs. *Open to 02.00, to 22.30 Sun.* Charge for downstairs bar *Tue-Sat.*

**Brief Encounter** **4 F3**
41 St Martin's Lane WC2. 071-240 2221. Ever-popular European-style bar. Very crowded, with alcove seating on the ground floor and a piano in the downstairs bar. Reduced price nightclub tickets over the bar.

**Bromptons** **6 B3**
294 Old Brompton Rd SW5. 071-373 6559. Smart video bar with DJ and a dancefloor. Very popular late evening. Licensed *Mon-Thur to 00.30, to 01.00 Fri & Sat, to 22.30 Sun.*

**Champion** **3 C3**
1 Wellington Terrace W11. 071-229 5056. Large bar and snuggery frequented by an older crowd. Popular with male gay locals.

**City of Quebec** **4 A2**
12 Old Quebec St W1. 071-629 6159. Gay bar on two levels. Comfortable and relaxing pub where the absence of loud music is welcomed.

**Coleherne** **6 B3**
261 Old Brompton Rd SW5. Well-established and vibrant gay men's pub. A favourite on the leather scene.

**Comptons** **4 E2**
53 Old Compton St W1. 071-437 4445. Large Soho pub. Comfortable seating and friendly bar staff. Cheap entry flyers available over the bar.

**Drill Hall** **4 E1**
16 Chenies St WC1. 071-631 1353. Busy bar in an arts centre with theatre and restaurant. Women-only every *Mon. Open to 23.00.*

### Eliza's                                                    1 F3
The Eliza Doolittle, 3 Ossulston St NW1. Relaxed and friendly women-only bar with music and dancing. *Open Fri & Sat to 23.00.*

### George IV
7a Ida St, Poplar E14. 071-537 7796. Amateur dramatic productions take place here once a month intermingled with drag cabaret every *Wed, Fri & Sat.* Large bar with pool table. Hot food and coffee is available at all times.

### King's Arms                                               4 D2
23 Poland St W1. 071-734 5907. Friendly gay men's pub in the centre of town. Downstairs is usually busy; if you want a quiet drink stay upstairs.

### King William IV
77 Hampstead High St, Hampstead NW3. 071-435 5747. Traditional pub with oak panelling. Wide cross-section of people gather here, a male preserve. Beer garden open in *summer.*

### The Locomotion                                           4 E3
18 Bear St WC2. 071-839 3252. This relaxed diner/bar locates a bit of 1950s America near crowded Leicester Square. Polished steel fittings and erotic black and white photographs on the walls. Food available in the downstairs bar.

### Market Tavern                                            7 C5
Market Towers, 1 Nine Elms Lane SW8. 071-622 5655. Thought of by many as the best gay pub in south London, it has a spacious, pleasant interior and friendly clientele. There are men-only nights *Mon & Wed. Open Mon-Thur to 02.00, to 03.00 Fri & Sat, to 24.00 Sun.*

### Queen's Head                                             6 F3
27 Tyron St SW3. 071-589 0262. Traditional pub with three bars, two of which attract a mixed gay crowd. *Open all day.*

### Royal Oak
62 Glenthorne Rd, Hammersmith W6. 081-748 2781. Suede and brocade decor in this plush pub. Good food. Drag acts *Sat & Sun.*

### Royal Vauxhall Tavern                                    7 F3
372 Kennington Lane SE11. 071-582 0833. A famous drag pub with DJ and live shows nightly. Very popular with a mixed crowd of gay men.

### Village Soho                                             4 E3
81 Wardour St W1. 071-434 2123. Newer, bigger sister of Village West One, with three bars on two levels. Winner of *The Pink Paper's* Best Bar Of The Year award. Food, tea and coffee served all day.

### Village West One                                         4 E2
38 Hanway St W1. 071-436 2468. Slickly decorated with a Mediterranean feel, there's a laid-back atmosphere and murals of well-toned and semi-clothed young men. Tables outside. *Open to 02.00, to 22.30 Sun.*

---

## RESTAURANTS

### First Out Coffee Shop                                    4 E2
52 St Giles High St WC2. 071-240 8042. Gay and lesbian Continental-style coffee house. Hot and cold meals, teas, coffees, pastries. The location means it is usually very busy. *Open Mon-Sat to 23.30, to 19.00 Sun.* No credit cards. **£**

**Papagaio**                                          **3 C3**
1 Wellington Terrace W2. 071-221 6702. Popular Brazilian basement
restaurant with excellent food and a predominantly gay clientele.
Live music *Fri & Sat. Open to 23.00. Closed Sun.* A.V. **££**

**Roy's**                                             **6 B5**
306b Fulham Rd SW10. 071-352 6828. A very gay restaurant with a
lively atmosphere, particularly good for party groups. The extrovert
waiters provide entertainment along with other occasional cabaret
acts. Mainly English cuisine; try the Aylesbury duck in honey and
lemon sauce, or the tender rack of English lamb with strawberry tart
to finish. (Reserve) *open Mon-Sun to 23.30.* A.Ax.Dc.V. **££**

# ENTERTAINMENT

In London there is something to entertain everyone – the Royal Ballet
and the Royal Opera Company have their homes here, you can catch
up with the latest sounds in rock, folk and jazz, watch one of the
hundreds of films and plays on offer, or enjoy some slapstick and satire
at one of the capital's many cabaret venues. And with almost 600
new theatre productions opening each year, you are spoilt for choice!

## LIVE ENTERTAINMENT
### CLASSICAL MUSIC, OPERA, BALLET & DANCE

**Barbican Hall**                                     **5 C1**
Barbican Centre, Silk St EC2. 071-638 8891. Recorded information:
071-628 2295. This is the base of the London Symphony Orchestra
which offers three one-month-long seasons during the year.
Excellent acoustics. Also opera, light classical music and jazz. Box
office *open Mon-Sun 10.00-20.00.* A.Ax.V.

**Blackheath Concert Halls**
23 Lee Rd, Blackheath SE3. 081-318 9758. Box office: 081-463
0100. Anything from chamber music to opera to jazz.  Box office
*open Mon-Sat 08.00-19.00.* A.V.

**British Music Information Centre**                  **4 C2**
10 Stratford Place W1. 071-499 8567. A reference library for British
20th century classical during the day, you can hear free recitals here
*on Tue & Thur at 19.30.*

**Central Hall**                                      **4 E5**
Storey's Gate SW1. 071-222 8010. This ornate building is the Chief
Methodist Church, built 1905-11. Its large hall is used for organ
recitals and orchestral concerts. Box office *open Mon-Fri 09.00-
17.00.* No credit cards.

### Coliseum                                                4 F3

St Martin's Lane WC2. 071-836 3161. Built in 1904, with a splendidly ornate interior, the Coliseum is London's largest theatre, seating 2400. Home of the English National Opera and host to visiting dance and ballet companies every summer. Standby tickets are sold at reduced prices on the day of the performance. Box office *open Mon-Sat 10.00-20.00*. A.Ax.Dc.V.

*The Coliseum on St Martin's Lane*

**Conway Hall**       **4 G1**
Red Lion Sq WC1. 071-242 8032. Two halls, one of which is famous for hosting celebrated *Sun eve* chamber music concerts from *Oct-Apr*. No telephone box office or credit cards.

**Institute of Contemporary Arts (ICA)**       **4 E4**
Nash House, The Mall SW1. 071-930 3647. Recorded information: 071-930 0493. Dynamic, innovative dance performed in the Institute's 200-seat theatre. Also three galleries, two cinemas, bookshop, video library, bar and restaurant. Box office *open Mon-Sun 12.00-21.30*. A.Ax.Dc.V.

**The Place**       **1 F4**
17 Duke's Rd WC1. 071-387 0031. One of the most innovative and modern dance venues. It is home to the London Contemporary Dance School and London Contemporary Dance Theatre, so you're likely to find yourself rubbing the lycra-clad shoulders of professional dancers in the audience. Box office *open Mon-Fri 12.00-18.00 (or up until start of performance)*. A.V.

**Purcell Room**       **5 A4**
South Bank SE1. 071-928 8800 for bookings. 071-928 3002 for information. Chamber music and solo concerts. Generally performances which require more intimate surroundings. Box office *open Mon-Sun 10.00-21.00*. A.Ax.Dc.V.

**Queen Elizabeth Hall**       **5 A4**
South Bank SE1. 071-928 8800 for bookings. 071-928 3002 for information. Chamber music, choral concerts, opera and dance, poetry readings, bands and films. Seating for 1100. Box office *open Mon-Sun 10.00-21.00*. A.Ax.Dc.V.

**Riverside Studios**
Crisp Rd, Hammersmith W6. 081-748 3354. Regular contemporary dance performances by visiting companies. Box office *open Mon-Sun 12.00-20.00*. A.V.

**Royal Albert Hall**       **3 E5**
Kensington Gore SW7. 071-589 8212. Recorded information: (0898) 500252. Victorian domed hall named after Prince Albert, built 1871. The first ever gramophone concert was held here in 1906. Now rock, folk and jazz feature, but pride of place goes to classical music – and particularly to the Proms, a series of concerts by a variety of orchestras, ensembles and individuals from all over the world. These concerts, for which tickets are sold at subsidised prices, have been held *every summer* since they were moved from the bombed Queen's Hall in 1941. They culminate in the famous Last Night of the Proms in *Sep*. Box office *open Mon-Sun 09.00-21.00*. A.V.

**Royal College of Music**       **3 E6**
Prince Consort Rd SW7. 071-589 3643. Founded by the Prince of Wales in 1882, the college is now a prestigious centre of musical excellence. In term-time students perform chamber, orchestral and choral concerts in their own theatre. Standards are high, admission is free. Phone for details.

**Royal Festival Hall**       **5 A4**
South Bank Centre SE1. 071-928 8800 for bookings. 071-928 3002 for information. Built in 1951 for the Festival of Britain. Seats 3000. Orchestral and choral concerts, opera and ballet. Box office *open Mon-Sun 10.00-21.00*. A.Ax.Dc.V.

*Royal Opera House, Covent Garden*

**Royal Opera House**                                          **4 F2**
Bow St WC2. 071-240 1066. Recorded information: 071-836 6903.
Credit card bookings: (0898) 600001. The home of the Royal Ballet
and the Royal Opera Company is the most lavish and famous theatre
in London and the greatest stage for British opera and ballet. Sixty-
five tickets are reserved for sale at the box office in Floral Street from
*10.00 on the day of the performance only* (except for gala nights). If
the performance is a sell-out, 50 standing-room tickets are made
available in the foyer at *19.00*. Be warned – queues have been
known to start at dawn! For the unlucky ones without tickets, there
are occasional live broadcasts on a huge screen in Covent Garden
Piazza. Box office *open Mon-Sat 10.00-20.00*. A.Ax.Dc.V.

**Royalty**                                                   **4 G2**
Portugal St, off Kingsway WC2. 071-494 5090. Built in 1911 as the
London Opera House, it was intended as a rival to the Royal Opera
House in Covent Garden. The 1000-seat capacity and large stage
make it increasingly popular as a dance venue. Box office *open Mon-
Sat 10.00-20.00*. A.Ax.V.

**Sadler's Wells**                                            **2 C4**
Rosebery Ave EC1. 071-278 8916. Recorded information: 071-278
5450. Once a spa – the original well is under a trap door at the back
of the stalls. Visiting opera, ballet and dance companies often pack
this 1500-seat theatre. When possible, 50 stalls seats are held
back for sale at reduced prices on the day of the performance and
go on sale at *10.30* in the box office. Phone for availability. Box office
*open Mon-Sat 10.30-19.30 (or 18.30 if no performance)*. A.Ax.Dc.V.

**St James's Church**     **4 D3**
Piccadilly W1. 071-734 4511. Recitals by young musicians, plus various festivals. Tickets on the door. Phone for details. No credit cards.

**St John's, Smith Square**     **7 E1**
Smith Sq SW1. 071-222 1061. A unique 18thC church now used for solo recitals, chamber, orchestral and choral works. Restaurant; art exhibitions in the crypt. Box office *open Mon-Fri 10.00-17.00 (to 19.30 on night of performance).* A.V.

**Wigmore Hall**     **4 C2**
36 Wigmore St W1. 071-935 2141. Well-loved by artists and audiences alike for its wonderful acoustics and intimate atmosphere. Stages all kinds of classical music. Tickets are usually cheap, but those for popular concerts go very quickly. Box office *open Mon-Sat 10.00-20.30.* A.Ax.Dc.V.

---

### JAZZ, FOLK & ROCK

Britain is world-famous for its contemporary music scene and London is the hub of the industry, attracting well-known bands and soloists as well as those trying to make the charts. There is a vast number of different places to go to hear live bands from huge concert arenas to shady basement clubs. The major concert halls are listed below along with some of the more established and popular smaller venues. Consult *Time Out, City Limits* or *New Musical Express* to find out who's playing when, or phone the *Evening Standard* Gig Line on (0891 555196) for a complete listing of concerts and events.

### MAJOR VENUES

**Academy**     071 924 9999
211 Stockwell Rd, Brixton SW9. 071-326 1022. A splendid, atmospheric rock venue. The bars are well staffed, and the sloping floor means you can still see the band, even if you're marooned at the back. *Open to 23.00 on night of performance.* Box office *open Mon-Fri 10.00-19.00, Sat 11.00-18.00. Closed Sun.* A.Dc.V.

**Apollo Theatre, Hammersmith**
Queen Caroline St, Hammersmith W6. 081-741 4868. Formerly the Hammersmith Odeon, this is west London's legendary live music venue. Plays host to a wide range of musical talents. Box office *open 10.00-18.00. Closed Sun.* A.Ax.V.

**Astoria**     **4 E2**
157 Charing Cross Rd WC2. 071-434 0403. Large auditorium for live music – anything from hard rock to classical. Restaurant and bars. *Open Mon-Sun, licensed to 03.00.* A.Ax.Dc.V.

**Dominion**     **4 E2**
Tottenham Court Rd W1. 071-580 9562. Seating-only theatre-style venue in central London for big-time performers. The plush fittings and spaciousness ensure a comfortable night out. *Open to 22.30.* Box office *open Mon-Sat 10.00-18.00. Closed Sun.* A.V.

**Earl's Court Exhibition Centre**     **6 A3**
Warwick Rd SW5. 071-385 1200. Box office 071-373 8141. Massive hall for top pop and rock stars. A.V.

*Marquee*

## Marquee 4 E2

105 Charing Cross Rd WC2. 071-437 6603. One of the original rock clubs; in the 1960s any rocker worth his salt played in the Marquee's original building on Wardour Street. Nowadays the club – and its bands – tend to be less prestigious, but it's still a popular and lively spot. *Open to 24.00, to 03.00 Thur-Sat, to 22.30 Sun.* Box office *open Mon-Fri 10.00-18.00, Sat & Sun 12.00-18.00.* A.V.

## National Ballroom, Kilburn

234 Kilburn High Rd, Kilburn NW6. 071-328 3141. Used as a ball-room by the local Irish community, this theatre also stages big rock acts. Check *Time Out* or *City Limits* for details. No credit cards.

## Palladium 4 D2

8 Argyll St W1. 071-494 5038. World-famous home of the Sunday night TV series, this charming West End theatre is sometimes used for exclusive shows by big name acts. Check *Time Out* or *City Limits* for details. A.Ax.V.

## Royal Albert Hall 3 E5

Kensington Gore SW7. 071-589 8212. Has a varied selection of artistes throughout the year. A.V.

## Town & Country Club

9-17 Highgate Rd, Kentish Town NW5. 071-284 0303. One of the best live music venues in London. This authentic 1930s theatre with its chandeliers and balconies retains its old-fashioned atmosphere. Views are excellent, and there's plenty of room for even the most energetic of dancers. Rock, folk, world and jazz. *Open to 23.00.* A.Ax.Dc.V.

## Wembley Arena

Empire Way, Wembley, Middx. 081-902 1234. Enormous capacity auditorium for really major concerts. A.Ax.Dc.V.

**Wembley Stadium**
Empire Way, Wembley, Middx. 081-900 1234. Open-air and used only for the real megastars, this is London's largest pop venue. Check *Time Out* or *City Limits* for details. A.Ax.Dc.V.

## SMALLER VENUES

**Africa Centre**　　　　　　　　　　　　　　　　　　**4 F3**
38 King St WC2. 071-836 1973. Popular venue for African and London-based black bands. Basement restaurant. *Open Fri & Sat 22.00-03.00.* No credit cards.

**Bass Clef**　　　　　　　　　　　　　　　　　　　　**2 G4**
35 Coronet St, off Hoxton Sq N1. 071-729 2476. A very popular venue to hear jazz, Latin American and African music. Cool, relaxed atmosphere. Good restaurant. *Open Mon-Sat 19.30-02.00, to 24.00 Sun.* A.Ax.Dc.V.

**Bull & Gate**
389 Kentish Town Rd, Kentish Town NW5. 071-485 5358. Small, established venue behind the pub, staging a mixed bag of indie and rock bands, including new faces. *Open Mon-Sat 20.00-23.00, to 22.30 Sun.* No credit cards.

**Cecil Sharpe House**　　　　　　　　　　　　　　　**1 C2**
2 Regent's Park Rd NW1. 071-485 2206. Regular live folk bands, including some big names, perform in the huge dance hall. Check *Time Out* or *City Limits* for details. No credit cards.

**Dover Street Wine Bar**　　　　　　　　　　　　　　**4 D4**
8-9 Dover St W1. 071-629 9813. Live music – predominantly jazz, but also some blues and soul. Restaurant. *Open Mon-Thur 17.30-03.00, Fri & Sat 22.00-03.15. Closed Sun.* A.Ax.Dc.V.

**The Grand**
St John's Hill, Clapham Junction SW11. 071-738 9000. Credit card hotline: 081-963 0940. Newly converted theatre offering indie, rock and reggae for up to 600 people. Best to book in advance. Phone for details. A.V.

**Hackney Empire**
291 Mare St, Hackney E8. 081-985 2424. Famous for its variety shows, this magnificently renovated East End music hall occasionally stages live music and benefit gigs. Phone for details. A.V.

**Jazz Café**　　　　　　　　　　　　　　　　　　　　**1 D2**
5 Parkway NW1. 071-284 4358. All kinds of jazz performed to mixed audiences at this extremely popular art deco Camden venue. Balcony restaurant serving Mediterranean food plus café menu downstairs. *Open Mon-Thur & Sun 19.00-24.00, to 02.00 Fri & Sat.* A.V.

**Mean Fiddler**
24-28a Harlesden High St, Willesden NW10. 081-965 2487. Seated bar areas, a dancefloor and a balcony make for a great atmosphere in this north London venue. Stages well-known indie rock bands plus folk and country & western. *Open Mon-Sat 20.00-02.00, Sun 19.30-23.00.* A.V.

**100 Club**　　　　　　　　　　　　　　　　　　　　**4 D2**
100 Oxford St W1. 071-636 0933. Friendly and comfortable basement club, historically the home of British traditional jazz. Still remains one of the best places in London for 'trad', but also caters

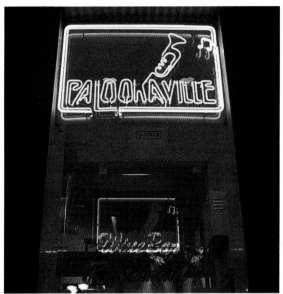

*Palookaville*

well for fans of modern jazz, blues, swing and sometimes rockabilly. *Open Mon-Thur 19.30-24.00, to 03.00 Fri, to 01.00 Sat, to 23.30 Sun.* No credit cards.

**Palookaville**                                                    **4 F3**
13a James St WC2. 071-240 5857. Spacious basement restaurant and wine bar serving a wide variety of bistro-style dishes to the accompaniment of modern or traditional live jazz from *21.00. Open 17.30-01.30, to 00.30 Sun.* A.Ax.Dc.V.

**Pizza Express**                                                  **4 E2**
10 Dean St W1. 071-437 9595. A basement restaurant where lively, mainly modern jazz is played. Some big names from both Britain and the USA. Admission charge depends on who is appearing. You don't have to eat to listen to the music. *Open Tue-Sun 21.30-01.00.* A.Ax.Dc.V.

**Pizza on the Park**                                              **4 B5**
11 Knightsbridge SW1. 071-235 5550. High-quality mainstream and traditional jazz played in this chic restaurant. Steaks, pasta and salads are served as well as pizzas. Book on *Fri & Sat. Open Mon-Sat 21.30-24.00.* A.Ax.Dc.V.

**Powerhaus**                                                      **2 C3**
1 Liverpool Rd N1. 071-837 3218. Credit card bookings: 081-963 0940. Packed Islington venue offering the best in new indie and rock. Recommended. *Open Mon-Thur 20.00-02.00, to 03.00 Fri & Sat, to 23.00 Sun.* A.V.

**Rock Garden**                                                4 F3
6-7 Covent Garden Piazza WC2. 071-240 3961. Beneath the restaurant of the same name, a selection of starry-eyed young bands play in a converted banana warehouse. You might hear tomorrow's stars – U2 and Dire Straits played here. *Open to 03.00*. A.Ax.V.

**Ronnie Scott's**                                             4 E2
47 Frith St W1. 071-439 0747. One of Europe's foremost jazz centres, and reputedly the best in London, attracting a succession of big-name jazz men and women. The atmosphere can be typically dark and smoky on a busy night. Tickets may be hard to come by, so book in advance. *Open to 03.00*. A.Ax.Dc.V.

**Sir George Robey**   .
240 Seven Sisters Rd, Finsbury Park N4. 071-263 4581. Large, dark pub venue staging indie and rock bands. *Open Mon-Sat 21.00-02.00, to 22.30 Sun*. No credit cards.

**Tenor Clef**                                                 2 G4
1 Hoxton Sq N1. 071-729 2440/2476. Intimate jazz bar above its larger sister, the Bass Clef. Also African, Latin and rare groove. *Open Mon-Sat 19.30-02.00, to 24.00 Sun*. A.Ax.Dc.V.

**T&C2**
20-22 Highbury Corner, Islington N5. 071-700 5716. The Islington branch of the legendary Town & Country Club, offering regular live music, cabaret and club nights. Check ticket availability in advance. *Open to 02.00*. Box office *open Mon-Fri 12.00-17.00, Sat 13.00-18.00*. A.Ax.Dc.V.

**Venue, New Cross**
2a Clifton Rise, New Cross SE14. 081-692 4077. Ticket hotline: 0891 200088. A former cinema and dance hall, now staging up to three bands per night *Thur-Sat*. Two dancefloors. Coach back to Trafalgar Square *Fri & Sat*. *Open to 02.00*. No credit cards.

**Vortex**
139-141 Stoke Newington Church St, Stoke Newington N16. 071-254 6516. Trendy jazz club above bookshop and art gallery. *Open Wed-Sat to 23.30, to 23.00 Sun. Closed Mon & Tue*. A.V.

---

**OPEN-AIR MUSIC**

---

There is nothing more pleasant or romantic on a warm summer's evening than being entertained under the stars. Open-air concerts range from brass bands in municipal gardens to opera in vast parks. Many are free, and any charge is usually nominal. Open-air pop concerts or festivals are also growing in popularity. For current programmes see *Time Out* or *City Limits*.

**Crystal Palace Bowl**
Crystal Palace Park SE26. 081-313 0527. Concerts featuring all types of music are held in *Jul & Aug* at the lakeside bowl, attracting enthusiastic crowds. Phone for details. Charge. A.Ax.Dc.V.

**Greenwich Park Open-air Theatre**
SE10. 081-858 2608. Brass bands entertain amidst the beautiful rolling parkland at Greenwich. *Sun & Bank hols 18.00-19.30 May-end Aug*. Free.

**Holland Park Theatre**                                          **3 A5**
Holland Park W8. 071-602 7856. Varied evening programme of opera, theatre, ballet and concerts from *Jun-Aug*. Phone for details. Charge. A.Ax.V.

**Hyde Park Open-air Theatre**                                    **4 B4**
W2. 071-262 5484. Military and brass bands play *Sun & Mon 18.00-19.30 May-end Aug*. Free.

**Kenwood**
Hampstead Lane NW3. Contact English Heritage (071-973 3426) for details. Prominent orchestras and singers give lakeside concerts in a beautiful setting. Climactic firework displays. Take a picnic to make the most of it. *Sat 19.30 Jun-Sep*. Charge. A.Ax.Dc.V.

**Marble Hill**
Richmond Rd, Twickenham, Middx. Contact English Heritage (071-973 3426) for details. Orchestral concerts, brass bands or jazz, sometimes accompanied by fireworks. *Sun 19.30 Jul & Aug*. A.Ax.Dc.V.

**Regent's Park**                                                 **1 B5**
NW1. 071-486 7905. Bands, mainly military and brass, perform in the bandstand *end May-end Aug*. Phone for details. Free.

**St James's Park**                                               **4 E5**
SW1. 071-930 1793. Brass and military bands entertain *Mon-Sun 17.30-19.00 end May-end Aug*. Free.

**Wimbledon Open-air Theatre**
Cannizaro Park, Westside, Wimbledon Common SW19. 081-540 0362. Enchantingly set in a walled garden in Cannizaro Park with seating for 500 and a varied programme of plays and opera *end Jul-Aug*. A.V.

---

## COMEDY AND CABARET

Alternative cabaret is now so popular in London that the word 'alternative' is a little out of date! From humble beginnings in the 1960s in the back rooms of pubs, 'new variety' really took off in the late '70s, when TV and radio began to tap the rich seam of talent coming from the thriving London scene. Cabaret provides some of the capital's cheapest, liveliest grass-roots entertainment, often covering topical political and social issues. Anything goes, from mime and dance to slapstick and satire. Improvisation nights – unscripted comedy from regular performers – can be hilarious, but beware, acts often go for audience participation in a big way! Pub venues remain popular, although there are now many purpose-built cabaret clubs with big-name bills. Some fringe theatres put on occasional shows, too. The major venues are listed below, but the circuit is ever-changing, with new places opening and one-nighters changing venue. Check *Time Out* or *City Limits* for details.

**081 Comedy Club**
The Tramshed, 51 Woolwich New Rd, Woolwich SE18. 081-317 8687. Good comedy and atmosphere. Bar and disco (included in price) until late. *Sat 21.15*.

**Aztec Comedy Club**
The Borderland, 47-49 Westow St, Bromley SE19. 081-771 0885.

Lively comedy club above a Mexican restaurant. Food served at your table. *Fri 21.30 & Sun 21.00*.

**Banana Cabaret**
The Bedford, Bedford Hill, Balham SW12. 081-673 8904. Great venue, rated highly on the cabaret circuit. Banana Cabaret gets in top comedians. *Fri & Sat 21.00*. Also in Acton on *Fri*; phone for details.

**Battersea Arts Centre (BAC)**
Old Town Hall, Lavender Hill, Battersea SW11. 071-223 2223. Adaptable theatre accommodates a lively mix of dance, cabaret and mime. Licensed café. *Sat 22.30*.

**Bearcat Club**
The Turk's Head, Winchester Rd, St Margaret's, Twickenham, Middx. 081-892 1972. Wide range of acts. *Mon 20.00*.

**Canal Café Theatre**                                              **3 D1**
The Bridge House, Delamere Terrace W2. 071-289 6054. Different cabaret shows *Mon 21.00, Tue-Sun 22.00*. Bar and restaurant. Newsrevue is a favourite, a topical comedy based on current affairs with sketches and songs. *Thur-Sun 22.00*.

**Cartoon at Clapham**
The Plough Inn, 196-198 Clapham High St, Clapham SW4. 071-738 8763. Strong line-ups at this large, comfortable pub venue. *Fri & Sat 21.00*. Bar until *midnight*. Collect reserved tickets by *20.45*.

**Chuckle Club**                                                    **2 A5**
The Marquis Cornwallis, 31 Marchmont St WC1. 071-476 1672. Top cabaret acts presented by compere Eugene Cheese. *Fri 20.30*. Also at The Shakespeare's Head, Carnaby St W1. (**4 D2**) *Sat 20.30*.

**Comedy Café**                                                     **2 G4**
66 Rivington St EC2. 071-739 5706. Open spot for new acts *Wed 21.30* (free entry); established acts *Fri & Sat 21.30*; black comedians at Cabarave *Tue 21.00*; Irish comedy night at Crack At The Café *Sun 20.00*. Bar until *01.00*. Food available.

*The Comedy Store*

**Comedy In Tatters**                                              **4 F4**
Tattershall Castle Paddle Steamer, Victoria Embankment WC2. 071-733 6322. London's only floating comedy club! *Sun 21.00.*

**Comedy Store**                                                  **4 E3**
28a Leicester Sq WC2. (0426) 914433. *The* London comedy venue where a lively array of comedians line up for a 2-3 hour show. The audience is encouraged to join in at the end. Improvisation from the famous Comedy Store Players *Wed 19.00 & Sun 20.00.* Food and drink available to 18s and over. *Thur 21.00, Fri & Sat 20.00 & 24.00.*

**Deadly Serious Comedy Club**
The Steamship, 24 Naval Row (off Cotton St), Tower Hamlets E14. 071-987 3474. Music, competitions, novelty acts. *Wed 20.30.*

**Downstairs at The King's Head**
2 Crouch End Hill, Crouch End N8. 081-340 1028. A fine selection of acts in this club below a popular Crouch End pub. Monthly try-out night *Thur 20.30.* Comedy *Sat & Sun 20.30.*

**East Dulwich Cabaret**
The East Dulwich Tavern, 1 Lordship Lane, East Dulwich SE22. 081-299 4138. Pub venue with quality comedy line-ups. *Fri & Sat 21.30.* Bar open until *midnight.*

**Gate Theatre Club**                                             **3 B3**
Prince Albert Pub, 11 Pembridge Rd W11. 071-229 0706. Improvised comedy shows. Late shows *Fri 22.00.*

**The Grace Theatre**                                             **6 F6**
The Latchmere, 503 Battersea Park Rd SW11. 071-228 2620. Custom-built theatre above a traditional pub. A good venue for satire, mime and alternative comedy. Can be relied on to stage the best of what is current on the revue circuit. Theatre bar. *Fri & Sat 22.00.* Improvisation *Thur 22.00.* Late bar.

**Guilty Pea**                                                    **4 E2**
The Wheatsheaf, 25 Rathbone Place WC1. 081-986 6861. Small above-a-pub venue offering new and established comedians. *Sat 20.45.*

**Hackney Empire**
291 Mare St, Hackney E8. 081-985 2424. Opulent and cavernous former home of East End music hall, lovingly restored for a new generation of variety. Definitely worth a visit. Phone for details of forthcoming shows.

**Jongleurs Battersea**
The Cornet, 49 Lavender Gardens, Battersea SW11. (0426) 933711. Booking: 071-924 2766. Very popular venue where the show comprises at least five acts – three comedians, a compere, visual acts, music and dance. A varied high-quality bill. Good wholesome food. Essential to book. *Fri 21.00, Sat 19.00 & 23.00, Sun 20.00.* Bar until *01.30.*

**Jongleurs Camden Lock**                                         **1 D1**
211-216 Chalk Farm Rd NW1. (0426) 933711. Booking: 071-924 2766. Newer Jongleurs venue where the show has the same formula of comedy and audience baiting as its Battersea counterpart. Seats 500. Restaurant. Spacious bar. Essential to book. *Fri 21.00, Sat 19.00 & 23.00, Sun 20.00.*

**Meccano Club**                                                  **2 D2**
The Market Tavern, 2 Essex Rd N1. 081-800 2236. Good comedy,

often from big names, in this pub basement venue. Improvisation a speciality. Food available. *Thur-Sun 21.00.*

**New Black Cat Cabaret**
The Samuel Beckett, Stoke Newington Church St, Stoke Newington N16. 081-806 8779. Good value variety night at popular watering hole. Food available. *Sun 21.00.* Bar until *23.30.*

**Oranje Boom Boom**                                                    **4 E3**
De Hems Dutch Coffee Bar, Macclesfield St W1. 081-694 1710. Stand-up comedy and variety from established and new acts. Licensed bar. *Wed 20.45.*

**The Players Theatre**                                                 **4 F4**
The Arches, Villiers St WC2. 071-839 1134. Traditional London music hall, presented by the Players Theatre Company. 'Late Joys' has been running since 1936! *Tue-Sun 20.15.*

**Pub Next Door**
The Samuel Pepys, 289 Mare St, Hackney E8. 081-985 2424. New variety comedy and 'open spots' for newcomers in this pub next door to the Hackney Empire. *Fri 22.00.* Talent night *Wed 21.30.*

**Punchline Comedy Club**
The Railway, West End Lane, West Hampstead NW6. 071-624 7611. Popular north-west London comedy venue. Late bar. *Sat 21.15.*

**Red Rose**
129 Seven Sisters Rd, Finsbury Park N7. 071-263 7265. One of north London's premier cabaret venues, featuring varied and consistently high-quality acts at low prices. Food available. *Fri & Sat 21.30.*

**Screaming Blue Murder**
Rose & Crown, 61 High St, Hampton Wick, Surrey. 081-339 0677. Comedy and music from new and established performers. *Wed & Fri 20.30.* Phone for details of other venues on *Mon & Thur.*

**T&C2**
20-22 Highbury Corner, Islington N5. 071-700 5716. Regular cabaret performances at spacious Islington offshoot of the Town & Country Club. Booking advisable. Food available. *Fri & Sat 20.30.* Bar until *02.00.*

**Up the Creek**
302 Creek Rd, Deptford SE10. 081-858 4581. Regular comedy, music and magic *Sat & Sun 21.00.* 'Cut price' show *Thur 21.00.* Late bar and Indian food.

# ARTS CENTRES

Many of these have appeared in London over the last decade. They put on shows – theatre, music, dance – usually have workshop facilities and give classes in a variety of arts skills.

**Barbican Centre**                                                     **2 E6**
Silk St EC2. 071-638 8891. Recorded information: 071-628 2295. Several arts venues in one – a concert hall, two theatres, three cinemas, a public library, an art gallery and sculpture court. In addition there is frequent entertainment in the foyer (free). Box office *open Mon-Sun 10.00-20.00.* A.Ax.V.

### Battersea Arts Centre (BAC)
Old Town Hall, Lavender Hill, Battersea SW11. 071-223 2223. A community arts centre with theatre, cinema, cabaret space, gallery, cafe and bookshop. Fringe and alternative theatre productions including local and touring companies. Regular weekend jazz and cabaret acts *Fri & Sat eves.* Box office *open Mon-Sun 10.00-22.00.* A.Ax.Dc.V.

### Brentford Watermans Arts Centre
40 High St, Brentford, Middx. 081-568 1176. Theatre, cinema, gallery, bar and restaurant. Wide range of productions; new work of all types is encouraged. Late-night cabaret *to 01.00 on alternate Sat.* Box office *open Tue-Sun 13.00-21.00.* A.Ax.V.

### Institute of Contemporary Arts (ICA)                    4 E4
Nash House, The Mall SW1. 071-930 3647. A good range of arts entertainment under one roof. Three galleries, a theatre, two cinemas, video reference library, arts bookshop, bar and restaurant. Membership required; day membership available (usually included in the ticket price). Box office *open Mon-Sun 12.00-21.30.* A.Ax.Dc.V.

### Riverside Studios
Crisp Rd, Hammersmith W6. 081-748 3354. Two studio theatres, cinema, gallery, bar and restaurant. Productions range from experimental theatre, performance art and dance to classic drama, plus a wide variety of music. Box office *open Mon-Sat 10.00-20.00, Sun 12.00-20.00.* A.Ax.V.

### South Bank Centre                                        5 A4
South Bank SE1. 071-928 8800. Recorded information: 071-633 0932. One of the best-known arts complexes in Britain with plenty of choice from film and theatre to music and dance. It houses the Royal Festival Hall, which hosts the English National Ballet Season every year, the Queen Elizabeth Hall, the Purcell Room, Hayward Gallery, the National Film Theatre and the Museum of the Moving Image. Restaurants, cafés and bars. Box office *open Mon-Sun 10.00-21.00.* A.Ax.Dc.V. The Royal National Theatre is also part of the South Bank complex and has three theatres: the Olivier, Lyttelton and Cottesloe. Box office: 071-928 2252 *open Mon-Sat 10.00-20.00.* A.Ax.Dc.V.

## THEATRES

London's great theatrical tradition is well established, and live theatre has been flourishing here for more than four centuries. The first regular playhouse, aptly named The Theatre, went up south of the Thames in 1576 – almost 14 years before Shakespeare started writing plays. Today, London has over 40 commercial theatres, principally in the West End, but with notable exceptions such as the Mermaid in the City, the Lyric at Hammersmith, and The Old Vic in Waterloo Road. There are also two major subsidised companies, the Royal National Theatre Company on the South Bank and the Royal Shakespeare Company, based at the Barbican Centre. Both operate mailing-list schemes which give early booking opportunities. The capital also has a thriving fringe scene where you can see anything from ex-West End shows to rare revivals by touring companies.

Performance details of all theatres appear in the national press (*The Times* and *The Independent* have particularly good listings), the *Evening Standard*, *Time Out* and *City Limits*. Seats may be booked at each theatre's own box office – either by telephone or in person – or through a ticket agency for West End shows. On the day of the performance unsold tickets for West End shows are available from:

**Society of West End Theatre (SWET)**          **4 E3**
**Half-Price Ticket Booth**
Leicester Sq WC2. Unsold tickets for evening performances available half-price from the pavilion on the south side of Leicester Square from *14.30-18.30 on day of performance*. You must book in person (maximum 4 tickets). No credit cards. Booking fee.

---

## TICKET AGENCIES

If you don't have the time, or the inclination, to go to the venue for tickets, the following agencies can shoulder the burden. Most will charge a commission.

**Albemarle of London**          **4 B2**
74 Mortimer St W1. 071-637 9041. A.Ax.Dc.V.
**Centre Point Tickets**          **4 E2**
105 Charing Cross Rd WC2. 071-434 1647. A.V.
**Fenchurch Booking Agency**          **5 C4**
94 Southwark St SE1. 071-928 8585. A.V.
**First Call**
071-240 7200. Bookings for all West End shows. A.Ax.Dc.V.
**Keith Prowse**
071-379 9901. Tickets for most West End shows. A.Ax.Dc.V.
**Theatre Tonight**
071-753 0333. Fast service for tonight's shows. A.V.
**Ticketmaster UK Ltd**          **4 E3**
48 Leicester Sq WC2. 071-379 4444. A.Ax.V.

---

## WEST END THEATRES

**Adelphi**          **4 F3**
Strand WC2. 071-836 7611. Musicals including *Me and My Girl*. A.Ax.Dc.V.
**Albery**          **4 F3**
St Martin's Lane WC2. 071-867 1115. Originally the New Theatre. Renamed in 1973. Musicals, comedy and drama. A.Ax.Dc.V.
**Aldwych**          **4 G3**
Aldwych WC2. 071-836 6404. Former London home of the Royal Shakespeare Company. Offers a wide programme of plays, comedies and musicals. A.Ax.Dc.V.
**Ambassadors**          **4 E2**
West St WC2. 071-836 6111. Small theatre, the original home of *The Mousetrap* until it moved to the nearby St Martin's. A.Ax.Dc.V.
**Apollo**          **4 E3**
Shaftesbury Ave W1. 071-494 5070. Old tradition of musical comedy. Now presents musicals, comedy and drama. A.Ax.V.

*Shaftesbury Avenue – Theatreland*

**Apollo Victoria**        **7 C2**
17 Wilton Rd SW1. 071-494 5070. This auditorium was completely transformed to accommodate the hit roller-skating railway musical *Starlight Express*. A.Ax.V.

**Barbican**        **2 E6**
Barbican Centre, Silk St EC2. 071-638 8891. Purpose-built for the Royal Shakespeare Company; the main auditorium is for large-scale productions in repertory and the Pit, a smaller studio theatre, is for new works. A.Ax.V.

**Cambridge**        **4 F2**
Earlham St WC2. 071-379 5299. Large theatre well suited to musical productions. A.Ax.V.

**Comedy**        **4 E3**
Panton St SW1. 071-867 1045. Good intimate theatre showing unusual comedy and small-cast plays. A.Ax.V.

**Criterion**        **4 E3**
Piccadilly Circus W1. 071-930 0314. Recently re-opened after being dark for two years due to extensive renovations. This listed building houses the only auditorium in London which is completely underground. A.V.

**Dominion**        **4 E2**
Tottenham Court Rd W1. 071-580 9562. One-time cinema, now mainly a rock concert venue which also features the occasional block-busting musical. A.Ax.Dc.V.

**Drury Lane (Theatre Royal)**        **4 G2**
Catherine St WC2. 071-494 5062. Operated under Royal Charter by Thomas Kiligrew in 1663, it has been burnt or pulled down and rebuilt

*Miss Saigon at the Theatre Royal, Drury Lane*

four times. Nell Gwynne performed here and Orange Moll sold her oranges. Garrick, Mrs Siddons, Kean and others played here. General policy now is vast musical productions like *Miss Saigon*. A.Ax.V.

### Duchess                                           4 G3
Catherine St WC2. 071-494 5075. Opened 1929. Plays, serious drama, comedy and musicals. A.Ax.V.

### Duke of York's                                    4 F3
St Martin's Lane WC2. 071-836 5122. Built by 'Mad (Violet) Melnotte' in 1892. Associated with names like Frohman, George Bernard Shaw, Granville Barker, Chaplin and the Ballet Rambert. Refurbished by the present owners, Capital Radio, for major productions. A.Ax.Dc.V.

### Fortune                                           4 F2
Russell St WC2. 071-836 2238. Small compared with its neighbour, Drury Lane. Intimate revues (Peter Cook and Dudley Moore shot to fame here in *Beyond the Fringe*), musicals and modern drama. A.Ax.Dc.V.

### Garrick                                           4 F3
Charing Cross Rd WC2. 071-494 5085. Built 1897. Notable managers included Bouchier and Jack Buchanan. A.Ax.V.

### Globe                                             4 E3
Shaftesbury Ave W1. 071-494 5065. A wide variety of successful plays and comedies. The third theatre of this name in London. A.Ax.V.

### Greenwich
Crooms Hill, Greenwich SE10. 081-858 7755. Stages a season of eight plays annually including new works, revivals and classics, often with famous names in the cast. Bar and restaurant. A.Ax.Dc.V.

### Haymarket (Theatre Royal)                         4 E3
Haymarket SW1. 071-930 8800. Originally built in 1721 as the little Theatre in the Hay, it became Royal 50 years later. The present theatre was built by Nash in 1821 and is sometimes enlivened by the ghost of Mr Buckstone, Queen Victoria's favourite actor-manager. He no doubt approves of the policy to present plays of quality. A.Ax.Dc.V.

### Her Majesty's                                     4 E4
Haymarket SW1. 071-494 5050. A fine Victorian baroque theatre

founded by Beerbohm Tree. Successes include *West Side Story, Fiddler on the Roof, Amadeus* and, most recently, Lloyd Webber's *Phantom of the Opera*. A.Ax.V.

**Lyric**                                                                                    **4 E3**
Shaftesbury Ave W1. 071-494 5045. Oldest theatre in Shaftesbury Avenue (built 1888). Eleonora Duse, Sarah Bernhardt, Owen Nares and Tallulah Bankhead all had long runs here. A.Ax.V.

**Lyric Hammersmith**
King St, Hammersmith W6. 081-741 2311. Rebuilt and restored to its original Victorian splendour inside a modern shell. Spacious foyers, bar and restaurant. Wide-ranging productions. A.Ax.Dc.V.

**Mermaid**                                                                                 **5 C3**
Puddle Dock, Blackfriars EC4. 071-410 0102. Plays and musicals. Restaurant and two bars overlooking the Thames. Ax.V.

**National**                                                                                **5 A4**
South Bank SE1. Box office: 071-928 2252. Complex of three theatres, the Olivier, Lyttelton and Cottesloe. Home of the Royal National Theatre Company. Stages a wide mixture of plays in repertory, including new works, revivals, Shakespeare and musicals. Also foyer entertainment. Restaurant, bars, exhibitions. A.Ax.Dc.V.

**New London**                                                                            **4 F2**
Drury Lane WC2. 071-405 0072. Can convert from a 900-seat conventional theatre to an intimate, theatre-in-the-round within minutes. Opened 1972 on the site of the old Winter Gardens. The hit musical *Cats* is well established here. A.Ax.V.

**Old Vic**                                                                                  **5 B5**
Waterloo Rd SE1. 071-928 7616. Built 1818. For a long time the home of the National Theatre Company. It now shows plays and musicals amid recreated Victorian decor. A.Ax.Dc.V.

**Palace**                                                                                   **4 E2**
Shaftesbury Ave W1. 071-434 0909. Listed building. Originally intended by Richard D'Oyly Carte to be the Royal English Opera House, but eventually became the Palace Theatre of Varieties.

*Les Misérables at the Palace Theatre*

Staged performances by Pavlova and Nijinski. Now owned by Sir Andrew Lloyd Webber whose musical *Jesus Christ Superstar* enjoyed a record run here; *Les Misérables* is its latest success story. A.Ax.V.

**Palladium**　　　　　　　　　　　　　　　　　　　　**4 D2**
8 Argyll St W1. 071-494 5038. Second in size to the Coliseum, it houses top variety shows, television specials and star-studded annual pantomimes. A.Ax.V.

**Phoenix**　　　　　　　　　　　　　　　　　　　　　**4 E2**
Charing Cross Rd WC2. 071-867 1044. A large theatre showing comedies, plays and musicals. A.Ax.Dc.V.

**Piccadilly**　　　　　　　　　　　　　　　　　　　　**4 E3**
Denman St W1. 071-867 1118. A pre-war theatre which showed the first season of 'Talkies' in Britain. A varied post-war history of light comedy, plays and musicals. Many Royal Shakespeare Company productions are staged here. A.Ax.Dc.V.

**Players**　　　　　　　　　　　　　　　　　　　　　**4 F4**
The Arches, Villiers St WC2. 071-839 1134. A theatre club, open to non-members, which stages regularly changing Victorian Music Hall productions; also Victorian pantomime and melodrama. Restaurant and bar. A.Ax.V.

**Playhouse**　　　　　　　　　　　　　　　　　　　　**4 F4**
Northumberland Ave WC2. 071-839 4401. Edwardian theatre used as a BBC studio and then closed in 1975. Restored to former glory and re-opened in 1987. Stages musicals, serious drama and comedies. A.Ax.Dc.V.

**Prince Edward**　　　　　　　　　　　　　　　　　　**4 F4**
Old Compton St W1. 071-734 8951. Started life as the 'London Casino' in 1936 and has also been a cinema. Now a large theatre where musicals are staged, including the hit show *Evita* which ran for 2900 performances. A.Ax.Dc.V.

**Prince of Wales**　　　　　　　　　　　　　　　　　**4 E3**
Coventry St W1. 071-839 5987. Rebuilt 1937, this large modern theatre has housed many musicals. A.Ax.V.

**Queen's**　　　　　　　　　　　　　　　　　　　　　**4 E3**
Shaftesbury Ave W1. 071-494 5040. Very successful between the wars. Still presents good drama and varied productions. A.Ax.V.

**Royal Court**　　　　　　　　　　　　　　　　　　　**6 G2**
Sloane Sq SW1. 071-730 1745. Home of the English Stage Company which produces many major experimental plays. A.Ax.V.

**St Martin's**　　　　　　　　　　　　　　　　　　　**4 E2**
West St WC2. 071-836 1443. Intimate playhouse with unusual polished teak doors. *The Mousetrap* continues its record run here having transferred from the Ambassadors. A.Ax.V.

**Savoy**　　　　　　　　　　　　　　　　　　　　　　**4 G3**
Strand WC2. 071-836 8888. Entrance in the forecourt of the Savoy Hotel. The first London theatre to be fully electrically lit and fire-proofed, it was, ironically, very badly damaged by a fire in 1990 and is closed until Autumn 1993. Produces a variety of plays, musicals and comedies. A.Ax.V.

**Shaftesbury**　　　　　　　　　　　　　　　　　　　**4 E3**
Shaftesbury Ave WC2. 071-379 5399. Permanent base of the Theatre of Comedy Company. A.Ax.Dc.V.

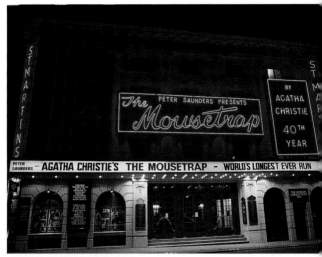

*The Mousetrap at St Martin's Theatre*

**Strand**                                           **4 F3**
Aldwych WC2. 071-930 8800. Large theatre presenting a mixture of straight plays, comedies and musicals. A.Ax.Dc.V.
**Vaudeville**                                 **4 F3**
Strand WC2. 071-836 9987. Listed building which originally ran farce and burlesque (hence the name), then became straight which, for the most part, it remains. A.Ax.Dc.V.
**Victoria Palace**                              **7 C1**
Victoria St SW1. 071-834 1317. Musicals, variety shows and plays. Once home of the Crazy Gang and the *Black and White Minstrel Show*, the musical *Buddy* is a recent success. A.Ax.V.
**Whitehall**                                     **4 F4**
14 Whitehall SW1. 071-867 1119. Splendid art deco interior. Now one of the Wyndham Theatres group staging varied productions. A.Ax.Dc.V.
**Wyndham's**                                  **4 F3**
Charing Cross Rd WC2. 071-867 1116. Small, pretty and successful theatre founded by Sir Charles Wyndham, the famous actor-manager. Plays, comedy and musicals. A.Ax.Dc.V.

---

### FRINGE THEATRES

Tickets for fringe shows range from £3-£10, so it's a lot cheaper than heading for the West End. Check *Time Out* or *City Limits* for what's on. The following venues present regular productions.
Day membership is usually only 50p-£1.00. As some of the venues listed are private clubs, it may be necessary to take out membership 48 hours in advance.

**Almeida**                                                    **2 D1**
Almeida St N1. 071-359 4404. Good reputation for off-beat productions. A.Ax.Dc.V.

**Arts**                                                       **4 F3**
6-7 Great Newport St WC2. 071-836 2132. A 340-seat theatre showing a variety of plays; also home of the Unicorn Theatre. Lounge and snack bar. A.V.

**Baron's Court Theatre**
Baron's Ale House, 28 Comeragh Rd, West Kensington W14. 071-602 0235. Exciting and innovative productions play to packed houses at this small theatre-in-the-round. **M**. No credit cards.

**Battersea Arts Centre (BAC)**
Old Town Hall, Lavender Hill, Battersea SW11. 071-223 2223. Fringe and alternative theatre productions including local and touring companies. **M**. A.V.

**Bear and Staff**                                             **4 E3**
37 Charing Cross Rd WC2. 071-724 3208. Small and friendly pub

theatre (only seats 30) staging open-ended runs of popular fringe shows. No credit cards.

**Bloomsbury**                                                          **1 F5**
15 Gordon St WC1. 071-387 9629. Part of London University and used by students for 12 weeks in the year. International plays, cabaret and opera. A.Ax.V.

**Bridge Lane**                                                         **6 E6**
Bridge Lane SW11. 071-228 8828. Professional companies offering new or neglected plays. Café and bar. **M**. A.V.

**Bush**
Bush Hotel, Shepherd's Bush Green W12. 081-743 3388. Premiere performances of British and international plays, some of which transfer to the West End. **M**. A.V.

**Café Theatre Club**                                                  **4 F2**
London Ecology Centre, 45 Shelton St WC2. 071-240 9582. New plays, modern classics and adaptations of novels, sometimes three in an evening. **M**. No credit cards.

**Canal Café Theatre**                                                 **3 D1**
The Bridge House, Delamere Terrace W2. 071-289 6054. Plays, burlesque and cabaret. Audience sits at tables – dinner optional but recommended. **M**. No credit cards.

**Cochrane**                                                           **2 A6**
Southampton Row WC1. 071-242 7040. Productions staged by such companies as the National Youth Theatre, National Youth Music Theatre, Practical Arts and Theatre with the Handicapped, Royal College of Music and The Old Vic Youth Theatre. A.V.

**Cockpit**                                                            **1 A5**
Gateforth St NW8. 071-402 5081. A studio theatre where avant-garde drama and music are presented principally by and for young people. Coffee and snack bar. A.V.

**Donmar Warehouse**                                                   **4 F2**
41 Earlham St WC2. 071-867 1150. Recently re-opened after substantial refurbishment, the Donmar welcomes touring companies, mounts its own productions and presents a mixture of fringe and West End theatre. A.Ax.V.

**Drill Hall**                                                         **4 E1**
16 Chenies St WC1. 071-631 1353. The plentiful spaces of the ex-Territorial Army drill hall are used in a variety of ways. Extensive fringe programme of drama, cabaret, music and opera. Bar and vegetarian restaurant in the basement. A.V.

**Duke's Head**
42 The Vineyard, Richmond, Surrey. 081-948 8085. Wide range of productions, including some ex-West End shows. No credit cards.

**Elephant**                                                           **5 D5**
Bridge House Pub, 30 Borough Rd SE1. 071-407 7501. Opposite the Goose & Firkin pub (for interval drinks!); new plays and classics. No credit cards.

**Etcetera**                                                           **1 D1**
Oxford Arms, 265 Camden High St NW1. 071-482 4857. Performances *six days a week*. Everything from comedy to tragedy

but mostly contemporary plays. *Sun evenings* one-off plays, music and poetry. **M**. No credit cards.

**Finborough**                                                            **6 B3**
Finborough Arms, 118 Finborough Rd SW10. 071-373 3842. New plays by resident or visiting companies. **M**. No credit cards.

**Gate Theatre Club**                                                     **3 B3**
Prince Albert Pub, 11 Pembridge Rd W11. 071-229 0706. British premieres of foreign works and rare revivals. **M**. No credit cards.

**Grace Theatre**                                                         **6 F6**
The Latchmere, 503 Battersea Park Road SW11. 071-228 2620. Quality productions of new work, contemporary drama classics, musicals. Established performers and visiting companies. Upstairs bar. **M**. A.V.

**Greenwich Studio**
Prince of Orange, 189 High Rd, Greenwich SE10. 081-858 2862. Quality productions of classics, new English and American writers and occasional cabaret. **M**. No credit cards.

**Hampstead**
Avenue Rd, Swiss Cottage NW3. 071-722 9301. One of the leading club theatres, dedicated to the presentation of new plays and the encouragement of new writers. Licensed bar. A.V.

**Hen & Chickens**
Hen & Chickens Pub, Highbury Corner, Islington N1. 071-704 2001. There is a resident company, but they also welcome regional companies bringing in plays by new writers. **M**. No credit cards.

**Institute of Contemporary Arts (ICA)**                                  **4 E4**
Nash House, The Mall SW1. 071-930 3647. Wide-ranging productions from dance and music to avant-garde and experimental theatre. **M**. A.Ax.Dc.V.

**Jackson's Lane**
Archway Rd, Highgate N6. 081-340 5226. Short runs of touring fringe shows plus circus and cabaret. Also live music. No credit cards.

**King's Head**                                                          **2 D2**
115 Upper St N1. 071-226 1916. Arguably the best-known and most widely reviewed of pub theatre, presenting musicals, revues, new plays, revivals. Tickets available for performance only or for dinner and performance, in which case you watch the show from your table. Pub itself has live music most nights. **M**. A.V.

**La Bonne Crêpe**
539 Battersea Park Rd, Battersea SW11. 071-228 5070. Well-established theatre set behind a restaurant. An inspiring mix of comedy, drama and music. Dinner available with the show. A.V.

**Lilian Baylis**                                                        **2 C4**
Sadler's Wells Theatre, Rosebery Ave EC1. 071-837 4104. Small studio theatre staging contemporary dance and high-quality productions by visiting drama companies and college groups. A.Ax.Dc.V.

**Link Theatre**                                                         **4 G1**
Holborn Centre, 3 Cups Yard, Sandland St WC1. 071-405 5334. Anything from Restoration and Shakespeare to new writing at this moveable-seating studio theatre that accommodates an audience of 50. No credit cards.

**Lyric Studio**
Lyric Theatre, King St, Hammersmith W6. 081-741 8701. Four floors of theatre, music and exhibitions with bar and café. Classics, modern, fringe and alternative cabaret. A.Ax.Dc.V.

**Man in the Moon**                                                      **6 D4**
392 King's Rd SW3. 071-351 2876/5701. Visiting companies present new plays and revivals. **M**. No credit cards.

**New End Theatre**
27 New End, Hampstead NW3. 071-794 0022. A good selection of hard-hitting and modern plays, plus late-night comedy. A.V.

**Old Red Lion**                                                        **2 D4**
418 St John's St EC1. 071-837 7816. Performances of a mixed bag of plays. Pub always has good food. **M**. No credit cards.

**Orange Tree**
1 Clarence St, Richmond, Surrey. 081-940 3633. Highly successful fringe theatre which started life above an early Victorian pub. Now in a new theatre offering a full range of productions – classics, revivals, new work and musicals. Bar. A.V.

**Questors**
Mattock Lane, Ealing W5. 081-567 5184. Plays by well-known writers plus some off-beat productions. Membership available. A.V.

**Riverside**
Crisp Rd, Hammersmith W6. 081-748 3354. Two studio theatres. Productions range from experimental theatre, performance art and dance to classic drama. A.V.

**Rudolph Steiner House**                                              **1 B5**
35 Park Rd NW1. 071-723 4400. A high standard of classic, modern and European productions by visiting companies. No credit cards.

**Shaw**                                                               **1 F4**
100 Euston Rd NW1. 071-388 1394. Modern theatre staging productions of special interest to students and young people. Bar and café. A.V.

**Theatre Royal Stratford East**
Gerry Raffles Sq, Stratford E15. 081-534 0310. New plays and musicals along with community projects. Bar and snacks available. A.V.

**Theatre Upstairs**                                                   **6 G2**
Royal Court Theatre, Sloane Sq SW1. 071-730 2554. New plays launched in a small studio space above the main theatre. A.Ax.V.

**Tom Allen Centre**
Grove Crescent Rd, Stratford E15. 081-519 6818. Touring companies, workshop productions, youth theatre and films. No credit cards.

**Tricycle Theatre**
269 Kilburn High Rd NW6. 071-328 1000. Lively fringe productions. Children's theatre on *Sat*. A.V.

**Tube Theatre**
071-586 6828. A comedian poses as a clumsy commuter. You follow and see the reaction! Now in its 22nd year, tube theatre has been labelled the 'longest running show under the West End'. Group bookings only. Minimum 12 people. No credit cards.

**Vanbrugh**                                                           **1 F6**
Malet St WC1. 071-580 7982. Theatre club presenting a range of

classic and contemporary drama by RADA students. Three theatres, bar. No credit cards.

**White Bear**                                                      7 G3
138 Kennington Park Rd, Kennington SE11. 071-735 8664. A cosy, well-equipped pub theatre with an interesting programme that includes rediscovered writers and little-known works. No credit cards.

**The Young Vic**                                                  5 B5
66 The Cut SE1. 071-928 6363. Theatre and studio theatre with the emphasis on the classics and good modern plays. Well-known names in the casts. A.Dc.V.

---

## OPEN-AIR THEATRES

Various parks in London stage one-off theatrical events in summer. To find out more about these, check *Time Out* and *What's On* in the summer months.

**Holland Park Theatre**                                            3 A5
Holland Park W8. Box office: 071-602 7856. Recorded information: 071-603 3436. Open-air theatre staging dance, opera and theatre productions *Jun-Aug*. The canopy covering is a definite attraction given the fickleness of the English summer! Seating for 600. A.Ax.Dc.V.

**Regent's Park Open-air Theatre**                                  1 C4
Inner Circle, Regent's Park NW1. Box office: 071-486 2431. In a magical setting enclosed within the park, this is delightful in good weather. Plays by Shakespeare (*A Midsummer Night's Dream* is a perennial favourite) and others alternate from *May-Sep*. Book in advance. Performances *Mon-Sat 20.00; and Wed, Thur & Sat 14.30.* A.Ax.V.

**Wimbledon Open-air Theatre**
Cannizaro Park, Westside, Wimbledon Common SW19. Box office: 081-540 0362. Enchantingly set in a walled garden in Cannizaro Park with seating for 500. Plays and opera *Jul & Aug*. A.V.

---

# CINEMAS

**Astral**                                                         4 E3
3-7 Brewer St W1. 071-734 6387.

**Camden Plaza**                                                   1 D2
211 Camden High St NW1. 071-485 2443. Quality films.

**Cannon Hampstead**
Pond St, Hampstead NW3. 071-794 4000. Three screens.

**Chelsea Cinema**                                                 6 E3
King's Rd SW3. 071-351 3742. Quality films, often foreign.

**Coronet Notting Hill**                                           3 B4
Notting Hill Gate W11. 071-727 6705.

**Curzon Mayfair**                                                 4 C4
Curzon St W1. 071-465 8865. Specially-selected new films in very plush surroundings.

*The Empire, Leicester Square*

**Curzon Phoenix**                                    **4 E2**
Phoenix Theatre, Charing Cross Rd WC2. 071-240 9661. Specially selected films.

**Curzon West End**                                   **4 E3**
93 Shaftesbury Ave W1. 072-439 4805. Specially selected films.

**Empire**                                            **4 E3**
Leicester Sq WC2. 071-437 1234. Three screens. Very large with the latest sound techniques.

**Gate Cinema**                                       **3 B4**
87 Notting Hill Gate W11. 071-727 4043. Quality art films.

**Lumière**                                           **4 F3**
42 St Martin's Lane WC2. 071-836 0691. Foreign and quality films.

**Metro**                                             **4 E3**
11 Rupert St W1. 071-437 0757. Two screens, foreign and quality films.

**MGM Baker Street**                                  **1 B6**
Station Approach, Marylebone Rd NW1. 071-935 9772. Two screens.

**MGM Chelsea**                                       **6 D4**
279 King's Rd SW3. 071-352 5096. Four screens.

**MGM Fulham Road**                                   **6 C3**
Fulham Rd SW10. 071-370 2636. Five screens.

**MGM Haymarket**                                     **4 E3**
63-65 Haymarket SW1. 071-839 1527. Three screens.

**MGM Oxford Street**                                 **4 E2**
18 Oxford St W1. 071-636 0310. Five screens.

**MGM Panton Street**                                 **4 E3**
Panton St SW1. 071-930 0631. Four screens.

**MGM Piccadilly**                                    **4 E3**
215-217 Piccadilly W1. 071-437 3561.

**MGM Shaftesbury Avenue**                            **4 E2**
135 Shaftesbury Ave W1. 071-836 6279.

**MGM Swiss Centre**                                  **4 E3**
Swiss Centre, Leicester Sq WC2. 071-439 4470. Four screens.

**MGM Tottenham Court Road**    **1 F6**
Tottenham Court Rd W1. 071-636 6148.
**MGM Trocadero**    **4 E3**
Trocadero, Piccadilly Circus W1. 071-434 0031. Smart new cinema
complex with seven screens.
**Minema**    **4 B5**
45 Knightsbridge SW1. 071-235 4225. Modern classics.
**Odeon Haymarket**    **4 E3**
Haymarket SW1. (0426) 915353.
**Odeon Kensington**    **3 B6**
Kensington High St W8. (0426) 914666. Six screens.
**Odeon Leicester Square**    **4 E3**
Leicester Sq WC2. (0426) 915683.
**Odeon Marble Arch**    **3 G2**
10 Edgware Rd W2. (0426) 914501.
**Odeon Mezzanine**    **4 E3**
Leicester Sq WC2. (0426) 915683. Five screens.
**Odeon Swiss Cottage**
Finchley Rd, Swiss Cottage NW3. (0426) 914098. Four screens.
**Odeon West End**    **4 E3**
Leicester Sq WC2. (0426) 915574.
**Plaza**    **4 E3**
Lower Regent St W1. 071-437 1234. Four screens.

**Prince Charles** 4 E3
Leicester Place, Leicester Sq WC2. 071-437 8181. Small cinema, latest releases.

**Renoir** 2 A5
Brunswick Sq WC1. 071-837 8402. Two screens, quality and foreign films.

**Screen on Baker Street** 1 B5
96 Baker St W1. 071-935 2772. Two screens.

**Screen on the Green** 2 D2
83 Upper St N1. 071-226 3520.

**Screen on the Hill**
203 Haverstock Hill, Belsize Park NW3. 071-435 3366. Quality films.

**UCI** 3 C2
Whiteleys, Queensway W2. 071-792 3332. Eight screens.

**Warner West End** 4 E3
Leicester Sq WC2. 071-439 0791. Five screens.

## REPERTORY CINEMAS

**Barbican** 2 E6
Level 1, Barbican Centre, Silk St EC2. 071-638 8891. Films often linked to Barbican exhibitions. Two screens.

**Electric** 3 A2
191 Portobello Rd W11. 071-792 2020. Everything from mainstream American to obscure imports shown.

**Everyman**
Holly Bush Vale, Hampstead NW3. 071-435 1525. Weekly classic revivals.

**Institute of Contemporary Arts (ICA)** 4 E4
Nash House, The Mall SW1. 071-930 3647. Two screens. Foreign and unusual theme films. Membership required; day membership available.

**National Film Theatre** 5 A4
South Bank SE1. 071-928 3232. Two screens. Rare foreign films, revivals of classics and seasons of notable directors' works.

**Phoenix**
52 High Rd, East Finchley N2. 081-444 6789. Recorded information 081-883 2233. European, American and Asian cinematic successes are shown, often in double bills. Children's cinema club on Saturday mornings.

**Rio Cinema Dalston**
107 Kingsland High St E8. 071-254 6677. Recorded information 071-254 6677. Everything from acclaimed European films to cult American pictures shown as double bills. Children's film club on Saturday morning.

**Ritzy Cinema Club**
Brixton Rd, Brixton SW2. 071-737 2121. Classics, mainstream films and documentaries from Europe, Hollywood and Australia are shown in double bills here. Late shows at weekends.

**Riverside Studios**
Crisp Rd, Hammersmith W6. 081-748 3354. Themes to coincide with studio theatre productions.

**Scala** 1 G4
275-277 Pentonville Rd N1. 071-278 8052. Double bills.

## POETRY READINGS

The Poetry Library, Theatre Level, Red Side, Royal Festival Hall, South Bank Centre SE1, 071-921 0664, prints detailed lists of poetry competitions in and around London. *Open Mon-Sun 11.00-20.00.* The following venues are well established and hold regular meetings. The Poetry Society is the most widely known.

### Apples & Snakes
Contact: 071-639 9656. Performance poetry in cabaret style. Different programme each week. Venues listed in press.

### Camden Voices                                                        1 E3
Working Men's College, Crowndale Rd NW1. 071-485 3830. Meet on *Wed 19.00-21.00 in term time* for readings, discussions on contemporary poetry, and a workshop for members to air their own work.

### City Lit                                                            4 F2
Stukeley St, Drury Lane WC2. Contact: 071-430 0542/3. Runs evening classes on contemporary poetry, verse speaking and the writing of poetry.

### Institute of Contemporary Arts (ICA)                                4 E4
Nash House, The Mall SW1. 071-930 3647. Occasional lectures, readings and discussions by distinguished poets.

### Pentameters
Three Horseshoes Pub, Heath St, Hampstead NW3. 071-435 6757. Arranges readings by distinguished poets at regular intervals.

### Poetry Round                                                        6 B2
Barkston Hotel, Barkston Gdns SW5. 071-373 7851. Weekly poetry forum. *Mon 20.00.*

### Poetry Society                                                      4 F2
22 Betterton St WC2. 071-240 4810. Holds regular poetry readings. Contact the Advice and Information Officer on the above number for details of forthcoming events.

## TV SHOWS

If you want to be part of the audience of your favourite TV show, or watch any of the other shows in a studio, write enclosing a sae and preference of programme to one of the following:

### BBC Radio & Television                                              4 C1
Ticket Unit, Broadcasting House, Portland Place W1.

### London Weekend Television                                           5 B4
Kent House, Upper Ground SE1.

# EATING OUT

In the following chapter, we have divided the restaurants into categories by nationality and theme so that you can find exactly the right place to fit into your evening out.

For a more comprehensive guide to eating in London, see Nicholson's *London Restaurant Guide* which lists over 700 places to eat and more than 30 national cuisines.

Most restaurants are confined by law to serving alcohol with meals during the usual licensing hours, that is until *23.30*. Some restaurants do however have extended licences until *after midnight*.

A service charge of 12½ % is often automatically included in the bill, but it is not enforced by law. Pay according to what you feel the service you have received warrants.

For reliable information on restaurants and eating out contact Restaurant Services (081-888 8080) or Direct Dining (071-287 3287) who will give free advice and can make table reservations.

### Symbols and abbreviations
🚪 Pre-theatre restaurant
❰ Late-closing restaurant which serves food *after midnight*

An index to pre-theatre and late-closing restaurants appears at the end of this chapter on pages 116-7.

## AFRICAN AND CARIBBEAN

### Afric-Carib
1 Stroud Green Rd, Finsbury Park N4. 071-263 7440. Specialists in authentic Nigerian dishes. Try chicken, beef or fish served with yams and plantain or an egusi dish (meat cooked in oil with crushed melon seeds). Very informal atmosphere encouraged by abundant quantities of African palm wine and music. *Open to 23.30.* A.V. **£**

### ❰ Brixtonian Backayard                     4 F2
4 Neal's Yard, off Neal St WC2. 071-240 2769. A large, bright restaurant with comfortable furniture and a menu inspired by the West Indies. Sweet potato and salmon patties, deep fried salt cod, chicken Columbo and fried snapper with red bean sauce are some of the tempting dishes. *Open to 24.00. Closed Sun & Mon.* A.V. **££**

### Brixtonian Restaurant
11 Dorrell Place, off Nursery Rd, Brixton SW9. 071-978 8870. French Caribbean cuisine in a charming white dining room with wooden floors. Each month dishes from a different island are featured. Creole shark, salmon with red pepper sauce and tropical fruit sorbets for dessert. *Open to 23.30. Closed Sun & Mon.* A.V. **££**

**Cottons Rhum Shop, Bar & Restaurant**    **1 C1**
55 Chalk Farm Rd NW1. 071-482 1096. First-class Jamaican home cooking served in a relaxed atmosphere. Try Port Antonio fried chicken, Jamaican hard dough bread, crab, carrot cake. Cocktails and rum are accompanied by reggae music in the bar. *Open to 23.15. Closed Sun.* A.V. **££**

**◖ Cuba**    **3 B6**
11-13 Kensington High St W8. 071-938 4137. This restaurant/bar is a relaxed and friendly place to discover Cuban cuisine. You can enjoy tapas dishes with your pre-dinner rum cocktail, then sit down to Cuban meatloaf, lobster tails served with a sweet creole sauce, or boniato (a sweet potato, filled with shredded beef in the same traditional creole sauce, accompanied with black beans, rice and plantains). Finish with a strong Cuban coffee. *(Reserve) open to 01.00, to 23.00 Sun.* No credit cards. **££**

**◖ Plantation Inn**
337-339 High Rd, Leytonstone E11. 081-558 6210. A ray of Caribbean sunshine, with pictures of islands adorning the walls and plenty of plant life. Slick service and adventurous food including chicken gumbo montego, fried plantain and breadfruit. *Open to 24.00, to 23.00 Sun. Closed Mon.* A.Ax.Dc.V. **££**

**◖ A Taste of Africa**
50 Brixton Rd, Brixton SW9. 071-587 0343. A lively, sometimes raucous establishment offering Nigerian specialities. Good egusi dishes and plenty of Nigerian beer to wash them down. *Open to 24.00.* A.Ax.Dc.V. **££**

## AMERICAN

**◖ Big Easy**    **6 D4**
332-334 King's Rd SW3. 071-352 4071. Self-styled as an 'American Bar-B-Q and Crabshack', here you can stock up on spicy shrimps, crab claws, ribs, chicken, brisket with barbecue beans and coleslaw. There are frozen cocktails, shooters and chasers accompanied by live music several nights a week. *Open to 24.00.* A.Ax.Dc.V. **££**

**◖ Blues Brothers**
50 Clapham High St, Clapham SW4. 071-622 0070. An up-market American restaurant with live music *at weekends*. Lively menu; the gumbo ya ya (stewy soup) is delicious. Then try Dixie meatloaf or maw maw's piquant chicken. Friendly service. Pavement seating on summer evenings. *Open to 24.00, to 22.30 Sun.* A.Ax.Dc.V. **££**

**Christopher's**    **4 G3**
18 Wellington St WC2. 071-240 4222. This building was reconstructed in 1863 to house the first licensed casino in Victorian London. The entrance hall to the restaurant, the curving staircase and domed ceiling are very dramatic. Not a burgers, fries and apple pie American restaurant. Enjoy rack of lamb, breast of chicken and fillet of beef. *Open to 23.30. Closed Sun.* A.Ax.Dc.V. **£££**

**Criterion Brasserie**    **4 E3**
Piccadilly Circus W1. 071-925 0909. Housed in a Victorian entertain-

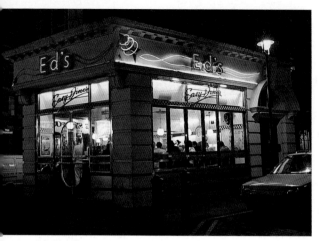

*Ed's Easy Diner*

ment complex, this opulent restaurant is worth visiting just for the surroundings. The cuisine on offer is Cal-Ital, a blend of American and Italian food. Dishes include veal parmesan sandwich, Caesar salad and fried spaghetti. *Open to 23.30*. A.Ax.Dc.V. **££**

**Deals and Deals West**

Deals, Chelsea Harbour, off Lots Rd SW10. 071-376 3232     **6 D6**

Deals West, 14-16 Foubert's Place W1. 071-287 1001.     **4 D2**

Owned by Viscount Linley and Patrick Lichfield, these are both lively, popular restaurants decked out like a Southern diner with bare wood and brickwork. Spare ribs, burgers and good salads ('Raw Deals'!) followed (if you have room) by huge portions of chocolate cheesecake and mud pie. Friendly service. *Open to 23.00, to 23.30 Fri & Sat*. A.Ax.V. **££**

**◖ Ed's Easy Diner**     **4 E2**

12 Moor St, off Old Compton St W1. 071-439 1955. An American-style diner with counter-top jukeboxes and bar seating. Hamburgers and fries dominate but there are also club sandwiches and salads. Don't expect to linger; their turnover is very fast. Imported US beers and thick milkshakes. *Open to 24.00, to 01.00 Fri & Sat*. No credit cards. **£**

**▣ Fatboy's Diner**     **4 F3**

21-22 Maiden Lane WC2. 071-240 1902. A 1940s American chrome dining carriage right in the heart of Covent Garden. Lively and noisy offering huge, tasty burgers to fill you up before the show. Fries, hot dogs and ice-cream floats as well. *Open 11.00-24.00, to 22.30 Sun*. No credit cards. **££**

**◖ Hard Rock Café**     **4 C5**

150 Old Park Lane W1. 071-629 0382. One of the best hamburger joints in London. Houses one of the largest collections of American

memorabilia in the world. Burgers and steaks are excellent; other favourites include grilled cheese, BLT and roast beef sandwich. Non-stop loud rock music. Expect to queue as this is a perennially popular spot. *Open to 00.30.* Ax.V. **££**

### Henry J. Bean's (But His Friends All Call Him Hank) Bar & Grill
**6 E3**

195-197 King's Rd SW3. 071-352 9255. A vast, jolly place modelled on a typical American bar/grill. Celebrity photographs and advertising signs line the walls. Potato skins, nachos, smokehouse burgers, fried chicken are tasty and good value. Garden at the rear. *Open to 23.15, to 22.00 Sun.* No credit cards. **££**

### ◖ Joe Allen
**4 G3**

13 Exeter St WC2. 071-836 0651. In a converted warehouse, London's 'Joe Allen' follows the pattern of its New York and Paris counterparts. Here you'll find checked tablecloths and brick walls hung with theatre posters. American-style cuisine includes steaks, chilli and pecan pie. Always crowded with people from the entertainment and showbiz world. *(Reserve) open to 00.45, to 24.00 Sun.* No credit cards. **£**

### ◖ Johnny Rockets
**6 D3**

140 Fulham Rd SW10. 071-370 2794. A British branch of an LA institution, this is a lively, noisy American diner, with chrome counters, burgers, fries, peanut and jello sandwiches, shakes and malts. The jukebox choices at your fingertips are occasionally accompanied by a song and dance routine from the staff! Handy for the MGM cinema on Fulham Road. No smoking. *Open to 24.00.* No credit cards. **£**

### ◖ Maxwell's
**4 F3**

17 Russell St WC2. 071-836 0303. Loud rock music and a lively atmosphere ensure this is a permanently busy place. Good burgers, steaks and salads, delicious desserts. The bar staff will make up any cocktail, whether it's on their list or not. *Open to 24.00, to 01.00 Fri & Sat.* A.V. **££**

*Maxwell's*

### ❏ Old Orleans                                          4 G3
29 Wellington St WC2. 071-497 2433. Huge portions of Deep South food from this busy, friendly restaurant will undoubtedly keep you going for the evening. Seafood gumbo, Deep South ribs, blackened snapper, vast hamburgers, followed by chocolate fudge brownies. *Open 11.00-23.00.* A.Ax.Dc.V. **££**

### ❏ Parsons                                             6 D3
311 Fulham Rd SW10. 071-352 0651. Relaxed and informal with a spacious interior. Large portions of pasta, steaks, burgers, fries and ribs served by friendly and cheerful staff make this a constantly popular spot. *Open to 00.30, to 24.00 Sun.* A.Ax.Dc.V. **££**

### PJ's                                                   6 E2
52 Fulham Rd SW3. 071-581 0025. Popular with young Fulhamites, here you are surrounded by polo memorabilia. The cuisine includes seafood chowder, barbecued ribs, grills, crab cakes and several European-influenced dishes. *Open to 23.45, to 23.30 Sun.* A.Ax.Dc.V. **££**

### ❏ PJ's Grill                                           4 G3
30 Wellington St WC2. 071-240 7529. American-style grill restaurant offering dishes from all areas of the United States. Creole fish cakes, New Orleans seafood gumbo, jumbo shrimp piri piri, with pecan pie to follow. Good value pre-theatre menu (*Mon-Sat*) includes two courses and coffee. Lively and friendly staff. *Open 12.00-24.00.* A.Ax.Dc.V. Pre-theatre menu **£** A la carte **££**

### ❏ Rock Garden                                          4 F3
6-7 Covent Garden Piazza WC2. 071-240 3961. Ground and first floor restaurant with a relaxed and friendly atmosphere. Tuck in to rack of ribs, chef's salad, nachos, huge hamburgers and chocolate fudge cake. Live bands perform in the converted banana warehouse below. *Open to 24.00, to 01.00 Fri & Sat.* A.Ax.V. **££**

### Rock Island Diner                                      4 E3
2nd Floor, London Pavilion, Piccadilly Circus W1. 071-287 5500. Truly American 50s and 60s diner overlooking Eros with a 1954 Chevy above the bar. Dancing waiters and waitresses complete with bobby sox. Its own radio station, WRID, plays 50s and 60s hits. Grilled sandwiches, burgers, hot dogs, salads and chocolate brownies are the staples. Good range of beers and cocktails. *Open to 23.30, to 01.00 Fri & Sat, to 23.00 Sun.* A.Ax.Dc.V. **£**

### ❏ Smollensky's on the Strand                           4 F3
105 Strand WC2. 071-497 2101. Big, light and bustling restaurant offering grilled and barbecued steaks done seven different ways. Also lamb, chicken and vegetarian dishes. Rich desserts and cocktails. *Open to 24.00, to 01.00 Fri & Sat, to 22.30 Sun.* A.Ax.Dc.V. **££**

### Thank God It's Friday's
Large, loud and lively with an American-style bar. Superior burgers are the mainstay, but there's also chicken chimichanga and blackened Cajun chicken. *Open to 23.30, to 23.00 Sun.* A.Ax.V. **££**

6 Bedford St WC2. 071-379 0585                             **4 F3**
29 Coventry St W1. 071-839 6262.                           **4 E3**

# BRITISH

### Bozzies                                                   4 E2
17 Frith St W1. 071-437 3603. Basically an English restaurant, Bozzies boasts the largest range of regional English and continental sausages in London – twenty-one at the last count! All dishes are excellent value and served in a charming, friendly and relaxed atmosphere. *Open to 23.30. Closed Sun.* No credit cards. **£**

### Constant Grouse
825 Fulham Rd, Fulham SW6. 071-736 9429. A delightful place run by Australians! Deer-heads on the walls and exposed wooden beams are reminiscent of a traditional English pub. The set menu changes regularly with game a speciality when in season. Excellent service and good wine list. *Open to 23.00, to 23.30 Fri & Sat.* A.Ax.Dc.V. **££**

### English House                                              6 F2
3 Milner St SW3. 071-584 3002. Charming dining room with antique chairs and smart wall fabrics in the style of an English country house. Imaginative, traditional dishes such as chicken and almond salad with mango, casserole of wild mushrooms, apple and ginger pie. Specially selected wines. *Open to 23.30.* A.Ax.Dc.V. **£££+**

### Farringdon's                                               5 C2
41 Farringdon St EC4. 071-236 3663. Cosy and dark, dine 'underneath the arches' in the candlelit vaults of Holborn Viaduct. Queen Victoria opened them in 1869 and the place hasn't changed much since. Good traditional British cuisine includes beef Wellington, steak and kidney pie, venison and lobster. Cambridgeshire burnt cream is a calorific concoction well worth trying! *(Reserve) open to 23.00. Closed Sun.* A.Ax.Dc.V. **£££**

### Foxtrot Oscar                                              6 F4
79 Royal Hospital Rd SW3. 071-351 1667. Friendly restaurant well-liked by the locals. Chalked up on the blackboard are traditional British dishes such as smoked salmon, duck, steak and kidney pie, sausage 'n' mash. *Open to 23.30, to 22.30 Sun.* A.V. **££**

### The Greenhouse                                             4 C4
27a Hay's Mews W1. 071-499 3331. Comfortable atmosphere with lush green plants and overhead fans giving it a conservatory feel. Service is friendly and efficient. Simple English cooking enlivened by French and Italian flavours. Tender confit of duck on braised butter beans, grilled calf's liver with crispy bacon, creamed potatoes and onion gravy. Wonderful choice of traditional puddings. *Open to 22.45. Closed Sun eve.* A.Ax.Dc.V. **£££+**

### The Guinea                                                 4 C3
30 Bruton Place W1. 071-499 1210. Excellent range of steaks in an informal pub/restaurant atmosphere. Popular with businessmen savouring 12oz rumps, sirloins and fillets or the award-winning steak and kidney pie. Long, reasonably priced wine list and efficient service. *Open to 23.00. Closed Sun.* A.Ax.Dc.V. **£££**

### The Lexington                                              4 D3
45 Lexington St W1. 071-434 3401. This is a smart, simple restaurant, lined with high, dark green leather banquettes. The menu changes

twice a day and offers delights such as warm pigeon and parsnip soup; wild mushroom risotto with shaved parmesan; roast haunch of hare with savoy cabbage and creamed potatoes. *Open to 23.30. Closed Sun.* A.Ax.V. **£££**

**◖ Lindsay House**                                        **4 E2**
21 Romilly St W1. 071-439 0450. You must ring the doorbell of this 17thC town house to gain entry, but don't be put off – the staff are pleasant and efficient and the decor is elegant with rich draperies and traditional paintings. Superb cuisine – choose from carrot and orange soup, rack of lamb, calf's liver, strawberry charlotte and syllabub. Extensive wine list. *(Reserve) open to 24.00, to 22.00 Sun.* A.Ax.Dc.V. **£££+**

**Maggie Jones**                                           **3 B4**
6 Old Court Place, off Kensington Church St W8. 071-937 6462. Tiny, neat and pleasant with scrubbed pine tables and a country atmosphere. Home-made soups and pâtés and hearty portions of plain English cooking – fish pie and boiled beef and dumplings – are accompanied by robust, fresh vegetables. Apple crumble and treacle tart to follow. Friendly and jolly. *(Reserve) open to 23.30, to 23.00 Sun.* A.Ax.Dc.V. **£££**

**▢ Plummers**                                             **4 F3**
33 King St WC2. 071-240 2534. An Edwardian-style dining room with jazz playing in the background. Delicious lamb hotpot, steak and kidney pie, and tender lamb steaks. Set pre-theatre menu. *Open 17.30-23.30. Closed Sun.* A.Ax.Dc.V. **££**

**▢ Porters**                                              **4 F3**
17 Henrietta St WC2. 071-836 6466. A large, pillared dining room in which to sample good value, filling English pies – lamb and apricot, turkey and chestnut, traditional fish pie. Stilton or bread and butter pudding to follow. The perfect accompaniment to a night in one of London's traditional theatres. *Open 12.00-23.30.* A.V. **££**

**◖ Quality Chop House**                                   **2 D6**
94 Farringdon Rd EC1. 071-837 5093. A Victorian dining room housed in a building dating to 1869. Lively and usually crowded, here you can sample well-prepared traditional dishes – steaks, sausages, calf's liver with mashed potato and perfect vegetables. Bread and butter pudding or strawberries and cream to follow, depending on the season. *Open to 24.00, to 23.30 Sun.* No credit cards. **££**

**◖ Rules**                                                **4 F3**
35 Maiden Lane WC2. 071-836 5314. Rich in associations – Dickens, Thackeray, Edward VII and Lillie Langtry all dined here. Plush velvet seats and an atmosphere of British decorum are the backdrop for their speciality of game; they also have traditional dishes of jugged hare, pies and roast beef, or more inventive recipes such as smoked pheasant and apricots. *(Reserve) open to 24.00. Closed Sun.* A.Ax.Dc.V. **£££**

**▢ The Savoy Grill**                                      **4 G3**
The Savoy Hotel, Strand WC2. 071-836 4343. Elegant wood-panelled dining room serving traditional British dishes such as steak and kidney pie and breast of guinea fowl. Friendly waiters and excellent old-fashioned service. Pre-theatre menu. *Open 18.00-23.15. Closed Sun.* A.Ax.Dc.V. **£££+**

### Simpson's-in-the-Strand 4 F3
100 Strand WC2. 071-836 9112. An English institution with the atmosphere of an Edwardian club. Excellent fish and meat dishes – smoked salmon, dover sole, duck or saddle of mutton. Mouth-watering treacle roll, spotted dick to follow. Fine wines and vintage port. Correct dress essential. *(Reserve) open to 23.00. Closed Sun.* A.Ax.Dc.V. **£££**

### Tiddy Dols 4 C4
55 Shepherd Market W1. 071-499 2357. A unique, comfortable restaurant rambling over eight mid-18thC houses with low ceilings and winding staircases. Traditional fare includes pheasant pâté, beef Wellington, cock-a-leekie, and the original gingerbread Tiddy Dol. Entertainment comes in the form of a resident pianist, wandering minstrel and Mayfair town-crier. *(Reserve) open to 23.30.* A.Ax.V. **£££**

### ◖ Veronica's 3 B2
3 Hereford Rd W2. 071-229 5079. A small, unpretentious spot run by the eponymous Veronica Shaw. The menu concentrates on nationwide recipes from medieval to modern cuisine and may include mushrooms marinated in claret, 'duck 'n' spinage', guinea fowl in port, followed by excellent Stilton and unusual puddings. *(Reserve) open to 24.00. Closed Sun.* A.Ax.Dc.V. **£££**

### Waltons 6 E2
121 Walton St SW3. 071-584 0204. Unusual decor predominates here, accompanied by excellent traditional British and international dishes. Follow up seafood sausage with fillet of Dover sole then strawberry pavlova. The menus change frequently and there are good-value set menus. Smooth service and a notable wine list. *(Reserve) open to 23.30, to 22.00 Sun.* A.Ax.Dc.V. **£££+**

## CENTRAL EUROPEAN (Austrian, German, Swiss)

### Kerzenstüberl 4 B2
9 St Christopher's Place, off Marylebone Lane W1. 071-486 3196. Authentic, hearty Austrian food with dishes such as Leberknödel soup, Bauernschmaus, Goulasch, Sacher Torte, Apfelstrudel. Lively accordion music, dancing and singing, and you can drink until 01.00. *Open to 23.00. Closed Sun.* A.Ax.Dc.V. **££**

### ▣ Marché 4 E3
Swiss Centre, 1 Swiss Court (off Leicester Sq) WC2. 071-434 1791. An imaginative serve-yourself restaurant with Swiss hot and cold buffets. Everything is made to order – grills, fresh vegetables, salads, raclette, fondues, ice-cream and home-made breads. Pleasant, relaxed atmosphere. *Open 11.00-24.00 Mon-Sat, 10.30-22.30 Sun.* A.Ax.Dc.V. **££**

### ◖ Old Vienna Budapest 4 C3
94 New Bond St W1. 071-629 8716. Lavishly decorated Austrian restaurant with a small dancefloor and an accordionist and singer. Specialities from Hungary and Austria include sweet and sour herring, roast pork with dumplings, veal goulash. *Open to 01.00, to 22.30 Sun.* A.Ax.Dc.V. **££**

**St Moritz**  4 E3
161 Wardour St W1. 071-734 3324. Typical Swiss decor, kitted out like a ski hut in the famous resort. Cheese and beef fondues are the house speciality. Also try smoked trout with horseradish, veal with rosemary and rösti. Swiss chocolates accompany the coffee. There's a nightclub downstairs *open every night. Open to 23.30. Closed Sun.* A.Ax.Dc.V. **££**

**Tiroler Hut**  3 C2
27 Westbourne Grove W2. 071-727 3981. Very lively with traditional German entertainment – yodellers, accordion players, cowbell shows and plenty of diner participation in the singing. Good, hearty fare includes Bauernschmaus with Schnaps, roast pork, Sauerkraut and dumplings. *Open to 00.30, to 23.30 Sun.* A.Ax.V. **££**

## CHINESE

For an abundance of Chinese restaurants head for Chinatown, and in particular Gerrard Street (**4 E3**). The following is a selection throughout London:

**◖ Canton**  4 E3
1 Newport Place WC2. 071-437 6220. Good Cantonese food, served with briskness. *Open to 00.45, to 01.45 Fri & Sat.* A.V. **£**

**China Jazz**  1 D2
29-31 Parkway NW1. 071-482 3940. Light and spacious restaurant with delicacies such as pickled Chinese cabbage and hand-made Peking noodles. Live music every night ensures a lively, noisy atmosphere. *Open to 23.30, to 23.00 Sun.* A.V. **£££**

**◖ Chuen Cheng Ku**  4 E3
17 Wardour St W1. 071-437 1398. Friendly and well patronised by Chinese customers. Cantonese cooking and large portions of delicious fish dishes such as whole bass in ginger, shrimp and marinated prawns, as well as interestingly named dishes such as duck's feet with fish lips. *Open to 24.00, to 23.15 Sun.* A.Ax.Dc.V. **£**

**Dragon Gate**  4 E3
7 Gerrard St W1. 071-734 5154. The first restaurant to bring hot, spicy Szechuan cuisine to London's Chinatown, and still the best at it. Three floors of bizarre Swiss-oriental decor are the background for sliced pork with garlic and chilli, tea-smoked duck. Pancakes or almond curd to follow. *Open to 23.30.* A.Ax.Dc.V. **££**

**Good Earth**  6 E3
91 King's Rd SW3. 071-352 9231. Old-fashioned decor and courteous service at this predominantly Cantonese restaurant. There are two menus, one with no meat dishes and the other a haven for omnivores – both are excellent value. Other branches. *Open to 23.30, to 22.30 Sun.* A.Ax.Dc.V. **££**

**Ken Lo's Memories of China**  7 A2
67 Ebury St SW1. 071-730 7734. Windows etched with Tang dynasty horses illuminate the interior and the menu features regional specialities – Shanghai sea bass, Szechuan crispy beef and Cantonese

*Chinatown*

seafood with black bean sauce. *Open to 23.00. Closed Sun.* A.Ax.Dc.V. **£££+**

**Lee Ho Fook**                                                       **4 E3**
15 Gerrard St W1. 071-734 9578. Renowned Cantonese cooking, very popular with the local Chinese. Huge portions at reasonable prices – shrimp in black bean sauce, duck stew with abalone, suckling pig, lobster. *Open to 23.30, to 22.30 Sun.* A.Ax.Dc.V. **£**

**Ley-On's**                                                          **4 E3**
56 Wardour St W1. 071-437 6565. Long-established Cantonese restaurant and a popular place with the regulars. Large and airy (the basement used to be a Chinese cinema), the service is friendly and the food well above standard. Try stuffed aubergine, crispy wun tun or steamed eel with black bean sauce. *Open to 23.30.* A.Ax.Dc.V. **£££**

**Ming**                                                              **4 E2**
35 Greek St W1. 071-734 2721. Innovative cuisine combines with pleasant, soothing decor for a memorable evening. Try lamb ta tsai mi, various fish dishes, Chinese-style ratatouille. Friendly service. *Open to 23.45. Closed Sun.* A.Ax.Dc.V. **££**

**Mr Chow**                                                           **3 F5**
151 Knightsbridge SW1. 071-589 7347. Very much on the see and be seen scene. Celebrities sit upstairs. Authentic Beijing and classic food – velvet chicken and Mr Chow's noodles with red meat sauce. *Open to 23.45.* A.Ax.Dc.V. **£££**

**Mr Kai of Mayfair**                                                 **4 B4**
65 South Audley St W1. 071-493 8988. A modern, stylish Chinese restaurant with simple decor and creative cuisine such as Peking

duck, chilli beef in bird's nest. Efficient and pleasant service. *Open to 23.30*. A.Ax.Dc.V. **£££+**

**◖ Mr Kong**                                                            **4 E3**
21 Lisle St W1. 071-437 7341. One of the best Chinese restaurants in London, renowned for its seafood and unusual dishes. *Open to 01.45, to 24.00 Sun*. A.V. **££**

**Now & Zen**                                                            **4 F3**
4a Upper St Martin's Lane WC2. 071-497 0376. You walk over a thick, glass gangplank to enter this restaurant, one of the Zen chain. Stylish, unusual decor and a modern menu. Beef in spicy coconut milk, chicken with walnuts and chilli. Efficient service. *(Reserve) open to 23.30, to 23.00 Sun*. A.Ax.Dc.V. **£££+**

**Pearl of Knightsbridge**                                               **3 G5**
22 Brompton Rd SW1. 071-225 3888. Simple, modern decor and a calm, luxurious atmosphere in which to sample well-prepared and unusual dishes such as drunken chicken with jellyfish, Shanghai bean and minced pork, noodles with sesame seeds. Efficient service and good value set menus. *Open to 23.30*. A.Ax.Dc.V. **££**

**Poons**
Wind-dried meats and sausages are the speciality at this unpretentious family-run chain of restaurants. The Lisle Street branch was the original one and is unlicensed (no corkage charge). The extensive menus also include good seafood and vegetable dishes. *Open to 23.30. Closed Sun*. No credit cards. **££**
4 Leicester St WC2. 071-437 1528.                                        **4 E3**
27 Lisle St WC2. 071-437 4549.                                           **4 E3**

**The Tank**                                                             **5 C1**
57 Charterhouse St EC1. 071-251 4129. A wine bar and restaurant decked out like an aquarium. Specialities include Szechuan and Peking-style cooking – try lamb and cucumber soup, drunken fish in rice wine. Good value set menus and charming service. Exotic snacks also available to accompany a tipple in the wine bar. *Open to 23.30. Closed Sat & Sun*. A.Ax.Dc.V. **££**

**▣ Wong Kei**                                                           **4 E3**
41 Wardour St W1. 071-437 8408. Large, cheap and cheerful Cantonese restaurant. Don't be put off by the attitude of the staff – they are abrupt with everyone and do not seem programmed to answer questions! Expect to share a table. Singapore fried noodles have a fame of their own here. Free Chinese tea. *Open 12.00-23.30*. No credit cards or cheques. **£**

**Zen Central**                                                          **4 C4**
20 Queen St W1. 071-629 8089. Located in Mayfair, this is the smartest of the Zen chain. Large, carefully-prepared menu. *(Reserve) open to 23.00*. A.Ax.Dc.V. **£££+**

## EAST EUROPEAN (Russian, Hungarian, Polish)

**◖ Borshtch 'n' Tears**                                                 **3 G6**
46 Beauchamp Place SW3. 071-589 5003. Crowded, informal and lively with a party atmosphere, popular with young people. Large portions of borshtch, beef Stroganoff, chicken Dragomiroff and

blinis served with Russian vodkas to the accompaniment of live Russian music. *Open to 01.15, to 00.15 Sun.* Ax. **££**

**Daquise**     **6 D2**
20 Thurloe St SW7. 071-589 6117. Good, authentic Polish fare popular with Polish émigrés and British alike. Simple and inexpensive dishes such as borshtch, bigos, kratsky, and sausages. *Open to 23.30.* No credit cards. **££**

**Gay Hussar**     **4 E2**
2 Greek St W1. 071-437 0973. Old-fashioned, wood-panelled rooms in which to sample wild cherry soup, stuffed cabbage, pike with beetroot sauce. Hungarian wines. Sophisticated clientele. *Open to 23.00. Closed Sun.* Ax. **££**

**Kaspia**     **4 C3**
18 Bruton Place W1. 071-493 2612. In comfortable, plush surroundings behind a caviar shop, this restaurant serves only fish and caviar. Three set-price menus include the Sanka, Troika and Trois Caviars, and there are other specialities of smoked salmon, blinis and quails' eggs. Russian and Polish vodkas and champagnes. *(Reserve) open to 23.30. Closed Sun.* A.Ax.Dc.V. **£££+**

**(( Luba's Bistro**     **3 F6**
6 Yeoman's Row SW3. 071-589 2950. Authentic Russian cooking in down-to-earth surroundings. Excellent value. Try kooliebaiaka (salmon pie), zrazra (chicken with vegetables), golubtzy, pojarsky and sanric for dessert. Unlicensed so bring your own wine (no corkage charge). *Open to 24.00. Closed Sun.* A.V. **££**

**(( Otchi**     **3 G1**
43 Crawford St W1. 071-724 8228. The decor evokes Russia before the revolution in this relaxed basement restaurant. Pirozki, caviar, shashlik, meat balls, chicken Kiev are the staples. Set menus available. Live gypsy music every night. *Open to 24.00.* A.Ax.Dc.V. **££**

## FISH

**Bentley's**     **4 D3**
11-15 Swallow St W1. 071-734 4756. Founded in 1916 and unchanged for over half a century, Bentley's is the only restaurant to have its own oyster bed. Offers a wide variety of excellent fish dishes, plus oysters, prawns and crab. *(Reserve) open to 22.45. Closed Sun.* A.Ax.Dc.V. **£££+**

**🖾 Café Fish**     **4 E3**
39 Panton St, off Haymarket W1. 071-930 3999. Pleasant and informal with blackboard menus listing a wide selection of fish which you can have shallow fried, deep fried, charcoal grilled or steamed. Cover charge includes hot pâté and French bread. Good cheese board and wine list. Snacks, oysters and mussels available in the wine bar downstairs. *Open 17.30-23.30. Closed Sun.* A.Ax.Dc.V. **££**

**La Croisette**     **6 B4**
168 Ifield Rd SW10. 071-373 3694. Ingeniously lit basement restaurant, packed with fashionable people. Fresh fish including monkfish, turbot and cod and the largest seafood platter you have ever seen. Good range of cheeses and desserts to follow. Efficient, friendly Gallic service. *Open to 23.30. Closed Mon.* A.Ax.Dc.V. **£££**

**La Gaulette** **1 E6**
53 Cleveland St W1. 071-580 7608. Delightful and friendly restaurant specialising in tropical fish prepared Mauritian style with some Chinese influences. Try vara vara with aubergine, halibut in champagne, turbot mistral. Set menus available. Wine bar. *Open to 23.30. Closed Sun.* A.Ax.Dc.V. **£££**

**Green's Restaurant & Oyster Bar** **7 D1**
Marsham Court, off Marsham St SW1. 071-834 9552. Traditional English-style restaurant and an excellent oyster bar. A good place for politician spotting as it is a favourite with those in the nearby Houses

of Parliament. Try smoked eel with horseradish, smoked salmon with blinis, dressed crab. Efficient service and a good wine list. *Open to 23.00, to 22.30 Sun. Closed Sat.* Restaurant **£££** Oyster Bar **££**

**L'Hippocampe** 4 E2

63 Frith St W1. 071-734 4545. The name is French for seahorse (although you won't find them on the menu!). Soothing decor with a frieze of undulating waves is the background for a variety of fresh fish presented in imaginative ways – seafood ravioli, langoustine wrapped in Parma ham, and their legendary bouillabaisse. Service is charming. *Open to 23.30. Closed Sun.* A.Ax.Dc.V. **£££**

**Lucullus** 3 F5

48 Knightsbridge SW1. 071-245 6622. A superb array of fresh fish greets you on your entrance to this elegant restaurant. Your choice of lobster, crab, langoustine, monkfish, turbot, sea bass, red mullet (the list is endless!) can be prepared in a variety of ways. Gourmet specials include salmon stuffed with broccoli mousse in filo pastry with champagne sauce. *Open to 23.30.* A.Ax.Dc.V. **£££**

**Manzi's** 4 E3

1 Leicester St WC2. 071-734 0224. Perennially popular, old-fashioned and somewhat regal restaurant now run by the fourth generation of the Manzi family. They offer a wide range of fish and shellfish as well as simpler dishes such as salmon or turbot, grilled or poached. Service is bustling and erratic. *(Reserve) open to 23.30, to 22.30 Sun.* A.Ax.Dc.V. **£££**

**Sheekey's** 4 F3

28 St Martin's Court WC2. 071-240 2565. Established in 1898, this is one of London's oldest fish restaurants. Has a grand reputation for excellent oysters, lobster and turbot. Also more unusual dishes such as finnan haddock and spinach pie, fish cakes with lobster sauce. Situated in the heart of theatreland, it's ideal for after-theatre suppers. *Open to 23.15. Closed Sun.* A.Ax.Dc.V. **£££**

**Wheeler's**

A well-known chain dating back over 100 years to the fish shop in Old

*Sheekey's fish restaurant*

Compton Street which today is one of the many London branches. Although each restaurant has its own character, there are certain similarities: green painted exteriors, leaded windows, panelling and plush surroundings. Many have an oyster bar and all offer a range of well-prepared fresh fish and shellfish including oysters, mussels, scallops, smoked salmon, smoked eel, plaice, turbot, crab and salmon. Specialities include lobster and sole. Service is cheerful and the restaurants inspire a loyal following. We list several branches below. In general the restaurants are *open to 23.00. Closing days vary.* A.Ax.Dc.V. **£££**

**Alcove**                                                        3 B6
17 Kensington High St W8. 071-937 1443.
**Carafe**                                                        6 F1
15 Lowndes St SW1. 071-235 2525.
**Vendome**                                                       4 C3
20 Dover St W1. 071-629 5417.
**Wheeler's St James's**                                          4 D4
12a Duke of York St SW1. 071-930 2460.
**Wheeler's Old Compton Street**                                  4 E2
19 Old Compton St W1. 071-437 2706.

# FRENCH

**The Ark**                                                       3 C4
122 Palace Gardens Terrace W8. 071-229 4024. Cosy and friendly atmosphere with good provincial French food in surroundings reminiscent of a ramshackle Swiss chalet. Menu changes daily and may include soupe à l'oignon, moules marinières, wild rabbit, fruits de mer, crème brûlée. *(Reserve) open to 23.15.* A.Ax.V. **££**
**L'Artiste Assoiffe**                                            3 A3
122 Kensington Park Rd W8. 071-727 4714. Authentic French food in what looks like a private house. Perennial favourite of celebrities and Portobello Road Market traders who come to sample filet Dijon, entrecôte au poivre, foie de veau de gourmets. Genial service. *(Reserve) open to 23.00. Closed Sun.* A.Ax.Dc.V. **££**
**Le Bistingo**                                                   4 E2
57 Old Compton St W1. 071-437 0784. Excellent value bistro serving French and Italian provincial cooking in a relaxed atmosphere. The blackboard menu usually includes fresh pasta, scampi, mussels, steak au poivre. Follow with crêpes, bananes au rhum. Set menus are particularly good value. *Open to 23.30. Closed Sun.* A.Ax.Dc.V. **££**
**Boulestin**                                                     4 F3
The Garden Entrance, 1a Henrietta St WC2. 071-836 7061. Splendid restaurant opened in the 1920s. Luxurious club-like atmosphere heralds a menu offering sumptuous dishes such as crabe à l'artichaut, balottine de turbot farcie au homard, tulipe de sorbets. Fine wines and dignified service. *Open to 23.15. Closed Sun.* A.Ax.Dc.V. **£££+**
◖ **La Brasserie**                                                6 E2
272 Brompton Rd SW3. 071-584 1668. Probably one of the closest things to a real French brasserie in London. Always very busy but the long-aproned waiters are very efficient. Menu includes onion soup

and boeuf bourguignon, and the wine list is exclusively French. *Open to 24.00.* A.Ax.Dc.V. **££**

### ☐ Café des Amis du Vin                    4 F2
11 Hanover Place, off Long Acre WC2. 071-379 3444. Very popular, lively spot with a wine bar in the basement, café on the ground floor and the restaurant on the first floor. An intimate atmosphere in which to enjoy first-class regional French cuisine such as chicken with shallots, ragoût of seafood. Set pre-theatre menu. *Open 18.00-23.30. Closed Sun.* A.Ax.Dc.V. **££**

### ☐ Café Flo                    4 F3
51 St Martin's Lane WC2. 071-836 8289. Charming and friendly chain of French-style brasseries offering a variety of reasonably priced set menus. Very close to theatres in St Martin's Lane and Shaftesbury Avenue. *Open 09.00-23.30 Mon-Sat, 08.30-22.30 Sun.* A.Ax.Dc.V. **£-££**

### ☐ Café du Jardin                    4 G3
25 Wellington St WC2. 071-836 8769. Spruce café with a large basement dining room offering Mediterranean-style cuisine. The à la carte menu includes cous-cous, moules marinières, salade niçoise. The pre-theatre menu includes two courses and unlimited coffee. *Open 17.30-23.30, to 22.30 Sun.* A.Ax.Dc.V. Pre-theatre menu **£** A la carte **££**

### The Capital                    3 G5
The Capital Hotel, 22 Basil St SW3. 071-589 5171. Classic French cuisine in a softly lit, gracious atmosphere. Feather-light quenelles, duck ballotine with rillettes, tarte tatin, carré d'agneau persille. Excellent selection of clarets. Set price and à la carte menus. *(Reserve) open to 23.00.* A.Ax.Dc.V. **£££+**

### Chez Nico                    4 C1
35 Great Portland St W1. 071-436 8846. Classic, rich French cuisine prepared by the eminently skilful hands of famous chef Nico Ladenis. Sea bass à la provençale, scallops and game dishes are his specialities. Efficient Gallic service and charming surroundings. Expensive wine list. *(Reserve) open to 23.00. Closed Sat & Sun.* A.Dc.V. **£££+**

### The Connaught                    4 B3
The Connaught Hotel, Carlos Place, off Mount St W1. 071-499 7070. Known as one of the grandest hotel dining rooms in the world. Old-fashioned panelling, mirrors and chandeliers are the setting for the famous Connaught terrine, oeufs de cailles Maintenon, langoustines and excellent game. Impeccable food, fine wines and a formal atmosphere with service by tail-coated waiters. Jacket and tie must be worn. Attracts the famous and well-connected. *(Reserve) open to 22.15.* A.V. **£££+**

### Daphne's                    6 E2
112 Draycott Ave SW3. 071-589 4257. Classical menu with international influences results in lobster thermidor, rack of lamb with herbs, poulet fumé, good grills, fish and game. Follow with the excellent cheeseboard or the Grand Marnier soufflé. Pleasant, airy surroundings with lots of plants and friendly service. *(Reserve) open to 23.30. Closed Sun.* A.Ax.Dc.V. **£££**

### ☐ L'Epicure                    4 E2
28 Frith St W1. 071-437 2829. Famous for its flambeaux, and some-

thing of a Soho institution. First-class cuisine, with excellent flambéd dishes including châteaubriand, crêpes de volaille, crêpes Suzette to follow. Pre-theatre set menu. *(Reserve) open 18.00-23.15. Closed Sun.* A.Ax.Dc.V. **£££**

**L'Escargot**                                                           **4 E2**
48 Greek St W1. 071-437 6828. A secluded dining room upstairs and a brasserie on the ground floor. First-class cuisine from a frequently changing menu with unusual dishes such as grilled peppers with anchovies, calf's liver with sage. Snail-shaped chocolates accompany the coffee! Excellent wine list and efficient service. *(Reserve) open to 23.15. Closed Sun.* A.Ax.Dc.V. Restaurant **£££** Brasserie **££**

**L'Escargot Doré**                                                     **3 C5**
2 Thackeray St W8. 071-937 8508. Whitewashed walls, tiled floor and potted plants provide a relaxed, informal atmosphere in which to sample a typically French menu – magret of duck with honey, escargots in garlic butter. Oyster bar in the basement. Good value set menus. Extensive range of wines. *Open to 23.30. Closed Sun.* A.Ax.Dc.V. **££**

**Frederick's**                                                         **2 D2**
106 Camden Passage N1. 071-359 2888. Choice of surroundings at this well-established restaurant – the airy white-walled conservatory at the back or, for more intimate soirees, the candle-lit tables at the front. Innovative menu – veal medallion with crab, chicken sausage with pistachios. Good value set menus. *(Reserve) open to 23.30. Closed Sun.* A.Ax.Dc.V. **£££**

**Le Gavroche**                                                         **4 B3**
43 Upper Brook St W1. 071-408 0881. Run by the famous duo Albert and Michel Roux and renowned for faultless, imaginative haute cuisine and a luxurious atmosphere. Papillotes de saumon fumé Claudine, tournedos vigneronne, soufflé Suissesse, daube de boeuf, excellent patisseries and superb cheeseboard are presented with polished, courteous service. Magnificent wine list – regrettably rather highly priced. A favourite with politicians and royalty. *(Reserve) open to 23.00. Closed Sun.* A.Ax.Dc.V. **£££+**

**Le Gothique**
The Royal Victoria Patriotic Building, Fitzhugh Grove, Trinity Rd, Wandsworth SW18. 081-870 6567. Housed in what was once an orphanage, a hospital and a home to the secret services, the walls of this restaurant are covered with historical photographs. Carefully prepared cuisine – snails with garlic mushrooms, gigot d'agneau, and exquisite chocolate mousse to follow.. *Open to 22.30. Closed Sun.* A.Ax.Dc.V. **£££**

**Harvey's**
2 Bellevue Rd, Wandsworth SW17. 081-672 0114. A south London restaurant with an excellent reputation. The chef, Marco Pierre White, has a huge following and his classic French cuisine is simple and adventurous. Tagliatelle of oysters, red mullet with truffle oil, roasted Bresse pigeon with thyme, terrine of fresh fruit. Good selection of French wines. *(Reserve) open to 23.00. Closed Sun & Mon.* A.V. **£££+**

**Au Jardin des Gourmets**                                              **4 E2**
5 Greek St W1. 071-437 1816. Famous for many years for its cellar which still harbours old and rare clarets (and is now climate-con-

trolled!). Ambitious menu in elegant surroundings; warm scallops on potato salad, sauté du foie gras, tournedos, sautéed sweetbreads in puff pastry. Very good cheeseboard. *(Reserve) open to 23.15. Closed Sun.* A.Ax.Dc.V. **£££**

**Langan's Bistro**     **4 C1**
26 Devonshire St W1. 071-935 4531. The first restaurant of the late, legendary Peter Langan. Original Hockneys and Prockters decorate the walls, while Japanese parasols open above your head. Mussel salad, lamb cutlets with piquant sauce, sauté of chicken with avocado, and Mrs Langan's renowned chocolate pudding to follow. Efficient service. *(Reserve) open to 23.30. Closed Sun.* A.Ax.Dc.V. **££**

**Langan's Brasserie**     **4 C4**
Stratton House, Stratton St W1. 071-493 6437. Opened by Peter Langan and Michael Caine – a vast L-shaped room with a buzzing atmosphere and stylish surroundings carefully contrived to impart decaying splendour. Still a fashionable place to be seen in. Changing menu may include oyster mushrooms, spinach soufflé with anchovies, black pudding. Live music *every night. (Reserve) open to 23.00,* to 24.00 *Sat. Closed Sun.* A.Ax.Dc.V. **£££+**

**◻ Magno's Brasserie**     **4 F3**
65a Long Acre WC2. 071-836 6077. Very slick, French establishment situated close to several theatres. Various dishes from the à la carte menu, such as poached chicken and spinach or fillet of pork with prunes, are included on the excellent value pre-theatre set menu, which includes two courses and coffee. Friendly Gallic service. *Open 17.30-23.30. Closed Sun.* A.Ax.Dc.V. Pre-theatre menu **£** Restaurant **£££**

**Ninety Park Lane**     **4 B3**
Grosvenor House Hotel, Park Lane W1. 071-409 1290. Pleasant surroundings in which to enjoy superb haute cuisine favouring Oriental-influenced dishes such as langoustines poached in Thai spices. Also more traditional dishes such as pan-fried foie gras, saddle of rabbit. Exhaustive (and expensive) wine list and very efficient service. Frequented by royalty and film stars. *Open to 22.45. Closed Sun.* A.Ax.Dc.V. **£££+**

**One Ninety Queen's Gate**     **3 D6**
190 Queen's Gate SW7. 071-581 5666. Run by Antony Worrall-Thompson, famous for his impeccable, inventive cuisine. Predominantly fish; try the crumbly crab and corn fish cakes or the saffron and mussel risotto. Mediterranean-style meat dishes too. Interesting and reasonably priced wine list. Less formal **Bistrot 190** next door (see under *Modern European). Open to 23.30. Closed Sun.* A.Ax.Dc.V. **£££+**

**La Poule au Pot**     **7 A2**
231 Ebury St SW1. 071-730 7763. Cheerful and crowded with a country kitchen style – brass and copper saucepans hang from the walls. Robust, provincial cooking such as ratatouille, beef bourguignon, gigot of lamb, coq au vin, crème brûlée, tarte aux pommes. Genial service. *Open to 23.15. Closed Sun.* A.Ax.Dc.V. **£££**

**◖◖ Le Renoir**     **4 E3**
79 Charing Cross Rd WC2. 071-734 2515. Friendly, efficient and right in the heart of theatreland. The menu is arranged in price

brackets so all starters cost the same, as do main courses and desserts. Good French cooking includes grilled trout, grilled duck, steak frites and some simpler dishes such as croque-monsieur and omelettes. *Open 11.30-01.00.* A.Ax.Dc.V. **££**

**Rue St Jacques**                                              **4 D1**
5 Charlotte St W1. 071-637 0222. A plush, elegant restaurant popular with media folk. Complex combinations and unusual ingredients result in delights such as roast monkfish with lentils, terrine of crab meat in lobster sauce, superb game dishes and passion fruit soufflé. Polished service. *(Reserve) open to 23.00. Closed Sun.* A.Ax.Dc.V. **£££+**

**La Tante Claire**                                            **6 F4**
68 Royal Hospital Rd SW3. 071-352 6045. Highly-regarded and beautiful restaurant offering innovative, perfectly executed French cuisine. Pig's trotters stuffed with sweetbreads are chef Pierre Koffman's speciality, or try filet d'agneau en papillotte, filet of venison in bitter chocolate. The tarte tatin is legendary. *(Reserve) open to 23.00. Closed Sat & Sun.* A.Ax.Dc.V. **£££+**

**Thierry's**                                                  **6 D4**
342 King's Rd SW3. 071-352 3365. Popular bistro with classic dishes such as cassoulet, moules, saddle of hare, fish soup with rouille, soufflé au fromage. Pleasant atmosphere and helpful staff. *(Reserve) open to 23.00, to 22.30 Sun.* A.Ax.Dc.V. **£££**

## GREEK, TURKISH AND CYPRIOT

**Beotys**                                                     **4 F3**
79 St Martin's Lane WC2. 071-836 8768. An old-fashioned atmosphere like a Victorian dining room. Stuffed vine leaves, kalamarakia, moussaka, baklava and kadeifi. International wine list. Perfect for after-theatre dining. *Open to 23.30. Closed Sun.* A.Ax.Dc.V. **££**

**⟨⟨ Four Lanterns**                                           **1 E6**
96 Cleveland St W1. 071-387 0704. Friendly, traditional restaurant serving exceptionally good grilled fish, meats and kebabs. Also unusual meze dishes, fresh salads and a varied selection of wines and retsina. *Open to 24.00. Closed Sun.* A.Ax.Dc.V. **££**

**⟨⟨ Hellas**                                                  **1 E2**
158 Royal College St NW1. 071-485 8386. Traditional fare in this excellent restaurant. Unusually wide choice of vegetarian meze, with interesting, immaculately presented dishes such as spinach with rice, vegetarian meatballs, Greek salad and houmous. Congenial service and atmosphere. *Open to 24.00. Closed Sun.* A.Ax.Dc.V. **££**

**⟨⟨ Mega Kalamaras**                                          **3 C3**
76-78 Inverness Mews, off Inverness Place W2. 071-727 9122. Also **Micro Kalamaras** 66 Inverness Mews W2. 071-727 5082. Two relaxed and informal restaurants sharing the same kitchen. **Micro** is smaller, less expensive and unlicensed (with no charge for corkage). **Mega** is larger, has a more mellow atmosphere and a more extensive menu. Superb national dishes such as spanakotyropitas (paper thin pastry with spinach and cheese) and tsirosalata (smoked strips of salted fish) are combined with more inventive choices such as arti-

choke hearts with broad beans, okra with leeks. Pleasant, unhurried service in both restaurants. **Mega** *open to 24.00. Closed Sun.* **Micro** *open to 23.30. Closed Sun.* A.Ax.Dc.V. **££**

**Psistaria**                                                                4 D6
82 Wilton Rd SW1. 071-821 7504. Excellent food, good service and a pleasant, calm atmosphere in light, airy surroundings (quite a rarity for a Greek restaurant!). Psistaria means 'grill', and grilled meat and fish are the specialities. Try monkfish kebab, game (when in season) and the impressive dessert trolley. *Open to 23.30. Closed Sun.* A.Dc.V. **££**

**◖ Venus Steak House**
366-368 Bethnal Green Rd, Bethnal Green E2. 071-739 2650. Traditional East End steak house serving up good char-grilled steaks to loyal customers. As much a social experience as a meal. *Open to 00.30, to 01.30 Sat.* A.Ax.Dc.V. **££**

**◖ Village Taverna**                                                        6 C4
198 Fulham Rd SW10. 071-351 3799. Family-run, popular local restaurant relying on good, traditional cooking in a relaxed and friendly atmosphere. Try kleftiko, Greek salad, calamares, washed down with good value wines. A great spot to head for after a visit to the MGM cinema nearby. *Open to 01.00.* A.Ax.Dc.V. **££**

**White Tower**                                                              4 E1
1 Percy St W1. 071-636 8141. Founded in 1938, this is the oldest Greek restaurant in London. Still exudes an old-fashioned, refined atmosphere which is reflected in the service. The cuisine is Greek-based but with Middle Eastern influences and there's a lot to choose from – feathery light taramasalata, chicken liver pâté, chicken pilaff, stuffed courgettes, shashlik, duck with bulgur. *Open to 22.30. Closed Sun.* A.Ax.Dc.V. **£££**

# INDIAN

There are many Indian restaurants in London and its suburbs, too many to list here. Below are those that offer more unusual dishes and/or good value for money:

**Bombay Bicycle Club**
95 Nightingale Lane, Balham SW12. 081-673 6217. A charming restaurant serving unusual dishes with mild, subtle flavours. Try lamb with butter, onion and tomatoes, or fish in light, spicy batter. *Open to 23.30. Closed Sun.* A.Ax.Dc.V. **££**

**◖ Bombay Brasserie**                                                       6 C2
Bailey's Hotel, Courtfield Close, Courtfield Rd SW7. 071-370 4040. Regarded by many as the best Indian restaurant in London, this is a fashionable venue in colonial style with a pianist to entertain. Ceiling fans and potted palms are the background for first-class regional cuisine, including Bombay thali, chicken dhansak, Goan fish curry. *Open to 24.00.* A.Dc.V. **£££**

**Chutney Mary**                                                             6 C5
535 King's Rd SW10. 071-351 3113. London's first Anglo-Indian restaurant where chefs from different regions recreate the dishes

from colonial days amid colonial decor – wicker chairs, ceiling fans and palms. Curried mango soup, lamb patties with chutney, Bombay bangers, bread and butter pudding and mango ice-cream. Accompany the meal in the traditional manner, with Madeira. *(Reserve) open to 23.30, to 22.00 Sun.* A.Ax.Dc.V. **££**

**Copper Chimney**      **4 D3**
13 Heddon St W1. 071-439 2004. Large, elegant restaurant with excellent cuisine, beautifully presented. Delicately flavoured rice with lentils, traditional dhals, and lassi to drink. Polite, courteous service. *Open to 23.30. Closed Sun.* A.Ax.Dc.V. **££**

**⟨ Diwan-E-Khas**      **1 E5**
45 Grafton Way W1. 071-388 1321. Cavernous interior and sub-dued lighting in which to sample very reasonably priced dishes. Excellent tandooris from north India, Moghul chicken or lamb and thalis – a selection of small dishes including tandoori chicken, prawn bhoona and Moghul mutton with nuts. *Open to 24.00.* A.Ax.Dc.V. **£**

**Gopal's of Soho**      **4 E2**
12 Bateman St, off Frith St W1. 071-434 1621. High-quality cooking in pleasant surroundings in the middle of busy Soho. Basmati rice accompanies succulent, spicy chicken and lamb dishes. Good wine list. *Open to 23.30, to 23.00 Sun.* A.Ax.Dc.V. **££**

**⟨ Khan's**      **3 C2**
13 Westbourne Grove W2. 071-727 5420. The vast dining hall, with its oriental arches and palm tree pillars, was formerly a Lyons tea house. Cheap, cheerful, noisy and always busy with excellent north Indian cuisine. Specialities include kofti dilruba (spiced curried meat-balls) and matter paneer (white cheese with peas and herbs). Service is bustling and erratic. *Open to 24.00.* A.Ax.Dc.V. **£**

**⟨ Light of India**      **6 D3**
276 Fulham Rd SW10. 071-352 5416. Romantic, candlelit atmo-sphere with special Mughlai dishes such as murgh massalum and khurzi chicken which can be ordered the day before. Also good tan-doori dishes – staff are willing to show you the clay ovens. *(Reserve) open to 24.00.* A.Ax.Dc.V. **££**

**Mumtaz**      **1 A4**
4-10 Park Rd NW1. 071-723 0549. One of the most lavishly decorat-ed Indian eateries in town. Wide vegetarian selection and good tan-doori dishes. Also a large variety of unusual dishes such as paneer pakoras, baby chicken with cream, saffron and almonds. *Open to 23.30, to 23.00 Sun.* A.Ax.Dc.V. **£££**

**Ravi Shankar**      **1 E5**
133 Drummond St NW1. 071-388 6458. A vegetarian Indian restaurant, part of a successful chain offering mainly south Indian dishes. Bhel pooris, rava dosa, vegetable curry, dahl. It shares a kitchen with **Chutneys**, 124 Drummond St NW1. 071-388 0604. *Open to 23.00.* A.Ax.Dc.V. **£**

**Red Fort**      **4 E2**
77 Dean St W1. 071-437 2525. A trend-setter in Bangladeshi fish dishes and now one of the most acclaimed Indian restaurants in the world. Attractive, luxurious surroundings and excellent cooking make it perennially popular. Try quails in mild spice or chicken

karahi. Elegant bar for pre-dinner drinks and handy for pre-theatre eating. *(Reserve) open to 23.30.* A.Ax.Dc.V. **££**

**Saheli Brasserie** 4 F2
35 Great Queen St WC2. 071-405 2238. Country house decor, unusual for an Indian restaurant, is the attractive setting for well-prepared north Indian cuisine. Good value set menus and handy for the nearby theatres. *Open to 23.30. Closed Sun.* A.Ax.Dc.V. **££**

**Salloos** 4 B5
62 Kinnerton St SW1. 071-235 4444. Luxurious oriental decor in a mews away from the bustle of Knightsbridge. Authentic Pakistani cooking with dishes from the era of the Moghul emperors – chicken jalfrezi, bataire masala, lamb barra, good tandooris. *Open to 23.15. Closed Sun.* A.Ax.Dc.V. **£££**

**Standard** 3 C2
21 Westbourne Grove W2. 071-727 4818. Above standard cooking for below standard prices. The menu includes over 80 specialities – tandoori and vegetarian dishes and fish masala. Follow up with kulfi – a cone-shaped, spiced ice-cream. *(Reserve) open to 23.50.* A.Ax.Dc.V. **££**

**◖ Tandoori of Chelsea** 6 D3
153 Fulham Rd SW3. 071-589 7617. Pleasant decor and soft music combined with a high standard of regional cooking using traditional tandoor clay ovens. Lamb and chicken are marinated with herbs and spices before cooking. Tandoori chicken, rogan gosht, fish curry. *Open to 24.00, to 23.30 Sun.* A.Ax.Dc.V. **££**

**▢ Veeraswamy** 4 D3
99-101 Regent St (entrance in Swallow St) W1. 071-734 1401. London's oldest Indian restaurant (established 1927) with refined, elegant decor and atmosphere. Large choice of curries, kebabs and tandooris from north India and some more unusual dishes such as Goan chicken with coconut, mutton dhansak. Pre-theatre set menu. *Open 18.00-23.15, to 22.00 Sun.* A.Ax.Dc.V. **£££**

**Viceroy of India** 1 B5
3 Glentworth St NW1. 071-486 3401. Elegant and refined, with fountains in the foyer and a varied and exciting menu – chicken pakora, fish masala, good tandooris, saag kamal kakari (spinach and lotus roots), several varieties of nan. Polite service. *Open to 23.30, to 23.00 Sun.* A.Ax.Dc.V. **££**

## INEXPENSIVE

The following are places where you can eat cheaply and well. Cafés serving 'sausage, egg and chips' are not included here, nor are the international fast food chains which can be found on nearly every High Street. This list prizes all styles of cooking and atmosphere where you can get good value for money. See under other nationalities, particularly *American, Chinese, Indian* and *Italian*, for restaurants serving cheaper meals.

**Alpino** 1 C6
42 Marylebone High St W1. 071-935 4640. Pleasing Italian atmosphere in this alpine-style restaurant. Always busy and crowded

with quick, efficient service offering generous portions of pasta, fish and chicken dishes. *Open to 23.00. Closed Sun.* A.Ax.Dc.V. **£**

**❑ Ambrosiana Crêperie**                                                    **6 C4**
194 Fulham Rd SW10. 071-351 0070. A huge selection of savoury and sweet crêpes. Interesting combinations including garlic sausage, peppers and asparagus, and figs, walnuts and ice-cream. Lively atmosphere with bright decor and loud music. *Open to 24.00.* No credit cards. **£**

**❑ Café Crêperie**                                                          **4 B2**
26 James Street W1. 071-935 8480. Noisy and busy café with tables outside on the pavement. In the basement restaurant you can enjoy a delicious galette of bacon, cheese, sour cream and chives, followed by a sweet crêpe with chocolate sauce and cream. *Open to 24.00.* A.Ax.V. **£**

**Chelsea Bun Diner**                                                        **6 C4**
9a Limerston St SW10. 071-352 3635. Fresh, attractive, bustling restaurant serving enormous portions of pasta and vegetarian dishes, burgers, omelettes and all-day breakfasts. Unlicensed, so bring your own (no corkage charge). *Open to 23.30.* No credit cards. **£**

**Chelsea Kitchen**                                                          **6 E3**
98 King's Rd SW3. 071-589 1330. Part of the Stockpot (see below) group. The daily menu offers healthy portions of moussaka, goulash or spaghetti, followed by jelly and ice-cream, apple crumble or sponge puddings. Licensed. *Open to 23.45, to 23.30 Sun.* No credit cards. **£**

**Diwana Bhel Poori House**                                                  **1 E5**
121 Drummond St NW1. 071-387 5556. Good value Indian vegetarian food. Try the thali, a set meal which includes a variety of delicacies, masala dosa, and bhel poori dishes. Friendly and always bustling. *Open to 23.30.* A.Dc.V. **£**

**❑ Gaby's Continental Bar**                                                 **4 E2**
30 Charing Cross Rd WC2. 071-836 4233. Busy Middle Eastern café with bar stools or banquette seating. Salt beef, pastrami, felafels, houmous and baklava in generous quantities. *Open to 24.00, to 22.00 Sun.* No credit cards. **£**

**Mustoe Bistro**                                                           **1 B2**
73 Regent's Park Rd NW1. 071-586 0901. Small bistro popular with the residents of Primrose Hill. Aubergine and yoghurt or eggs Madras to start, followed by garlic or pepper steak. Good dessert trolley. *(Reserve) open to 23.00, to 22.30 Sun.* No credit cards. **£**

**My Old Dutch**                                                            **4 G1**
131 High Holborn WC1. 071-242 5200. Traditional Dutch farmhouse decor in which over 100 generous-sized savoury and sweet pancakes are offered. Very good value. Licensed. *Open to 23.45.* A.Ax.Dc.V. **£**

**Pollo**                                                                   **4 E3**
20 Old Compton St W1. 071-734 5917. Extremely busy Italian restaurant serving huge helpings of pasta, meat and fish dishes. Zabaglione is recommended to follow. Expect to share a table. *Open to 23.30. Closed Sun.* No credit cards. **£**

**❑ Le Shop (the Veritable Crêperie)**                                       **6 D4**
329 King's Rd SW3. 071-352 3891. The oldest crêperie in town,

serving typical sweet or savoury Breton crêpes – lots of combinations or create your own. English and French cider to wash it all down. Classical music plays in the background. *Open to 24.00.* A.V. **£**

**Stockpot**                                                            **3 G5**
6 Basil St SW3. 071-589 8627. Crowded, noisy and excellent value (unusual for this area of London) offering home-made soups, moussaka, toad-in-the-hole, apple crumble and treacle pudding. Other branches. *Open to 23.00, to 22.30 Sun.* No credit cards. **£**

## INTERNATIONAL

**Blakes**                                                              **6 C3**
Blakes Hotel, 33 Roland Gdns SW7. 071-370 6701. An opulent basement restaurant offering a blend of east and west cuisine. Sashimi, chicken tikka, satay, rack of lamb, mousseline of lobster, guinea fowl – all presented in generous portions. Fashionable with actors and musicians. *(Reserve) open to 23.30.* A.Ax.Dc.V. **£££+**

**◖ Boardwalk**                                                        **4 E2**
18 Greek St W1. 071-287 2051. Lively, stylish restaurant (on the site of Bill Stickers) with a waterfall cascading in the middle. Well-presented dishes include satay, deep fried Camembert, burgers, swordfish, lamb cutlets with rosemary, cauliflower gratin, cheese fries. Friendly service. *Open to 01.00, to 02.00 Fri & Sat, to 23.30 Sun.* A.V. **££**

**◖ Le Caprice**                                                       **4 D4**
Arlington House, Arlington St SW1. 071-629 2239. Stylish and elegant, tucked behind The Ritz, with efficient, smooth service and black and white decor. The menu is influenced from all corners of the world – bang bang chicken, salmon fishcakes, brandade of cod, roulade de chocolat. French, Italian and Californian wines. A fashionable hangout for the artistocracy and people from the media world. *Open to 24.00.* A.Ax.Dc.V. **£££**

**Mélange**                                                            **4 F2**
59 Endell St WC2. 071-240 8077. Stylish surroundings and an inventive menu make this a very popular spot. Handy for nearby theatres and offering unusual dishes such as Thai-style fish cakes, grilled polenta with Gorgonzola, warm lemon chicken salad with chilli. *Open to 23.30. Closed Sat & Sun.* A.Ax.V. **££**

**▣ Phood**                                                            **4 D2**
31 Foubert's Place W1. 071-494 4192. Pale pink and matt black interior with an eclectic menu including Thai fishcakes, eggs Benedict, several vegetarian choices, fresh fruit brûlé. Steak sandwiches and salads also on the snack menu *(17.30-19.30).* Only a short step across Soho to theatreland. *Open 11.00-23.00. Closed Sun.* A.Ax.V. A la carte menu **£££** Snack menu **£**

**Pomegranates**                                                       **7 C4**
94 Grosvenor Rd SW1. 071-828 6560. Highly original and adventurous restaurant with a truly cosmopolitan menu. Welsh, Turkish, Malaysian and Greek dishes happily rub shoulders with Chinese, Italian and French cuisine. All prepared from first-class ingredients. Multi-national wine list. *(Reserve) open to 23.15.* A.Ax.Dc.V. **£££+**

**Portobello Gold** 3 A2
95 Portobello Rd W11. 071-727 7898. Lively, noisy bar and restaurant with loud music and friendly staff. Caribbean-style decor sets off an interesting menu with stir-fries, pasta dishes, nachos with salsa, bananas and chilli in bacon. Several types of Tequila and rum available from the bar. *Open to 23.00. Closed Sun.* A.Ax.V. **££**

**La Reash Cous-Cous House** 4 E2
23 Greek St W1. 071-439 1063. Not all cous-cous, despite the name. A variety of other dishes from the Middle East and north Africa at this friendly, smart establishment. Good value meze including a vegetarian version and a set pre-theatre menu which offers two courses, or meze, and coffee. *Open 12.00-24.00.* A.V. Pre-theatre menu **£** A la carte **££**

**La Reserve** 6 B5
422 Fulham Rd SW6. 071-385 8561. Chic, minimalist surroundings in a new hotel in fashionable Fulham. The menu includes Thai, West Coast and Italian combinations – char-grilled aubergine, bruschetta with onions, fettucine with salmon, Thai beef salad, rocket and pancetta salad with corn bread croutons. *Open to 23.15.* A.Ax.Dc.V. **££**

**South of the Border** 5 C4
8 Joan St SE1. 071-928 6374. Farmhouse decor in this spacious restaurant in a converted mattress factory. Indonesian, Japanese and Australian dishes – rijstafel, tempura prawns, surf 'n' turf, home-made ice-cream. *Open to 23.30. Closed Sun.* A.Ax.Dc.V. **££**

**Sydney Street** 6 E3
4 Sydney St SW3. 071-352 3433. In a handsome town house, a basement restaurant specialising in Australian fish mixed with international recipes. Hungarian chilled papaya and yoghurt soup, smoked woodsquab, rösti, inoki mushrooms. Congenial service and a good selection of wines. *Open to 23.30. Closed Sun.* A.Ax.V. **££**

**The Wilds** 6 B5
356 Fulham Rd SW10. 071-376 5553. An unusual mixture of African and European cuisine is reflected in the burnished walls and swagged wall-hangings. Memorable dishes such as Gruyère and spinach crêpes, spicy shrimp salad with chillis. *(Reserve) open to 23.30. Closed Sun.* A.V. **£££**

## ITALIAN

**Arlecchino** 3 B4
8 Hillgate St W8. 071-229 2027. Behind Notting Hill Gate station, in a converted Kensington cottage, is this tiny, inviting, busy restaurant. Minestrone, costoletta di vitello del priore, fresh vegetables, fraises Romanoff. Italian wines. Friendly service. *Open to 23.30. Closed Sun.* A.Ax.Dc.V. **£££**

**Bertorelli's** 4 F3
44a Floral St WC2. 071-836 3969. A popular and unpretentious ground floor restaurant and basement café. Traditional, well-presented food ranges from Parma ham with olives to pasta, pizzas and veal dishes. Italian and Californian wines. *Open to 23.00. Closed Sun.* A.Ax.Dc.V. Café **£** Restaurant **£££**

### Café Italien des Amis du Vin                    4 D1
19 Charlotte St W1. 071-636 4174. Brasserie, wine bar and more formal dining room (the Bertorelli) in which to sample classic dishes. Salads and pasta in the wine bar; a wider selection in the brasserie ranging from pasta to steak, grilled tuna, bresaola, calf's liver, veal escalope, carpaccio; more formal and elegant version in the Bertorelli Room. French, Italian and Californian wines and champagnes. *Open to 23.00. Closed Sun.* A.Ax.Dc.V. Brasserie and Bertorelli Room **££** Wine bar **£**

### 🔲 Café Pasta                    4 E3
184 Shaftesbury Ave WC2. 071-379 0198. Light, airy and relaxed offering a good variety of pasta dishes and salads. Daily specials and also sandwiches and cakes. *Open 09.30-23.30, to 22.30 Sun.* No credit cards. **£**

### Café Tempo                    6 E3
235 King's Rd SW3. 071-376 5796. A good, straightforward pasta place with clocks on the walls showing the time in various other parts of the world. Traditional dishes include rigatoni all'matriciana, linguine con vongole and some good grills. *Open to 23.30.* A.Ax.V. **£**

### 🔲 Cucina d'Arte                    4 E3
The Trocadero, Piccadilly W1. 071-734 0122. Minimalist decor amid the trendy shops of Fusion underground at the Trocadero. They offer all the pasta you can eat for a very reasonable price. Varied selection. Guaranteed to keep your stomach from rumbling halfway through the performance! *Open 12.00-24.00.* A.Ax.V. **£**

### 🔳 Eleven Park Walk                    6 C4
11 Park Walk SW10. 071-352 3449. Where the high-fashion photographers, designers and models wine and dine. A stylish cellar restaurant with a strong Mediterranean feel. Home-made pastas are the speciality; also game, salmon, veal, trout and tasty crudités with hot bagna calda sauce. *(Reserve) open to 24.00. Closed Sun.* A.Ax.Dc.V. **£££**

### 🔳 La Famiglia                    6 C4
5 Langton St SW10. 071-351 0761. Lively and very popular. High standard of cooking – pasta e fagioli, sea bream with fennel, tiramisu – which in summer (if the weather permits) is served in the garden at the back under awnings. *Open to 24.00.* A.Ax.Dc.V. **££**

### Gritti                    4 F3
11 Upper St Martin's Lane WC2. 071-836 5121. Smart restaurant offering a mainly traditional menu. Mozzarella, tomato and avocado salad, veal escalope, calf's liver in white wine, tiramisu, zabaglione. Italian and French wines and charming, attentive service. *Open to 23.15. Closed Sun.* A.Ax.V. **£££+**

### L'Incontro                    7 A3
87 Pimlico Rd SW1. 071-730 6327. Sumptuous, comfortable restaurant with a wealthy clientele enjoying Venetian cooking. Salt cod with olive oil, cuttlefish in ink with polenta. Excellent (but expensive) Italian wines. *(Reserve) open to 23.30, to 22.30 Sun.* A.Ax.Dc.V. **£££+**

### Leoni's Quo Vadis                    4 E2
26-29 Dean St W1. 071-437 4809. Pretty pastel dining room in one of Soho's oldest buildings and home to Karl Marx when he was writing

*Das Kapital*. The specialities are rich, traditional Italian dishes with plenty of cream such as chicken in brandy and cream. Excellent courteous service. *(Reserve) open to 23.15, to 22.30 Sun.* A.Ax.Dc.V. **£££**

### Mimmo d'Ischia                                                7 A2
61 Elizabeth St SW1. 071-730 5406. Bright, exciting restaurant with autographed photos of famous stars posing with the ebullient owner, Mimmo. Try the Italian mixed hors d'oeuvres, scampi in brandy and cream, scallopine bella valeria, fusilli with veal. Rich desserts. Speedy service. *(Reserve) open to 23.30. Closed Sun.* A.Ax.Dc.V. **£££**

### Osteria Antica Bologna
23 Northcote Rd, Battersea SW11. 071-978 4771. Friendly and relaxed with rustic surroundings. The menu concentrates on regional dishes and specialises in cuisine from Sicily. Try bruschetta, potatoes roasted with garlic, fresh grilled sardines, a variety of polenta dishes. *Open to 23.00. Closed Sun.* A.V. **££**

### Palms Pasta on the Piazza                          · 4 F3
39 King St WC2. 071-240 2939. Very popular and usually crowded with both young and old popping in from Covent Garden. Good value pasta dishes as well as grills and huge salads. Excellent starters such as gazpacho and deep fried Camembert. Extremely friendly staff. *(No reservations) open to 23.30.* A.V. **££**

### The Pavilion                                              4 D2
15 Poland St W1. 071-437 2745. Renowned for its daily-changing menu of unusual dishes. Featuring rarely more than one pasta dish, the sauces are inventive and the menu dominated by seafood. *(Reserve) open to 23.00. Closed Sat & Sun.* A.Ax.Dc.V. **£££**

### ▣ Prima Pasta                                           4 F3
30 Henrietta St WC2. 071-836 8396. One of a chain of pasta places with a good reputation. Various pastas – spaghetti, ravioli, fusilli, tortelloni, fettucine – come with a variety of tasty sauces. Extra large portions also available. Service is friendly and efficient. *Open 12.00-23.45, to 23.00 Sun.* A.Dc.V. **£**

### San Lorenzo                                            3 G6
22 Beauchamp Place SW3. 071-584 1074. This charming, family-run establishment has a fashionable clientele – this is said to be the Princess of Wales's favourite restaurant. The wine list is extensive and you can sit outside in summer. *(Reserve) open to 23.30. Closed Sun.* No credit cards. **£££**

### Signor Sassi                                            3 F6
Smart and lively restaurant with whitewashed walls and marble floors, giving it a Mediterranean feel. Excellent authentic cuisine is beautifully presented. Specialities are crespoline stuffed with ricotta and spinach, calf's liver with white wine and grapes. The wine list is expensive with a limited selection of Italian wines. *(Reserve) open to 23.30. Closed Sun.* A.Ax.Dc.V. **££**

### Topo Gigio                                             4 D3
46 Brewer St W1. 071-437 8516. Appetising Italian food at reasonable prices. Good minestrone, cannelloni, petti di pollo, veal escalopes. Helpful service. *(Reserve) open Mon-Sat to 23.15.* A.Ax.Dc.V. **££**

# JAPANESE

**Ajimura**                                                          **4 F2**
51-53 Shelton St WC2. 071-240 0178. Agreeable, simple Japanese restaurant with good set meals offering a selection of specialities, particularly sashimi and tempura. Sake or green tea is served to accompany the meal. *(Reserve) open to 23.00. Closed Sat & Sun.* A.Ax.V. **££**

**₢ Benihana**
100 Avenue Rd, Hampstead NW3. 071-586 7118. One of the Japanese/US chain of Hibachi restaurants, Benihana provides an elegant and enjoyable night out. Diners are seated round three sides of a rectangular grill, facing the chef, as he prepares, with much twirling and flashing of blades, grilled vegetables, seafood, chicken and beef. Short wine list to choose from or accompany your meal with sake. *Open to 24.00. Closed Mon.* A.Ax.Dc.V. **£££**

**Ikeda**                                                           **4 C3**
30 Brook St W1. 071-629 2730. Watch sushi chefs work at great speed in this charming restaurant with its own small courtyard. Set sashimi or tempura meal, or unusual seasonal specialities à la carte. *(Reserve) open to 22.30, to 22.00 Sat. Closed Sun.* A.Ax.Dc.V. **£££**

**Masako**                                                          **4 B2**
St Christopher's Place W1. 071-935 1579. A traditional Japanese restaurant with private (tatami) dining rooms, where you can sit on the floor and waitresses, dressed in kimonos, attend to your every need. They have a wide-ranging menu including set sukiyako and tempura meals. *Open to 22.00. Closed Sun.* A.Ax.Dc.V. **£££+**

**Nakano**                                                          **3 F6**
11 Beauchamp Place SW3. 071-581 3837. Simple, traditional restaurant serving imaginative dishes. The cuttle fish marinated in sake is very popular; for the more adventurous, grilled salmon head. *(Reserve) open to 23.00. Closed Mon.* A.Ax.Dc.V. **£££**

**Ninjin**                                                          **1 D6**
244 Great Portland St W1. 071-388 4657. This basement restaurant below a Japanese supermarket is inexpensive, comfortable and friendly; the perfect place to try Japanese food for the first time. Food is cooked at the table and served in generous portions. *Open to 22.00. Closed Sun.* A.Ax.Dc.V. **£**

**Suntory**                                                         **4 D4**
72 St James's St SW1. 071-409 0201. Popular with ministers and officials from the Japanese Embassy, this restaurant has an excellent reputation. Try teppan-yaki, sushi or sashimi; all exquisitely prepared. *(Reserve) open to 22.20. Closed Sun.* A.Ax.Dc.V. **£££**

**Wagamama**                                                        **4 F1**
4 Streatham St, off Bloomsbury St WC1. 071-323 9223. A Japanese noodle bar with simple decor and seating in rows. Not the place for an intimate dinner for two! Huge bowls of ramen noodle soup and fried rice or noodles with vegetable or seafood toppings served by super-efficient waiters and waitresses wielding hand-held computer pads. Non-smoking. *Open to 23.00. Closed Sun.* No credit cards. **£**

## KOREAN

**Arirang**                                                      **4 D2**
31-32 Poland St W1. 071-437 9662. London's oldest Korean restaurant where waitresses in Korean dress will steer you through a large menu including kimchee (hot pickled cabbage) and yuk hwe (beef strips with sugar, pear and spices). For dessert, special cut fruit. Sake, ginseng, Korean tea. Taped Korean music. *(Reserve) open to 23.00. Closed Sun.* A.Ax.Dc.V. **£££**

**Jin**                                                             **4 E2**
16 Bateman St W1. 071-734 0908. Authentic Korean restaurant with smart white and gold frontage. Specialises in set meals which are barbecued at the table. Lots of choice and friendly, helpful service. *(Reserve) open to 23.00. Closed Sun.* A.Ax.Dc.V. **££**

**Kaya Korean**                                                 **4 E2**
22-25 Dean St W1. 071-437 6630. Waitresses in full national costume will talk you through the menu at this traditional Korean restaurant. The seafood special is worth tasting. So is the sliced, seasoned venison, which you won't find on many Korean menus. *(Reserve) open to 23.00.* A.Ax.Dc.V. **££**

**Shilla**                                                          **4 D2**
58 Great Marlborough St W1. 071-434 1650. Charming formal service guides you through this restaurant's exciting speciality – barbecue dishes – with the barbecue at your own table and you as the chef. Delicious sauces accompany beef, chicken or seafood. Set menus available. *(Reserve) open to 22.30.* A.Ax.Dc.V. **££**

**◖ You Me House**
510a Hornsey Rd, Edmonton N19. 071-272 6208. Spacious and elegantly decorated. Good set menus. Try bintatok (Korean pizza topped with minced beef, spring onions, crab meat, garlic and mixed vegetables). Artistically cut fresh fruit for dessert. Good service. *(Reserve) open to 24.00. Closed Sun.* No credit cards. **££**

## MEXICAN & TEX-MEX

**◖ Arizona**                                                    **1 D2**
2a Jamestown Rd NW1. 071-284 4730. Big, lively Tex-Mex restaurant near Camden Lock, popular with young locals as a prelude to a night out. Very good value and the rooftop terrace is an ideal spot for warm nights. *Open to 24.00, to 23.00 Sun.* A.Ax.V. **£**

**◖ Break for the Border**                                       **4 D2**
8 Argyll St W1. 071-734 5776. Evoking memories of the gold-rush – a huge establishment with an open saloon-style bar serving reasonably cheap beers and cocktails. The food is traditional Tex-Mex – nachos, chilli, tacos, enchiladas, fajitas. *(Reserve) open to 24.00.* A.V. **££**

**Café Pacifico**                                                **4 F2**
5 Langley St WC2. 071-379 7728. Crowded cantina in a converted warehouse. No booking at night, but have a cocktail while you wait. Young, faithful clientele. Large bar, helpful staff and generous portions.

Guacamole, nachos, enchiladas, quesadillas, tostadas, chilaquiles. Fresh pineapple or helados to finish. *Open to 23.45, to 22.45 Sun.* A.V. **££**

**Chiquito**                                                         **4 E3**
20 Leicester Sq WC2. 071-839 6925. Large, bright restaurant on two floors, decorated with artefacts and colourful wall-hangings. Fresh ingredients and mild spices are used to prepare this traditional north Mexican cuisine. Pollo Moterez, enchiladas, tacos, guacamole, chimichangas (by request) and to follow, Mexican fried ice cream. Four different Margaritas are available; also imported Mexican beer. *(No reservations) open to 23.45, to 22.45 Sun.* A.Ax.Dc.V. **£££**

**La Cucaracha**                                                    **4 E2**
12 Greek St W1. 071-734 2253. London's first Mexican restaurant, in the cellars of a converted monastery. Decorated in hacienda style with alcoves and a covered terrace. Try the Mexican national dish, mole poblano de guajolote (roasted turkey in a cocoa nut sauce) or avocado Mexicano (baked and stuffed with crabmeat). Finish with copa vallarta (sorbet with fresh melon and mango). *(Reserve) open to 23.30.* Closed Sun. A.Ax.Dc.V. **££**

**Down Mexico Way**                                                 **4 D3**
25 Swallow St, off Regent St W1. 071-437 9895. Originally a Spanish restaurant owned by the Martinez family. The decor has been kept as it was with floors and walls covered in hand-painted tiles given to the family by King Juan Carlos. An interesting menu including nachos, ceviche, jalapeno muffins, mesquite smoked dishes and plenty of choice for vegetarians. Mexican hot chocolate. Tequila slammers and Chilean wine. *(Reserve) open to 23.45, to 22.30 Sun.* A.Ax.V. **££**

**Texas Lone Star West**                                           **3 C3**
117 Queensway W2. 071-727 2980. One of a chain of frontier-style restaurants with rough wood, heaps of straw, a lively atmosphere and Tex-Mex dishes. Burgers, ribs and steaks combine with guacamole, tacos and burritos from across the border. Cocktails too. *Open to 23.15.* No credit cards. **£**

## MIDDLE EASTERN

**❑ Al Hamra**
31-33 Shepherd Market W1. 071-493 1954. Very elegant Lebanese restaurant, with Viennese blinds and a huge chandelier. Long, comprehensive list of meze dishes followed by a variety of charcoal-grilled meats and sweet, sugary desserts. Lebanese wine or arak to drink. Very friendly service. *Open to 24.00.* A.Ax.Dc.V. **£££**

**❑ Divan**                                                         **3 F1**
228 Edgware Rd W2. 071-724 7257. Smart, bright pastel interior, giving this restaurant a rather international quality, far removed from the usual kebab shop. Electronic keyboard music and a young clientele. Excellent cuisine; the hot and cold meze dishes are recommended, as is the freshly made bread. Desserts are well worth leaving room for. *Open to 24.00.* Closed Sun. A.Ax.Dc.V. **££**

**Efes Kebab House**                                               **4 D1**
80 Great Titchfield St W1. 071-636 1953: Behind the take-away

counter lies a smart restaurant decorated in subtle Islamic style. Very efficient traditionally-dressed staff serving slightly westernised Turkish food. Generous starters, fresh salads and a great choice of dishes. Seating outdoors. *(Reserve)* open to 23.30. *Closed Sun.* A.Ax.Dc.V. **££**

**◖ Fakhreldine**                                                    **4 C4**

85 Piccadilly W1. 071-493 3424. The grandest and perhaps best known of London's Middle Eastern restaurants. Swish and opulent furnishings and excellent views of Green Park make it very popular. A spectacular range of 55 mezes means there definitely will be something for everyone. *(Reserve)* open to 01.00, to 24.00 Sun. A.Ax.Dc.V. **££**

**◖ Hafez**                                                          **3 B2**

5 Hereford Rd W2. 071-229 9398. This small, intimate Persian restaurant serves delicious authentic traditional food, well presented and served with a smile. The fresh Persian bread cooked in the large ovens at the front of the restaurant is still hot when it reaches your table. Chelo-kebab, houmous, feta cheese, sabzi, kebabs. *Open to 24.00.* No credit cards. **££**

**◖ The Lebanese Restaurant**                                        **3 F2**

60 Edgware Rd W2. 071-262 9585. Eat genuine Lebanese dishes in an oriental atmosphere. Mirrors, arches, dim wall lights and carved chairs inlaid with brass. Montabar (baked aubergine with sesame sauce, lemon, olive oil and garlic) and kibbeh (fresh raw lamb pourri served with spices and wheat) are worth trying. Various kebabs. For dessert try usmalieh (pieces of shredded wheat in cream and syrup) and finish off with proper mint tea made with mint leaves. Arabic music. *Open to 24.00.* A.Ax.Dc.V. **££**

**◖ Maroush III**                                                    **4 A2**

62 Seymour St W1. 071-724 5024. This luxurious, ever-popular Lebanese restaurant is part of the Maroush chain which always maintains high standards. Large selection of mezes and meat dishes – habra nayah (fresh raw meat served with spices) and kibbeh nayah ourphaliyeh (raw meat pureed with crushed wheat, onions and spices served with fried meat on the side). Arabic pop videos. *Open to 01.00.* A.Ax.Dc.V. **££**

**The Olive Tree**                                                   **4 E3**

11 Wardour St W1. 071-734 0808. Popular stop-off before or after the cinema. The food here is very reasonably priced and there is an impressive choice of vegetarian dishes. Pitta with felafel, served with huge, fresh, delicious salads. *(Reserve)* open to 23.00, to 21.00 Sun. A.V. **£**

**◖ Phoenicia**                                                      **6 A1**

11-13 Abingdon Rd W8. 071-937 0120. Intimate Lebanese restaurant with water jets and a spotlit internal garden. Specialities are mezes and charcoal grills. Katayaf with honey, nuts and cream to follow. *Open to 24.00.* A.Ax.Dc.V. **££**

**◖ Sofra**                                                          **4 C4**

18 Shepherd St W1. 071-493 3320. One of the most popular Turkish restaurants in London, with its light, pleasant atmosphere and the healthiness of the food which is a preoccupation of the owner. Large selection of hot and cold mezes. Fine houmous dolma, tabouleh, broad beans cooked in olive oil and dill served with

yoghurt, garlic and coriander. The dessert trolley is not to be missed. Prompt and friendly service. *Open to 24.00.* A.Ax.Dc.V. **££**

**Tageen**                                                    **4 F3**
12 Upper St Martin's Lane WC2. 071-836 7272. Successful restaurant decorated in true Moroccan style – coloured glass lamps, Moroccan tablecloths and tableware, and the food comes to the table in authentic north African cooking pots. Harira to start with – a thick and spicy soup. The main dishes are all wonderfully marinated, tangy or pleasantly spiced. Willing and friendly staff. *Open to 23.30. Closed Sun.* A.Ax.Dc.V. **££**

## MODERN EUROPEAN

**Alastair Little**                                           **4 E2**
49 Frith St W1. 071-734 5183. Fashionable restaurant with an imaginative, frequently-changing menu. Tempting and delicious results. *(Reserve) open to 23.00. Closed Sat & Sun.* A.V. **£££**

**The Belvedere**                                            **3 A4**
Holland Park W8. 071-602 1238. The Belvedere restaurant occupies the original summer ballroom of Holland Park. The interior has been revamped in a stylish, unfussy way, overlooking the gardens. The cuisine is carefully prepared and beautifully presented. Specialities are caramelised onion tart, salad of rocket, potatoes and truffles, roasted sea bream, black leg chicken with polenta mash and lentils, and fruit soup. *(Reserve) open to 22.30. Closed Sun eve.* A.Ax.V. **££-£££**

**Bibendum**                                                  **6 E2**
Michelin House, 81 Fulham Rd SW3. 071-581 5817. A delightful blue and cream restaurant on the first floor of the unusual 1910 Michelin building. The long menu of simple, elegant and inventive French and English dishes is renowned. Carefully chosen wine list. *(Reserve) open to 23.00, to 22.30 Sun.* A.V. **£££+**

**❰❰ Bistrot 190**                                           **3 D6**
190 Queen's Gate SW7. 071-581 5666. Simple, hearty, modern cuisine served at this inexpensive and popular brasserie. Try the grilled cuttlefish, red pepper sauce, rocket leaves and chips, or the chicory tart tatin with duck livers. The lemon tart to follow is highly recommended. *(No reservations) open to 00.30 Mon-Sat, to 23.30 Sun.* A.Ax.Dc.V. **£**

**Boyd's**                                                    **3 B4**
135 Kensington Church St W8. 071-727 5452. Crisp linen and masses of plants add to a fresh, pleasant atmosphere. Luxurious menu includes warm quail and raspberry salad with toasted walnuts, or rib-eye Scotch beef marinated in orange, olive oil and garlic with wild mushrooms and watercress. *Open to 23.00. Closed Sun.* A.Ax.V. **£££**

**The Brackenbury**
129 Goldhawk Rd W6. 081-748 0107. This double-fronted restaurant, decorated in pink and green, has a faithful local following, attracted to the robust menu of solidly flavoured food. Very affordable prices and a constantly changing menu. All very tempting – potato pancakes filled with salmon caviar and crème fraîche, roast hake with

pesto mash, followed by a rich, thick prune and Armagnac mousse. You can just have a drink in the wine bar but it's well worth eating too. *(Reserve) open to 23.00. Closed Sun & Mon.* A.V. **£-££**

**Chanterelle**                                            6 C3
119 Old Brompton Rd SW7. 071-373 5522. A distinctive Modern European menu in this popular, busy restaurant. Choose from marinated monkfish with avocado, roast Guinea fowl with mushrooms and bacon, and Toulouse sausages. The set-price menus change regularly and are excellent value. *Open to 23.30.* A.Ax.Dc.V. **££**

**The Halcyon**                                            3 A4
129 Holland Park Ave W11. 071-221 5411. A delightful restaurant with an international menu ranging from brasserie classics such as eggs Benedict, to grilled venison with celeriac. You can have a full meal or just a quick snack. *(Reserve) open to 23.00, to 22.30 Sun.* A.Ax.Dc.V. **££**

**Hilaire**                                               6 D2
68 Old Brompton Rd SW7. 071-584 8993. Bryan Webb, the chef here, is renowned for his excellent Modern European cuisine. Steak au poivre is one of his specialities. Choose from the set or à la carte menus. *Open to 23.00. Closed Sun.* A.Ax.Dc.V. **£££**

**◖ The Ivy**                                             4 F3
1 West St WC2. 071-836 4751. This busy, fashionable, wood-panelled restaurant serves excellent cuisine with impeccable service. Bang bang chicken, Caesar salad and salmon fishcakes, tomato and basil galette, tagliatelli nero with scallops and baby squid. Short, European wine list. *(Reserve) open to 24.00.* A.Ax.Dc.V. **££-£££**

**Julie's**
135 Portland Rd, Notting Hill W11. 071-727 4585. A well-loved local restaurant with a relaxed atmosphere and a reliable menu. Creative

*The Ivy*

dishes like Swabian noodles on field mushrooms. Menu changes daily. *(Reserve) open to 23.00, to 22.20 Sun.* A.V. **£££+**

**Kensington Place** 3 B4

201-205 Kensington Church St W8. 071-727 3184. Aimed at a young, trendy clientele, the decor here is very design conscious with diners on show through the vast windows. The menu offers the latest fashionable concoctions. Try ox tongue or partridge with cabbage. *(Reserve) open to 23.45.* A.Ax.Dc.V. **££**

**Leith's** 3 A3

92 Kensington Park Rd W11. 071-229 4481. A charming restaurant in a converted Victorian house run by Prue Leith, well known for her original, inventive Modern European cuisine. The menu ranges from old Beeton recipes to classic French cooking. Excellent dessert trolley and a good selection of British cheeses. *(Reserve) open to 23.30.* A.Ax.Dc.V. **£££+**

**【 Ménage à Trois** 3 F6

15 Beauchamp Place SW3. 071-589 4252. A haunt of the trendy and aristocratic who come here to sample classic cuisine. An escalope of salmon comes with roasted peppers and basil on braised rocket. A pianist plays discreetly in the background. *(Reserve) open to 24.00.* No credit cards. **££**

**Neal Street Restaurant** 4 F2

26 Neal St WC2. 071-836 8368. Designed by Sir Terence Conran, this is a chic and modern restaurant with a menu culled from recipes worldwide. Elegant decor matches the cooking – scrambled eggs with smoked eel, prawns wrapped in bacon. *(Reserve) open to 23.00. Closed Sat & Sun.* A.Ax.Dc.V. **£££**

**Odette's** 1 B1

130 Regent's Park Rd NW1. 071-586 5486. A plant-filled restaurant on several levels with a daily-changing menu and a great reputation. The pan-roasted Bresse pigeon stuffed with cabbage and foie gras is exquisite, as are the delicious puddings. *(Reserve) open to 22.45. Closed Sat & Sun.* A.Ax.Dc.V. **£££**

**192** 3 A3

192 Kensington Park Rd W11. 071-229 0482. This underground, post-modernist restaurant is spacious, cool and relaxed. Menu changes twice daily. Innovator of the warm salad – goat's cheese, scallops or pigeon with radicchio. Stir-fries, calf's liver, wild mushrooms and mouth-watering fish dishes. Inexpensive and carefully selected wine list. *(Reserve) open to 23.30, to 23.00 Sun.* A.Ax.V. **££**

**Smith's** 4 F2

25 Neal St WC2. 071-379 0310. A simple, spacious restaurant housed in a converted Victorian brewery and shared with Smith's Art Galleries. Specialises in British cuisine and the menu favours traditional meat and fish recipes. Popular with theatre-goers and local workers. *(Reserve) open to 23.30. Closed Sun.* A.Ax.Dc.V. **££**

**Stephen Bull** 4 A2

5-7 Blandford St W1. 071-486 9696. Large, bright and airy serving excellent Modern European cuisine. The menu is changed frequently but always has interesting and inventive dishes such as goat's cheese soufflé, fillet of brill with oyster mushrooms and rosemary. *(Reserve) open to 23.15. Closed Sun.* A.V. **£££**

**Turner's** 6 E2
87-89 Walton St SW3. 071-584 6711. Attractively decorated, this Modern European restaurant offers à la carte and very good value set menus. Specials include marinated scallops, crispy duck in ginger. Good but fairly expensive wine list. *(Reserve)* open to 23.00. *Closed Sat & Sun.* A.Ax.Dc.V. **£££**

## PIZZAS

**Chicago Pizza Pie Factory** 4 C2
17 Hanover Sq W1. 071-629 2669. Crowded with Chicago paraphernalia from street signs to old movie posters. American deep-pan pizzas are their speciality – they're vast, so take a friend! Carrot cake and ice-cream to follow. Non-smoking section. *(Reserve)* open to 23.00 Sun. A.Ax.V. **£**

**La Delizia** 6 E3
Chelsea Farmers' Market, Sydney St SW3. 071-351 6701. One of London's most authentic Italian pizzerias, in two huts with seating outside. Pizzas are made in the thin-and-crispy style, with traditional toppings. Relaxed atmosphere with young, friendly Italian staff. Open to 23.30. No credit cards. **£**

**◖ Kettners** 4 E2
29 Romilly St W1. 071-437 6437. Great atmosphere in this turn-of-the-century-style Soho landmark, which is part of the Pizza Express chain. Sample pizza and pasta while reclining in the sumptuous surroundings. Champagne bar and pianist *every evening*. *(No reservations)* open to 24.00. A.Ax.Dc.V. **££**

**Pappagalli's Pizza Inc** 4 D3
7-9 Swallow St (off Regent St) W1. 071-734 5182. Large, lively restaurant serving wholemeal and white flour deep-pan and thin-crust pizzas. Also offers pasta with a variety of sauces and an extensive salad bar. An impressive selection of drinks including

*Kettners restaurant and champagne bar*

*Soho Pizzeria*

frozen vodka in a variety of flavours. *Open to 23.00. Closed Sun.* A.V. **£**

**◖ Pizza Express** 1 G6

30 Coptic St WC1. 071-638 2244. One of a good-quality chain serving freshly-made Italian-style pizzas. The ovens are stategically placed so you can watch your pizza being cooked. Delicious desserts and ice-creams. *Open to 24.00.* A.Ax.V. **£**

**◖ Pizza on the Park** 4 B5

11 Knightsbridge SW1. 071-235 5550. Stylish and fashionable, specialising in interesting pizzas. Good, varied wine list and live music (jazz) *every night. (Reserve) open to 24.00.* A.Ax.Dc.V. **£**

**◖ Pizza Pomodoro** 3 F6

51 Beauchamp Place SW3. 071-589 1278. Tiny and very popular basement restaurant. Pizzas and pasta dishes. Live music *every night* and lively, unconventional staff, even at 1am! *Open to 01.00.* No credit cards. **£**

**◖ Pizzeria Condotti** 4 D3

4 Mill St W1. 071-499 1308. Authentic pizzas using only the best ingredients. Try the Condotti – topped with ricotta and Gorgonzola. Sophisticates from the art world and the nearby Bond Street galleries eat here. *Open to 24.00. Closed Sun.* A.Ax.Dc.V. **££**

**▣ Soho Pizzeria** 4 D3

16 Beak St W1. 071-434 2480. Large, modern dining room in black and red. Excellent value and in the heart of Soho, a good place to stock up with pizza before the night's entertainment. Rich, generous toppings on Italian-style pizzas plus calzone – a folded pizza. *Open 12.00-23.30.* A.Ax.V. **£**

## RESTAURANTS FOR PARTIES

### Anna's Place

90 Mildmay Park, Islington N1. 071-249 9379. Excellent home-made Swedish cooking at this homely restaurant. Great venue for a dinner

party with Scandinavian flair. Can seat up to 20 at a table. Adaptable set menu and the puddings are wonderful. No hire charge. *Open Tue-Sat to 22.45.* No credit cards. **£££**

**Antipasto e Pasta**

511 Battersea Park Rd, Battersea SW11. 071-223 9765. This cheerful pasta restaurant has a separate conservatory available for parties. Seats 35. Relaxing atmosphere. Tailor-made or set menu. No hire charge. *Open to 23.30.* A.Ax.Dc.V. **££**

**Bombay Palace**                                          **3 F2**

50 Connaught St W2. 071-723 8855. An up-market Indian restaurant with an adjoining party room. Cool and spacious. Seats 40. Excellent north Indian cuisine and superb service. Tailor-made or set menu. No hire charge. *Open to 23.30.* A.Ax.Dc.V. **££**

**Chin's**

311-313 New King's Rd, Fulham SW6. 071-736 8833. A luxury Chinese restaurant where you can hire the whole place or one of its feature rooms – the garden room, the waterfall room and the dragon room. Each seats up to 20. Adaptable set menu. Cantonese, Szechuan and Beijing cooking. No hire charge. *Open to 23.45.* A.Ax.V. **££**

**Dan's**                                                  **6 E3**

119 Sydney St SW3. 071-352 2718. A bright, airy restaurant. Hire the conservatory which leads out onto the garden (seats 34) or there is a smaller private room downstairs (seats 14). Set menu. No hire charge. *Open to 22.30. Closed Sun.* A.Ax.Dc.V. **£££**

**Dôme**

38-39 Hampstead High St, Hampstead NW3. 071-435 4240. You can have a completely private setting for a dinner party or buffet at this lively brasserie. Big windows lead out onto a private balcony and you even have your own bar. Seats 40. No hire costs but minimum charge £200. *Open to 23.00, to 22.30 Sun.* A.Ax.Dc.V. **££**

**❰❰ Mongolian Barbeque**

147 Upper Richmond Rd, Putney SW15. 081-780 9252. This lively restaurant has a separate dining room downstairs which seats 30. It's a great place for a noisy group looking for some fun! You help yourself to pieces of meat (turkey, chicken, lamb, pork, beef and fish). Add raw vegetables and your choice of sauces and the chef will barbecue it in front of you. No hire charge. *Open to 24.00.* A.Ax.V. **££**

**Nikita's**                                               **6 B4**

65 Ifield Rd SW10. 071-352 6326. A cavernous basement restaurant exquisitely decorated in red and gold. Hire the whole place or one of their private rooms; there is a wonderful room for 12, hidden away behind a decorated door, and there are also two cosy alcove areas for six, curtained off with heavy tapestry drapes. Russian food – try golubtzy (cabbage parcels filled with spiced meat, herbs and dried fruit) and of course caviar. Wide selection of vodkas. No hire charge. *Open to 23.30. Closed Sun.* A.Ax.V. **£££**

**Paulo's**

30 Greyhound Rd, Hammersmith W6. 071-385 9264. Friendly, Brazilian atmosphere for a lively, informal evening. There's a separate room in the basement for parties. Seats 20. Set menu or

main course buffet. Try camarao com xuxu (prawns with vegetables) or arroz e feijao (black beans and rice). Brazilian music and cocktails. No hire charge. *Open to 22.30*. No credit cards. **££**

## SOUTH EAST ASIAN

### Bamboo Kuning                                        3 G1
114 Seymour Place W1. 071-723 2920. Spacious, bamboo-shaded restaurant on two floors. Family-run kitchen offers a vast selection of South East Asian dishes. Try a four-course set meal, or experiment with ikan pangang (charcoal grilled fish). For dessert, try Malaysian aiskacang (sweetcorn and jelly in coconut milk and syrup). *(Reserve) open to 22.45*. A.V. **££**

### Bintang
93 Kentish Town Rd, Kentish Town NW1. 071-284 1640. Small, family-run establishment bringing the delights of sunny Malaysia to north London. Bamboo and palm matting, tropical fish tanks and flickering lights make a perfect setting for speciality dishes such as satay, seafood and chicken in sour sauce. *(Reserve) open to 22.30. Closed Sun & Mon*. No credit cards. **££**

### Desaru                                              4 E2
60-62 Old Compton St W1. 071-734 4379. A very busy Indonesian/Malaysian restaurant, convenient for the theatres in nearby Shaftesbury Avenue. Good noodle dishes, or try one of their fish specialities – kari ikan (fish curry) or ikan panggang (grilled fish in spicy coconut sauce). *Open to 23.45, to 22.00 Sun*. A.Ax.V. **££**

### Lemongrass Restaurant                               1 E1
243 Royal College St NW1. 071-284 1116. An eclectic restaurant serving Vietnamese, Thai, Cambodian and Chinese dishes. Try the vegetarian spring rolls or the samosas to start with, followed by the hot and spicy chicken Saigon or the highly recommended French steak cooked with crispy fried shallots, ginger and of course, lemon grass. *(Reserve) open to 22.45*. A.V. **££**

### Melati                                              4 E3
21 Great Windmill St W1. 071-437 2745. A very popular Indonesian restaurant with simple decor and good food. Try the satay or nasi goreng, beef rendang or ikan masak lemak (fish cutlets in coconut sauce). *(Reserve) open to 23.30, to 24.30 Fri & Sat*. A.Ax.Dc.V. **££**

### Nusa Dua                                            4 E2
11-12 Dean St W1. 071-437 3559. Cheerfully decorated Soho restaurant. Good for vegetarians – tofu saté, organic soya bean with peanuts, chillies and sweet soya sauce. Also pepes ikan (fish grilled in banana leaf). *(Reserve) open to 23.30. Closed Sun*. A.Ax.Dc.V. **£-££**

### ◖ Rasa Sayang                                       4 E3
3 Leicester Place, Leicester Sq WC2. 071-437 4556. Unpretentious restaurant serving authentic Singaporean, Indonesian and Malaysian food. Try the gado, prawns, orange chicken, ribs in tamarind sauce or kalio sotong (squid in coconut gravy). *(Reserve) open to 01.45, to 22.15 Sun*. A.Ax.Dc.V. **£-££**

**Singapore Garden**  **4 C4**
85 Piccadilly W1. 071-491 2222. Popular with business men, diplomats and the Malaysian royal family! Try the crispy, sugary seaweed, the mild fish curry and the sticky toffee bananas. Service is fast and attentive. Note the crisp, white linen, the hot towels and chocolates in ice to end the meal. *(Reserve) open to 23.30. Closed Sun.* A.Ax.Dc.V. **£££**

**◖ Singapura**
839 Fulham Rd, Fulham SW6. 071-736 9310. A family-run restaurant with an elegant atmosphere. They specialise in a blend of Indonesian, Singaporean and European cuisine, beautifully prepared and presented. There's live music in the *evenings*. Set menus are excellent value. *(Reserve) open to 24.00.* A.Ax.Dc.V. **££-£££**

## SPANISH AND PORTUGUESE

**Bar Gansa**  **1 D2**
2 Inverness St NW1. 071-267 8909. One of the best tapas bars in London. Excellent authentic tapas, modern decor and a lively crowd. Good wine list with several Spanish choices. Occasional live music. *Open to 23.00, to 22.30 Sun.* A.V. **£**

**◖ El Bodegon & Tapas Bar**  **6 C4**
9 Park Walk SW10. 071-352 1330. A small dark tapas bar in the basement and a restaurant on the ground floor. The food is well presented and the waiters charming. Gambas al pil-pil (prawns in a hot garlic sauce), zarzuela, paella. Year-round patio seating. *(Reserve) open to 24.00.* A.Ax.Dc.V. **££**

**◖ Caravela**  **3 F5**
39 Beauchamp Place SW3. 071-581 2366. Small, intimate basement restaurant with white walls and a ceramic mosaic floor. The menu offers an extensive range of seafood and fish, as well as a wide variety of meat. Freshly grilled sardines, king prawns piri piri or regional specialities like arroz a Nazare (a rice and seafood combination). Delicious torta de laranga, an orange roll dessert. Wine list exclusively Portuguese. Guitarist or fado singer *Tue-Sun*. *(Reserve) open to 01.00, Sun to 24.00.* A.Ax.Dc.V. **££**

**Casa Santana**
44 Golborne Rd, North Kensington W10. 081-968 8764. This Portuguese restaurant is a focal point for the Portuguese community, with its lively, jolly atmosphere and rustic feel. Hearty servings of traditional Portuguese stews and fish dishes and live guitar music *Fri-Sun. Open to 23.15.* A.Ax.Dc.V. **££**

**Galicia**  **3 A2**
323 Portobello Rd W10. 081-969 3539. Crowded restaurant with an upstairs gallery. The Spanish chef prepares authentic tapas. Dishes include marinated anchovies and pulpo Gallega (octopus served on a wooden plate with rock salt and pimentos). Good selection of Galician wines. *Open to 23.00. Closed Mon.* A.Ax.V. **££**

**◖ The Rock**
619 Fulham Rd, Fulham SW6. 071-385 8179. A simple and traditional

tapas bar and restaurant serving genuine Spanish food. Flamenco fans and posters of bull-fighters decorate the walls. A choice of 29 tapas dishes awaits you at the bar plus tortilla española, fresh sardines and piping hot chorizo. *Open to 01.00, to 23.30 Sun.* A.V. **£-££**

**La Rueda**
68 Clapham High St SW4. 071-627 2173. Wagon wheels (ruedas) form a central part of the decor at this noisy, lively and friendly bar/restaurant. A stockpile of wines stacked into the enormous false ceiling runs into hundreds of bottles, with over 72 Spanish varieties. Good traditional food such as paella, patatas bravas, prawns in garlic. *(Reserve) open to 23.00, to 22.30 Sun.* A.Ax.V. **£-££**

**Triñanes**
298 Kentish Town Rd, Kentish Town NW5. 071-482 3616. Basically a tapas ·bar serving the same food upstairs and down. Specials change weekly. If you feel like some traditional Spanish entertainment, this is the place to come as the owners perform as guitarist and flamenco dancer. *(Reserve) open to 02.00, to 01.00 Sun.* No credit cards. **££**

## THAI

**Bahn Thai**                                                    **4 E2**
21a Frith St W1. 071-437 8504. Stylish decor and high-quality authentic Thai food make this a very popular restaurant where the dishes are chilli-rated for spiciness! Vegetarians are well catered for. Try the fiery Thai whisky. *(Reserve) open to 23.15.* A.Ax.V. **££**

**Bangkok**                                                      **6 D2**
9 Bute St SW7. 071-584 8529. The first Thai restaurant to be established in London. Limited but excellent menu. Beef satay in peanut sauce and Thai noodles and chicken fried in garlic are favourites with the regulars. *(Reserve) open to 23.00. Closed Sun.* A.V. **££**

**❰❰ Blue Elephant**                                             **6 A5**
4-5 Fulham Broadway SW6. 071-385 6595. One of London's best Thai restaurants. The surroundings resemble a tropical jungle, and the food is beautifully presented, Royal Thai style, by unobtrusive waiters and waitresses in Thai costume. *(Reserve) open to 00.15, to 22.15 Sun.* A.Ax.Dc.V. **£££**

**Busabong Too**                                                 **6 C4**
1a Langton St SW10. 071-352 7414. A Thai restaurant with a loyal following. Low tables and cushions provide relaxed but elegant surroundings. Menu includes lots of spicy specialities. Charming attentive service. *(Reserve) open to 23.15.* A.Ax.Dc.V. **££-£££**

**Chiang Mai**                                                   **4 E2**
48 Frith St W1. 071-437 7444. Modelled on a traditional Thai stilt-house with an air of calm and serenity. Try beef with kaffir lime leaves and lemon grass soup. There's a set menu for those unfamiliar with Thai cuisine. *(Reserve) open to 23.00.* A.V. **££**

**Sri Siam**                                                     **4 E3**
14 Old Compton St W1. 071-434 3544. Popular Thai restaurant, attracting a fashionable crowd with its stylish interior and superb

food. The soups and stir-fry dishes are particularly popular. *Open to 23.15.* A.Ax.Dc.V. **££**

**Thai Pavilion**   **4 E3**

42 Rupert St W1. 071-287 6333. This four-storey restaurant has something to offer all tastes. Each floor is named after a Buddhist heaven; the basement, complete with fountain, is for relaxed dining; the ground floor is now a 'sateh' bar, similar to a snack bar. The first floor restaurant, with its waterfall, is for more cosy and intimate dining, while the second floor is in true, traditional style with low cushions. An interesting menu which is changed frequently – the Royal Thai is a mixture of prawns, asparagus and black mushrooms. *(Reserve) open to 23.15 Mon-Thur, to 23.30 Fri & Sat, to 22.30 Sun.* A.Ax.Dc.V. **££**

## VEGETARIAN

**Blah Blah Blah**

78 Goldhawk Rd, Shepherd's Bush W12. 081-746 1337. Imaginative and original restaurant/café. Tempting and mouth-watering menu – fennel and apple korma and ciabatta with olive paste, sesame crêpes filled with spinach, courgette and ricotta with a creamy mushroom and white wine sauce. Friendly service. Unlicensed but you may bring your own drinks. *(Reserve) open to 23.30. Closed Sun.* No credit cards. **£-££**

**de Las Casas**

153 Clapham High St SW4. 071-738 8760. A trendy restaurant/café with a local clientele, decorated in bright colours. Newspapers, chess and backgammon boards provided on request. Very relaxed atmosphere. Soups are a must, blue cheese and celery, followed by tofu and fennel goulash with rice or apple. Tempting cheesecakes, trifles and scrumptious cakes. Entertainment: jazz, flamenco (phone for details). *Open to 22.30. Closed Sun.* No credit cards. **£**

**◖◗ Fungus Mungus**

264 Battersea Park Rd, Battersea SW11. 071-924 5578. Not the most attractive name for this 1960s-style cluttered bar with a laid-back atmosphere. Efficient staff serve up international vegetarian food, which you can wash down with some very exotic beers. *Open to 24.00, to 22.30 Sun.* No credit cards. **££**

**Manna**   **1 B1**

4 Erskine Rd NW3. 071-722 8028. Good, reliable food in this authentic vegetarian restaurant. There are cool stone floors and pine tables which create a farmhouse kitchen atmosphere. Home-made food, including the bread, and welcoming and friendly service. *Open to 23.00.* No credit cards. **£**

**Mildred's**   **4 E2**

58 Greek St W1. 071-494 1634. Trendy glass-fronted café. Excellent vegetarian, vegan and some fish and seafood dishes on the daily-changing menu. They use organic produce where possible and no preservatives or additives. The vegetable stir-fry with noodles is very popular, either plain or with satay sauce. Follow with home-made brown bread ice cream. *Open to 23.00. Closed Sun.* No credit cards. **£**

## VIETNAMESE

### Mekong                                          7 C2
46 Churton St SW1. 071-834 6896. An unpretentious Thai/Vietnamese restaurant with a bistro-like atmosphere. Beautifully presented cuisine with a choice of vegetarian dishes and set-price menus. *(Reserve) open to 22.45.* A.V. **££**

### Nam Long at Le Shaker
159 Old Brompton Rd SW5. 071-373 1926. Behind the busy and noisy cocktail bar lies a peaceful and relaxed restaurant serving excellent food. Try the Vietnamese beef salad with coriander and mint or the butterfly king prawns. *(Reserve) open to 23.30. Closed Sun.* A.Ax.Dc.V. **££**

### Pho                                             4 E3
2 Lisle St W1. No phone. A very popular, thriving café-style restaurant, serving quick food at reasonable prices. The food is by no means pre-prepared; everything is cooked on the spot. 'Pho' means breakfast. *Open to 23.30.* No credit cards. **£**

### Saigon                                          4 E2
45 Frith St W1. 071-437 7109. A smart, comfortable Vietnamese restaurant in a cool, spacious building. There's a vast, imaginative menu ranging from simple spring rolls to green papaya salad. Good value set meals. *Open to 23.15. Closed Sun.* A.Ax.Dc.V. **££**

### Van Long                                        4 E2
40 Frith St W1. 071-439 1835. An attractive, modern Vietnamese restaurant. The set menus can be helpful for the uninitiated. The soups are excellent, almost a meal in themselves, and lemon grass features strongly. Superior seafood dishes, hot and sour seafood soup, fried seaweed with scallops, bang bang chicken with chilli sauce. *Open to 23.30. Closed Sun.* A.Ax.Dc.V. **££**

## PRE-THEATRE RESTAURANTS

## LATE-CLOSING RESTAURANTS

# DRINKING

Going for a drink is a national pastime in Britain, and you'd be hard pushed to find a street in London without at least one licensed venue! Continental-style pavement cafés, brasseries and bars are still springing up all over the capital, and the good old British pub is as popular as ever. Whether you fancy a glass of wine, an exotic cocktail, or just a quick pint, in London you're spoilt for choice. We have divided a selection of the best drinking spots around town into the following categories: bars, brasseries, pubs and wine bars.

Although traditional evening opening hours are *17.30-23.00 Mon-Sat, 19.00-22.30 Sun,* licensing laws have been relaxed so that pubs and bars can now open all day (look for the 🍷 symbol) from *11.00-23.00 Mon-Sat (no change to Sun opening hours).* Where there is no symbol they are *open traditional pub hours.* Any other variations to the above hours are stated at the end of each entry.

**B** – Bar food/snacks     **D** – Restaurant dinner
**£**=inexpensive food     **££**=medium priced     **£££**=top priced

## BARS

Cocktail bars have always been popular drinking spots in London. Cocktails are expensive, but you do get value for money, glamorous surroundings, possibly the odd famous face and bar staff with the expertise to concoct something with a flourish to suit your personal taste. They come into their own at 'cocktail hour', around *18.00* or *19.00*. Those run by the large West End hotels are the most reliable – they do not tend to serve food, but put more emphasis on the serious business of mixing drinks. Many of the other bars, however, do serve excellent food, which varies from a snack to a full meal. It is advisable to *check the price in advance*.

Most bars run a 'happy hour', generally one or two hours in the early evening when drinks are cheaper, often half-price.

### American Bar                                                    4 G3
Savoy Hotel, Strand WC2. 071-836 4343. Glass-topped cocktail bar in art deco style where you can sample expertly mixed cocktails like the dry martini, Royal Silver and Moonwalk. The barmen are happy to devise new concoctions should the enormous range not be to your satisfaction. Pianist *nightly*. Smart dress. A.Ax.Dc.V.

### ● Arizona                                                       1 D1
2-2a Jamestown Rd NW1. 071-284 4730. Very busy, lively video bar attached to a Tex-Mex restaurant. Bottled Mexican beers (served with the standard slice of lime) and an exuberant tequila girl who'll no doubt tempt you into the odd slammer or two! *Open to 24.00, to 22.30 Sun*. No credit cards.

### ● Athenaeum Bar                                                 4 C4
Athenaeum Hotel, Piccadilly W1. 071-499 3464. Mellow wood-panelled room for discreet drinking. This bar has one of London's biggest selections of malt whiskies. A.Ax.Dc.V.

### ● Bar Escoba                                                    6 D2
102 Old Brompton Rd SW7. 071-373 2403. Crowded Spanish-style bar/restaurant serving tapas and other snacks. Very popular with Spaniards and young locals. Fairly pricey. Live South American music on *Sun & Mon*. Small upstairs bar *open to 24.00*. A.Ax.Dc.V. **B** *to 23.00*.

### ● Bar Royale                                                    1 E2
111-113 Camden High St NW1. 071-911 0667. Flashy mirrored video bar with extremely skilled staff. This must be where Tom Cruise learned the ropes for his role in *Cocktail*! DJs at weekends. Entry charge *after 22.00 Fri & Sat. Open to 01.00, to 02.00 Fri & Sat, to 22.30 Sun*. V.

### ● Bar Sol                                                       4 F2
11-12 Russell St WC2. 071-240 5330. This jazz/latin venue is sure to be packed with people out for a good time. A wide range of Spanish and Mexican beers are served in wacky surroundings. A.Ax.Dc.V.

### ● Boardwalk                                                     4 E2
18 Greek St W1. 071-287 2051. Bright, smart decor and regular happy hours make this bar popular with the Soho media set. The restaurant has an unusual mix of American Deep South and French cuisine. *Open to 01.00, to 02.00 Fri & Sat. Closed Sun*. A.Ax.Dc.V. **B** *to 24.00*.

### Bracewell's Bar                                                 4 C4
Park Lane Hotel, Piccadilly W1. 071-499 6321. John Siddley designed this room highlighted with Chinese lacquer. Canapés, memorable classic cocktails and new ones prepared to individual choice. A.Ax.Dc.V.

### ● Break for the Border                                          4 D2
8 Argyll St W1. 071-734 5776. Good place to go if you are in a party mood and if you're with a large group of people. Two bars and a

restaurant. Great choice of margaritas; also shooters, mixed liqueurs and, of course, cocktails. If you feel like eating as well, choose from the American/Tex-Mex menu. *(Reservations for large parties only).* A.Ax.V. **B** *to 23.30.*

### 🍷 Brixtonian
11 Dorrell Place, off Nursery Rd, Brixton SW9. 071-978 8870. Very popular and trendy bar below a restaurant of the same name. The relaxed friendly atmosphere conjures up feelings of the Caribbean, helped along by the wide range of rums – over 200! *Open to 24.00 Mon-Wed, to 01.00 Thur-Sat, to 23.00 Sun.* A.V.

### 🍷 Café Pacifico
**4 F2**
5 Langley St WC2. 071-379 7728. This bar/restaurant built in a converted warehouse has a long and welcoming bar where you can

sit and drink margaritas, tequilas or Mexican beer to your heart's content. Latin music plays in the background and on Mexican festivals a traditional band plays the real thing. *Open to 23.45, to 22.45 Sun.* A.Ax.V. **B** *to 23.45.*

### 🍷 Café Royal
4 D3

68 Regent St W1. 071-437 9090. First opened in 1865 by Daniel Nicolas Thevenon, a Parisian wine merchant. The Domino Room became a fashionable meeting place from 1890 to the early 1920s for artists and writers such as Aubrey Beardsley, Oscar Wilde and Whistler and in the 1930s for J.B. Priestley and T.S. Eliot. The Grill Room still preserves the slightly decadent atmosphere of the old café. *Closed Sun.* A.Ax.Dc.V. **B** *to 22.45.*

### 🍷 Casper's
4 E2

2 St Anne's Court, off Dean St W1. 071-494 4941. Each of the tables in this lively bar/restaurant has a telephone enabling you to make contact with anyone on another table without revealing your identity! Bar *open to 23.00*, restaurant *to 00.15. Closed Sun.* A.V.

### 🍷 Churchill's Bar
4 A2

Churchill Hotel, 30 Portman Sq W1. 071-486 5800. Beautiful bar in Regency-style room. Murals of oriental sporting scenes blend subtly with the deep-red fittings. Dozens of elaborately mixed cocktails. *Closed Sun.* A.Ax.Dc.V.

### 🍷 Circa
4 C3

Landsdowne House, 59 Berkeley Sq W1. 071-499 7850. Glossy, stylish bar, on the ground floor of the Saatchi & Saatchi building, and popular with advertising people. Extensive wine list and tempting bar snacks. *Closed Sun.* A.Ax.Dc.V. **B** *to 22.30.*

### 🍷 Cuba Libre
2 D2

72 Upper St N1. 071-354 9998. Very popular bar and restaurant with live Cuban music; arrive early at weekends to ensure a seat. Chilean, Mexican and Portuguese wines, plus beers and cocktails. *Open to 02.00, to 24.00 Sun & Mon.* A.Ax.V. **D** *to 24.00.*

### The Dive Bar
4 E3

The King's Head, Gerrard St W1. 071-437 5858. In the basement of the King's Head bar is London's oldest cellar bar; it opened in 1934. Noisy, good music, with fairly unfavourable decor, or rather lack of it. Worth going for a good old traditional pint. No credit cards.

### 🍷 The Dug Out Café
4 E3

12a Irving St WC2. 071-925 0457. 'Dug out' in this context refers to the trench at the side of an American football pitch; hence all the American sport paraphernalia. Exotic and obscure cocktails are served by barmen proud of their know-how and skill. Cheapish beer. A.Ax.V. **B** *to 23.00, to 22.30 Sun.*

### 🍷 Freuds
4 F2

198 Shaftesbury Ave WC2. 071-240 9933. This bar is fitted out in earth colours and has a very relaxed atmosphere. Good meeting place for pre-club/theatre/cinema. Trendy, young clientele. Short cocktail list and imported beers. Jazz on *Sun.* No credit cards.

### Green's Champagne & Oyster Bar
4 D4

36 Duke St SW1. 071-930 4566. Drink champagne and snack on the finest oysters or fresh salmon fishcakes. Popular with internation-

al businessmen and all in all a very British experience. *Closed Sun.*
A.Ax.Dc.V. **B** *to 22.45.*

📮 **Henry J. Bean's (But His Friends All Call**       **6 E3**
 **Him Hank) Bar & Grill**
195-197 King's Rd SW3. 071-352 9255. Long wooden bar, with
high tables and stools and an extensive food counter. Cocktails on
request. A.Ax.V. **B** *to 22.30, to 22.00 Sun.*

📮 **ICA Bar**       **4 E4**
The Mall SW1. 071-930 3647. You need an ICA day pass to drink at
the bar here, but that gives you free entry to the current exhibition.
Relaxed, arty atmosphere and a paper-reading, chess-playing clientele. Delicious, wholesome food served in the café below. Pub prices
at the bar. No credit cards.

📮 **King's Bar, Hotel Russell**       **2 A5**
Hotel Russell, Russell Sq WC1. 071-837 6470. Very civilised, relaxed,
gentlemen's club-style bar, with high ceilings, wooden-panelling and
huge leather armchairs. Extensive choice of drinks. A.Ax.Dc.V.

📮 **Lillie Langtry Bar**       **4 A6**
Cadogan Hotel, Sloane St SW1. 071-235 7141. Charming intimate
cocktail lounge in the original drawing room where the 'Jersey Lily'
(mistress of Edward VII) entertained. The decor is aptly Edwardian,
suffused with delicate colours and feminine elegance. A.Ax.Dc.V.

📮 **Maxie's**       **3 G5**
143 Knightsbridge SW1. 071-225 2553. The original idea of serving
Chinese snacks has made this Knightsbridge wine bar extremely
popular. The wine list has been carefully selected to complement a
range of tasty delicacies such as duck pancakes and spring rolls.
There is also a restaurant area with a more expensive menu. *Closed
Sun.* A.Ax.V. **B** *to 22.45.*

📮 **Maxwell's**       **4 F3**
16-17 Russell St WC2. 071-836 0303. This Covent Garden restaurant/
bar/grill is very popular with office workers and tourists, always busy
and lively. There is a very good selection of inexpensive drinks, the
measures being American-sized, ie doubles! Highly-skilled barmen, just
waiting for a cocktail challenge. *Open to 24.00.* A.Ax.V. **B** *to 24.00.*

**Nautilus**       **4 E3**
3 Panton St SW1. 071-321 0197. Stylish Chinese-run cocktail bar on
two floors, decorated in black and white, with marble tables and
floors. Long list of expertly made cocktails, including house specialities.
Non-alcoholic cocktails and beers are also served. *Closed Sun.* A.Ax.V.

📮 **Old Orleans**
8 Queen's Road, Richmond, Surrey. 081-940 1306. A barbecue
smokehouse with a true taste of the Deep South. Good range of
cocktails and a lively atmosphere. A.Ax.V. **B** *to 22.00.*

**Rib Room Bar**       **6 F1**
Carlton Tower Hotel, Cadogan Place SW3. 071-235 5411. A popular
bar with a wide range of frothy cocktails and particularly good
martinis. Much frequented by the smart set. A.Ax.Dc.V.

**Rumours**       **4 G3**
33 Wellington St WC2. 071-836 0038. The main bar is in a large,
pillared room surrounded by mirrors – a former flower market, now

a fashionable setting in which to enjoy an imaginative range of modern and classic cocktails. Two basement bars. *Open to 23.00, to 22.00 Sun.* A.Ax.Dc.V.

📎 **Shuffles** 4 E2

3 Rathbone Place W1. 071-255 1098. This popular wine bar turns into a club later in the evening. Large murals of jazz singers and a snack menu which has 22 different varieties of sandwich. *Open to 03.00. Closed Sun.* A.Ax.V. **B** *to 22.00.*

📎 **TGI Friday's** 4 F3

6 Bedford St WC2. 071-379 0585. A large, loud and lively bar attached to an American-style burger restaurant. Wild cocktails and a fun atmosphere. *Open to 23.30, to 23.00 Sun.* A.Ax.V.

**Trader Vic's** 4 B4

Basement, London Hilton Hotel, Park Lane W1. 071-493 7586. The London branch of this famous international chain is every bit as sumptuous as its overseas counterparts. The decor is ocean-inspired and the cocktails are served with flowers floating in them. The cocktail menu is sure to bring a smile to the face of any connoisseur. *Open to 01.00, to 22.30 Sun.* A.Ax.Dc.V.

📎 **WKD Café** 1 D1

18 Kentish Town Rd NW1. 071-267 1869. This popular north London bar without doubt boasts one of the finest decors in town. The chairs are works of art, complementing the mixed media art exhibitions that line the walls. There's also dancing to live music and DJ sounds. *Open to 02.00 Wed-Sat, to 23.00 Sun.* A.Ax.V. **B** *to 24.00.*

# BRASSERIES

Continental-style bars and brasseries are to be found all over the capital. They offer good food (from snacks to three-course meals) and alcoholic drinks, which you can consume without having to eat, in informal, stylish surroundings. Out of a cast of hundreds we have listed good brasseries offering value for money and a pleasant atmosphere.

📎 **La Brasserie** 6 E2

272 Brompton Rd SW3. 071-584 1668. The most authentic French-style brasserie in London. Sophisticated but unpretentious with efficient service and a conventional menu blanquette de veau, avocado with celery and smoked salmon, onion soup, boeuf bourguignon. *Open to 24.00, to 23.30 Sun.* A.Ax.Dc.V. **£££**

📎 **Brasserie du Coin** 2 B5

54 Lamb's Conduit St WC1. 071-405 1717. A typical French brasserie with wooden floors and candlelit tables. You can get quick meals such as fresh filled baguettes at the counter or more leisurely classic French dishes such as moules marinières, boeuf bourguignon and good cheeses. Fixed menu available. The wine list is mostly French with some Portuguese and Italian alternatives. *Open to 22.30. Closed Sat & Sun.* A.Ax.Dc.V. **£-££**

📎 **Brasserie du Marché aux Puces**

349 Portobello Rd, North Kensington W10. 081-968 5828. Trendy and minimalist, with scrubbed wooden tables, this brasserie is pleas-

antly light and airy, due to its street-corner position. International menu with daily specials such as lamb shanks with root vegetables and excellent vegetarian alternatives. *Closed Sun*. No credit cards. **££**

● **Café des Amis du Vin**                                                    **4 F2**
11 Hanover Place, off Long Acre WC2. 071-379 3444. This extremely popular brasserie is sandwiched between a wine bar in the basement and the elegant Salon des Amis du Vin restaurant upstairs. The walls are adorned with photographs from the nearby Opera House. Several types of French sausage and excellent cheeses are on the reasonably priced menu. *Open to 23.30. Closed Sun.* A.Ax.V. **£**

● **Café Bohème**                                                             **4 E2**
13 Old Compton St W1. 071-734 0623. Pleasantly chaotic French-style brasserie/bar in the heart of Soho. Chic clientele and pavement tables. You may well spot a famous face here. *Open to 01.00, to 23.00 Sun.* A.Ax.V. **££**

● **Café Delancey**                                                           **1 D2**
3 Delancey St NW1. 071-387 1985. Relaxed, European-style brasserie with a sophisticated, bohemian appeal. Delicious cakes and unusual daily specials contribute to making this one of London's best brasseries. *Open to 24.00*. A.V. **£-££**

*Café des Amis du Vin*

**Café Flo**
A growing chain of chic Parisian-style cafés. Reasonably priced à la carte menus plus well-prepared set menus and a tasty range of puddings. A.V. **££**
- 205 Haverstock Hill, Belsize Park NW3. 071-435 6744.
- 127-129 Kensington Church St W8. 071-727 8142. **3 B4**
- 51 St Martin's Lane WC2. 071-836 8289. **4 F3**
- 334 Upper St N1. 071-226 7916. **2 D2**

**Café Italien des Amis du Vin** **4 D1**
19 Charlotte St W1. 071-636 4174. Good value, classic Italian dishes in this charming brasserie, which spills out onto the street in summer. Italian, French and Californian wines and champagnes. Also a restaurant and wine bar. Closed Sun. A.Ax.Dc.V. **££**

- **Café Météor**
158 Fulham Palace Rd, Hammersmith W6. 081-741 5037. Laid-back and friendly brasserie/restaurant with a wide range of snacks and more substantial dishes. The extensive selection of coffee is enough to placate any caffeine addict! Live music nightly. Open to 23.00. A.V. **£-££**

- **Café Pelican** **4 F3**
45 St Martin's Lane WC2. 071-379 0309. A narrow, sumptuous brasserie and French restaurant renowned for its impeccable service. Sample anything from a well put together croque-monsieur to à la carte specialities with gentle piano jazz in the background. Open to 02.00. Snack menu only from 23.00. A.Ax.Dc.V. **£-£££**

- **Café Rouge** **5 F4**
Hay's Galleria, Tooley St SE1. 071-378 0097. Sister to the Café Pelican, this brasserie is run on similar lines with wooden tables and classical French paintings adorning the walls. There's a French pizzeria upstairs. Open to 22.00. Closed Sat & Sun. A.Ax.Dc.V. **£-££**

**Café Royal Brasserie** **4 D3**
68 Regent St W1. 071-734 0981. Grand and elegant, the Café Royal has an excellent international menu which includes several good vegetarian dishes. A huge range of cocktails. Closed Sun. A.Ax.Dc.V. **££-£££**

**Camden Brasserie** **1 D2**
216 Camden High St NW1. 071-482 2114. A comfortable brasserie near the canal serving quality Mediterranean food. They're renowned for their excellent pommes frites. Exposed brickwork and an open fire in winter add to the relaxed ambience. Open to 23.30, to 22.30 Sun. A.V. **£-££**

- **Covent Garden Brasserie** **4 F3**
1 Covent Garden Piazza WC2. 071-240 6654. This Parisian-style brasserie provides a refuge from the hustle and bustle of the piazza, serving snacks such as nachos and mussels, plus more substantial French and Italian dishes. The wine list is mostly French, but includes bottles from Chile and California. A.Ax.Dc.V. **£**

**Dôme**
This successful chain of brasseries named after the famous Paris Dôme has branches all over London, distinguished by their brown and cream striped canopies. Friendly, lively atmosphere and standard brasserie fare. A.Ax.Dc.V. **£-££**
- 38-39 Hampstead High St, Hampstead NW3. 071-435 4240.
- 354 King's Rd SW3. 071-352 7611. **6 D4**
- 98-100 Shepherd's Bush Rd, Hammersmith W6. 071-602 7732.
- 341 Upper St N1. 071-226 3414. **2 D2**

### ☙ Fungus Mungus

264 Battersea Park Rd, Battersea SW11. 071-924 5578. The food served at this laid-back, 60s-style bar/restaurant is a lot more attractive than the name would suggest! Munch your way through an acclaimed international vegetarian menu (changes weekly) washed down with an exotic bottled beer or two, or a glass of Chilean wine. Live bands and guest DJs play in the bar area, where snacks are available. *Open to 24.00, to 23.30 Sun*. No credit cards. **££**

### HQs                                                       1 D1

West Yard, Camden Lock NW1. 071-485 6044. Unique canalside venue comprising a dancefloor, restaurant and two bars. Some of the best jazz funk and Latin American bands in London. It's best to reserve a table at weekends. *Open to 23.30, to 02.00 Fri & Sat*. A.Ax.Dc.V. **££**

### Joe's Café                                                 6 E2

126 Draycott Ave SW3. 071-225 2217. Striking black, white and chrome interior and an extremely suave clientele. The exquisite international menu includes such delicacies as quail salad and calf's liver, not to mention their Porkinson banger with mash. Fine cocktails. *Open to 23.30. Closed Sun*. A.Ax.Dc.V. **£££**

### ☙ Le Metro                                                4 A6

28 Basil St SW3. 071-589 6286. In the heart of fashionable Knightsbridge, below the L'Hotel hotel, Le Metro is a French country-style brasserie with candlelit tables and an extensive selection of good-quality, mostly French, wines. *Open Mon-Fri to 23.00*. A.Ax.V. **££**

### ☙ Opera Terrazza                                          4 F3

45 East Terrace, Covent Garden WC2. 071-379 0666. Part of a chain of trattoria distinguished by their bright blue and yellow decor and·

*Opera Terrazza, Covent Garden*

modern Italian menu. Housed in a replica of the old Flower Market Conservatory, near the Royal Opera House. Terrace seating overlooks
. the piazza. *Open to 23.30.* A.Ax.Dc.V. **££**

### The Oriel                                          6 G2
50-51 Sloane Sq SW1. 071-730 4275. Large, comfortable and well-situated French brasserie/wine bar/art gallery. The menu offers regional French cuisine that includes all the staples plus their special choux croutes and black pudding. A.Ax.Dc.V. **£-££**

### PJ's                                               6 E2
52 Fulham Rd SW3. 071-581 0025. A huge, trendy brasserie/bar very popular with the Fulham set. An international menu includes American and Creole dishes, and the wine list spans the globe from America to Australia to France. Great place to people watch. A.Ax.Dc.V. **££**

### Le Renoir                                          4 E3
79 Charing Cross Rd WC2. 071-734 2515. Brasserie/restaurant where the waiters are almost more French than those you'd find in France! Their steak and duck dishes are particularly popular. *Open to 01.30, to 24.00 Sun.* A.Ax.Dc.V. **££**

### Soho Brasserie                                     4 E2
23-25 Old Compton St W1. 071-439 9301. Once the haunt of Mick Jagger, this pub conversion has an arty French interior and a good-looking clientele to match. The tables outside are much sought after during the summer months as an excellent place to watch the world go by. Good bar snacks and more substantial meals at the rear. A.Ax.Dc.V. **££**

### Soho Soho                                          4 E2
11-13 Frith St W1. 071-494 3491. A glass-fronted wine bar/brasserie which spills out onto the pavement on warm summer evenings. Upstairs is a top-quality French restaurant; downstairs is a cheaper rotisserie, where wine is available in half bottles. *Open to 01.00. Closed Sun.* A.Ax.Dc.V. **£-££**

### Tearooms des Artistes
697 Wandsworth Rd, Wandsworth SW8. 071-720 4028. Despite its name, Tearooms is more of a brasserie/restaurant, specialising in vegetarian cuisine. There's a large upstairs area and a very pleasant garden attracting a friendly, bohemian clientele. Great atmosphere. *Open to 24.00. Closed Mon.* No credit cards. **££**

### Terrace Garden                                     4 D3
Le Meridien Hotel, 21 Piccadilly W1. 071-734 8000. It's well-worth paying a little extra to visit the Terrace Garden, not only for its well-prepared French menu but also for its fabulous location, in a conservatory overlooking one of the most famous landmarks in London – Piccadilly Circus. *Open to 23.30.* A.Ax.Dc.V. **££-£££**

### Tuttons Brasserie                                  4 F2
11-12 Russell St WC2. 071-836 4141. Right on the edge of the Covent Garden piazza, this is a large, airy brasserie with a good, reasonably priced English/international menu and a relaxed atmosphere. *Open to 23.30, to 24.00 Fri & Sat.* A.Ax.Dc.V. **£**

# PUBS

Most London pubs date from the 19th century, but many are up to 400 years old. An unlimited number of pubs can be found by the thirsty or curious imbiber, but of the thousands in London we have given a selection based on location or history. Pubs used to be very class-conscious places where the working men drank in the Public Bar, and the middle classes kept aloof in the Saloon or Lounge Bar. Go to the Public Bar if you like to play darts in an informal atmosphere and don't mind rudimentary furnishings. For more comfortable surroundings and softer lighting, go to the Saloon Bar or Lounge Bar. Real ale, beer brewed in the traditional manner, is now served in numerous London pubs. Many pubs serve snacks in the evening, some have more substantial bar food available, such as steak and kidney pie, lasagne, chilli con carne, and a few have restaurants. Times shown in this section refer to last orders for food. *Closed* refers to the whole pub. Most pubs do not accept credit cards in payment for drinks only.

### Admiral Codrington                                    6 E2
17 Mossop St SW3. 071-589 4603. Good Chelsea pub with wood panelling and a conservatory restaurant. Over 12 different whiskies available. Popular with resident Sloanes! **B D** *to 20.30.* **£**

### 🍷 Albert                                                     7 C1
52 Victoria St SW1. 071-222 5577. One of the oldest and grandest Victorian pubs in the area. Popular with MPs – there's even a division bell to remind them when it's time to return to the Commons! Carvery restaurant serving traditional English fare. Real ales served from hand pumps. **D** *to 21.30.* **££**

### 🍷 Albion                                                    2 C1
10 Thornhill Rd N1. 071-607 7450. Albion was the Celtic and then the Latin name for Britain, and this is indeed a wonderfully traditional pub. Hundreds of horse brasses, paintings by local artists and an open fire in winter. There's also a small rear garden and a sunny forecourt for summer drinking. **B** *to 21.30, to 21.00 Sun.* **££**

### 🍷 The Alma
499 Old York Rd, Wandsworth SW18. 081-870 2537. Large and decorative with a huge mahogany bar, table football and a well-reputed French restaurant at the back. **D** *to 22.30 Mon-Sat.* **££**

### 🍷 The Angel                                                 4 B2
37 Thayer St W1. 071-486 7763. Victorian oak-panelled pub on two levels, popular with nearby office workers. **B** *to 20.00 Mon-Sat.* **£**

### 🍷 Argyll Arms                                               4 D2
18 Argyll St W1. 071-734 6117. 300-year-old pub which has retained all its traditional features. The old manager's pulpit-like

*The Argyll Arms*

office still stands in the middle of the main bar. *Closed Sun.* **B D** *to 19.00.* **£**

### Baker & Oven                                     4 B1
10 Paddington St W1. 071-935 5088. Revamped Victorian pub with green, black and white decor. Restaurant and wine bar downstairs with live music and cabaret. **B D** *to 23.00, to 22.30 Sun.* **££**

### Barley Mow                                       5 C1
50 Long Lane EC1. 071-606 6591. Built on the site of a monastery, this 400-year-old inn specialises in real ale and bitters. Stylish Edwardian interior, exposed beams and wine bar upstairs. *Closed Sat & Sun.* **B** *to 21.30.* **£**

### Blackfriar                                       5 C3
174 Queen Victoria St EC4. 071-236 5650. Triangular-shaped building in the shadows of Blackfriars railway bridge. Stunning bronze and marble art nouveau interior with arched mosaic ceilings, marble columns and crouching alabaster demons. *Closed Sat & Sun.* **B** *to 22.00.* **£**

### Boot & Flogger                                   5 D4
10-20 Redcross Way SE1. 071-407 1184. Part of the chain of Davy's

wine bars; dusty barrels, old prints and sawdust-covered floors. Housed in a converted ham-smoking factory, with the original ovens in the basement. **B D** to 20.00 Mon-Fri. **£**

**🍷 Britannia**     **3 B6**
1 Allen St W8. 071-937 1864. Warm, friendly, traditional pub with a conservatory and plenty of seating. **B** to 21.30. **£**

**🍷 Buck's Head**     **1 D2**
202 Camden·High St NW1. 071-284 1513. Invariably crowded pub with large Victorian windows to be seen through. Generous helpings of nuts, olives and Japanese rice crackers are available at the bar.

**🍷 Bunch of Grapes**     **6 E1**
207 Brompton Rd SW3. 071-589 4944. Crowded Victorian pub. The glass 'snobscreens' separating the bars were originally installed so that the coachmen couldn't see how much the gentlemen were drinking! **B** to 22.00. **£**

**Cartoonist**     **5 B2**
76 Shoe Lane EC4. 071-353 2828. In the old heart of the newspaper world, this Victorian pub is lavishly wallpapered with original cartoons. Its outside sign is changed every year, the design being chosen from those submitted by cartoonists. Headquarters of the International Cartoonist Club. **B** to 23.00 Mon-Fri. **£**

**🍷 Cheshire Cheese**     **5 B3**
5 Little Essex St, off Milford Lane WC2. 071-836 2347. Intimate Jacobean pub with original oak beams, three bars and a resident ghost. Closed Sat & Sun. **B** to 23.00. **£**

**🍷 Cheshire Cheese, Ye Olde**     **5 B2**
Wine Office Court, off 145 Fleet St EC4. 071-353 6170. Rebuilt after the Great Fire, with low ceilings, oak tables and sawdust on the floor. Although new bars have been added, most of this pub hasn't changed much since those early days. Six bars. Traditional English fare. **D** to 21.30. **£**

**🍷 Cittie of York**     **5 A1**
22-23 High Holborn WC1. 071-242 7670. This late 17thC pub is broken up with cosy, wood-panelled cubicles where lawyers used to have confidential chats with their clients. Closed Sun. **B** to 21.30. **£**

**🍷 Coach & Horses**     **4 D2**
1 Great Marlborough St W1. 071-437 3282. This 18thC coaching inn stands on what was once the main road to Bath. Pavement benches for al fresco drinking and The Horse Box wine bar upstairs. Closed from 20.00 Sat and all day Sun.

**🍷 Coach & Horses**     **4 E2**
29 Greek St W1. 071-437 5920. Celebrated Soho institution famous for its landlord, Norman Balon – self-proclaimed as the rudest in London – and its literary regulars, including columnist Jeffrey Barnard, notorious for propping up the bar.

**🍷 Cock Tavern, Ye Olde**     **5 B2**
22 Fleet St EC4. 071-353 8570. Lawyers and nearby office workers have replaced the journalists who used to frequent this small tavern with literary and Dickensian associations. Pictures of 18thC London adorn the walls. Nell Gwynn, Pepys and Garrick once drank here. Closed Sat & Sun.

🍺 **County Arms**
345 Trinity Rd, Wandsworth SW18. 081-874 8532. Comfortable country-style pub looking out over Wandsworth Common. Beer garden and home-cooked bar meals. **B** to 22.00 Mon-Fri. **£**

🍺 **Crocker's**
24 Aberdeen Place, St John's Wood NW8. 071-286 6608. Originally known as Crocker's Folly because its founder, Frank Crocker, built it in 1897 on the mistaken assumption that Marylebone Street Station, with all its thirsty travellers, was about to be built nearby. His ghost is said to haunt it, still waiting for the trains to stop across the road. Vegetarians catered for. **B** to 21.45, to 21.30 Sun. **£**

**Cross Keys**                                        **6 E4**
2 Lawrence St SW3. 071-352 1893. Popular Chelsea local with friendly staff. Open fire in winter, real ales, enclosed garden and excellent home-made sausages! **B** to 23.00 Mon-Sat. **£**

🍺 **Crown**                                          **2 C2**
116 Cloudesley Rd N1. 071-837 7107. Friendly Islington pub with lots of polished wood, brass and glass. Video screen and regular quiz nights. Traditional pub grub. **B** to 21.30. **£**

🍺 **De Hems**                                        **4 E3**
11 Macclesfield St, off Gerrard St W1. 071-437 2494. Named after a Dutch licensee and serving Dutch specialities, this is a Victorian pub very popular with visitors.

🍺 **Dirty Dick's**                                   **5 F1**
202 Bishopsgate EC2. 071-283 5888. The original pub named after Nat Bentley, well-known 18thC miser of the famous ballad. Now fully refurbished and serving real ales. Mummified cats and mouse skeletons are, despite the name, safely enclosed in a glass case in the lower bar! **B** to 23.00, to 22.30 Sun. **£**

🍺 **Duke of Cumberland**
235 New King's Rd, Parsons Green SW6. 071-736 2777. Elegant and friendly Edwardian pub. At weekends the clientele includes rugby and football supporters from the nearby stadiums. Summertime drinking can be enjoyed on Parsons Green so long as you promise to return your glass.

🍺 **Eagle**                                          **2 E4**
2 Shepherdess Walk N1. 071-253 4715. Victorian music hall pub immortalised in the song *Pop Goes The Weasel*. People used to spend their money here after 'popping the weasel', ie after pawning their possessions. **B** to 21.30. **£**

🍺 **Empress of Russia**                              **2 D4**
362 St John St EC1. 071-837 1910. Cosy pub with subdued lighting, taped music and Sky TV. **B** to 22.30 Mon-Sat. **£**

**Ennismore Arms**                                    **3 F6**
2 Ennismore Mews SW7. 071-584 0440. Homely, relaxing mews pub with neo-Georgian decor and comfortable seating. Daily changing menu. **B** to 21.30 Mon-Fri. **£**

🍺 **Fitzroy Tavern**                                 **4 D1**
16 Charlotte St W1. 071-580 3714. Famous literary and artistic pub. Real ales and taped music. **B** to 21.30. **£**

🍺 **The Flask**
77 Highgate West Hill, Highgate N6. 081-340 7260. Dating back to

1663, this large, extremely popular tavern is named after the flasks people used to buy here to fill with water at the nearby Hampstead wells. Highwayman Dick Turpin once hid in the cellars and William Hogarth and Karl Marx both drank here. Crowded forecourt during summer months. **B** *to 21.00 Mon-Sat.* **£**

### ● The French   4 E2
49 Dean St W1. 071-437 2799. Good wines. French aperitifs and an antique dispenser for adding water to your Pernod. French dining room upstairs. Live jazz *every Sun.* **D** *to 22.30.* **££**

### ● The George   4 D2
55 Great Portland St W1. 071-636 0863. Popular Edwardian pub frequented by nearby BBC staff and college students. Excellent bar food and three own-brew ales. Taped music. **B** *to 21.00.* **£**

### ● The George   5 B2
213 Strand WC2. 071-353 9238. Originally a coffee house, this fine old timbered inn, built in 1723, stands opposite the Royal Courts of Justice. *Open to 21.00 Mon-Wed, to 23.00 Thur & Fri.* Carvery restaurant *open for parties only in the evening (phone for details).*

### ● George Inn   5 E4
77 Borough High St SE1. 071-407 2056. London's only surviving galleried coaching inn rebuilt in 1676 after the Great Fire of Southwark and mentioned in Dickens' *Little Dorrit.* Shakespeare plays are occasionally performed in the courtyard. Wine bar and choice restaurant serving à la carte and set meals. **B D** *to 21.00.* **££**

### Grenadier   4 B5
18 Wilton Row SW1. 071-235 3074. Once an officers' mess for the Duke of Wellington's soldiers. Full of military bric-a-brac – there's even a sentry box outside. Good food in the restaurant and mean Bloody Marys at the bar! Supposedly haunted by a soldier who was flogged to death for cheating at cards. **D** *to 22.00.* **££**

### ● The Guinea   4 C3
30 Bruton Place W1. 071-409 1728. Pleasant old pub hidden away in a narrow cobbled Mayfair mews. Originally known as the One Pound One, probably because of the cattle pound that is thought to have once stood nearby. Good but pricey English dining room. *Closed Sun.* **B D** *to 23.00 Mon-Sat.* **££**

### ● Hole in the Wall   5 B4
5 Mepham St SE1. 071-928 6196. Free house. Ten different real ales, two stouts, six lagers and bar-loads of beer fanatics. Built into the arches by Waterloo Station. **B** *to 22.30.* **£**

### ● Horse & Groom   1 D6
128 Great Portland St W1. 071-580 4726. Attractive 200-year-old mews tavern popular with BBC employees and local office workers. **B** *to 22.00* **£**

### Island Queen   2 D3
87 Noel Rd N1. 071-226 5507. Has without doubt the most outlandish decor of any pub in London. Giant papier-mâché caricatures of politicians and famous figures are suspended from the ceiling! The upstairs restaurant is light and sunny, with a smorgasbord on *Sun.* **D** *to 22.30 Thur-Sun.* **££**

### ● King of Bohemia
10 Hampstead High St, Hampstead NW3. 071-435 6513. Bow-fronted

Georgian pub. Fashionable meeting place for locals. Good home-cooked bar meals. **B** *to 23.00, to 22.30 Sun*. **££**

### Kings Arms    6 D3
190 Fulham Rd SW3. 071-351 5043. Fine solid Victorian pub on three floors. The tiles in the lounge are listed. Arty crowd. Good bar meals with daily specials. **B** *to 22.00 Mon-Sat*. **££**

### Lamb    2 B5
94 Lamb's Conduit St WC1. 071-405 0713. Extremely friendly Bloomsbury local with some intriguing music hall photographs and Hogarth prints. Reputed to have the best 'snobscreens' in London, and the largest pub dog! **B** *to 22.00*. **£**

### Lamb & Flag    4 F3
33 Rose St, off Garrick St WC2. 071-497 9504. A 300-year-old pub, originally known as the Bucket of Blood because of the bare fist fights arranged in the upstairs room. A less gruesome clientele these days, spilling out onto the forecourt in summer months.

### The Mayflower
117 Rotherhithe St, Shadwell SE16. 071-237 4088. This famous Tudor riverside inn was originally called the Shippe, but changed its name when the *Mayflower*, which carried the Pilgrim Fathers from this part of the Thames, reached America. Pleasant wooden veranda for summertime drinking. Extensive bar menu – 40 different dishes. **B** *to 21.00 Tue-Sun*. **£**

### Museum Tavern    4 F1
49 Great Russell St WC1. 071-242 8987. Located opposite the British Museum, this traditional tavern attracts a mixture of research students and sightseers. Karl Marx wrote and drank here. **B** *to 22.00*. **£**

### Old Bull & Bush
North End Rd, Hampstead NW3. 081-455 3685. Trendy young meeting place made famous by the music hall song. Housed in an attractive 17thC building once the country home of the painter William Hogarth. The small bar resembles a library. Occasional live jazz. Real ale. **B** *to 20.30*. **£**

### Phoenix & Firkin
Windsor Walk, Denmark Hill, Camberwell SE5. 071-701 8282. High-ceilinged pub with immense railway clocks and posters of 'the old days' on the railways. Huge iron spiral staircase leads up to a balcony area. Live jazz *Sun & Mon*. **B** *to 22.30*. **£**

### Printer's Devil    5 B2
98-99 Fetter Lane EC4. 071-242 2239. A printers' and journalists' pub, named after the traditional printer's apprentice. Notable collection of early prints and etchings. Plush pizza restaurant upstairs. **B** *to 22.30*. **££**

### Prospect of Whitby
57 Wapping Wall, Shadwell E1. 071-481 1095. Historical dockland tavern dating back to the reign of Henry VIII. Samuel Pepys and Rex Whistler drank here, as did 'hanging' Judge Jeffreys and so many thieves and smugglers that it was known as the Devil's Tavern. Continental cuisine in the terrace restaurant. Occasional live music. **D** *to 22.00 Mon-Sat*. **££**

### Queen's Elm    6 D3
241 Fulham Rd SW3. 071-352 9157. So-called because Elizabeth I took shelter under a nearby elm in 1567. Large Victorian pub serving real ales, good lagers and traditional hot and cold bar snacks. **B** *to 22.00*. **£**

### Queen's Head
13 Brook Green, Hammersmith W6. 071-603 3174. A 300-year-old

wayside inn, with wood panelling. The Marquis of Queensberry, who lived nearby, is thought to have mulled over the Queensberry rules of boxing here. Beer garden, open fireplace and good English cooking in the restaurant. **D** *to 21.30 Mon-Sat.* **££**

🍷 **Railway Tavern** **5 F1**
15 Liverpool St EC2. 071-283 3598. Packed with railway relics – models, prints, posters and timetables – a train spotter's paradise! The Games Room restaurant upstairs serves mainly pizzas. **D** *to 23.00 Mon-Fri.*

🍷 **Red Lion** **4 D4**
2 Duke of York St SW1. 071-930 2030. Plenty of Victoriana in this friendly pub. Beautifully preserved mirrors and rich mahogany panelling. *Closed Sun.* **B** *to 23.00.* **£**

🍷 **Red Lion** **4 C4**
1 Waverton St W1. 071-499 1307. Lovely 17thC Mayfair inn with Royal Academy prints and paintings inside. Mingle with models, actors and young businessmen. Restaurant serving international cuisine. **B D** *to 21.45.* **££**

🍷 **Rose & Crown** **4 C5**
2 Old Park Lane W1. 071-499 1980. 200-year-old country-style pub now surrounded by Park Lane houses. Colourful and comfortable with hessian-covered walls and velvet banquette seats. Good value sandwiches and basket meals. *Closed Sun.* **B** *to 22.00.* **£**

**Rossetti**
23 Queen's Grove, St John's Wood NW8. 071-722 7141. Large airy pub/restaurant/cocktail bar on three levels with Rossetti etchings on the walls. Brass railings, tiles and potted plants. Thai food in the restaurant. **B D** *to 23.00, to 22.30 Sun.* **££**

🍷 **Running Footman** **4 C4**
5 Charles St W1. 071-499 2988. This pub once had the longest name in London: 'I am the Only Running Footman'. Popular with band-boys and croupiers from the nearby clubs. A la carte restaurant serving English food. **D** *to 21.30.* **£££**

🍷 **Salisbury** **4 F3**
90 St Martin's Lane WC2. 071-836 5863. Glittering Edwardian pub in the heart of theatreland. Cut-glass mirrors, illuminated gilt statuettes and sumptuous red velvet seats.

**Scarsdale Arms** **3 A6**
23a Edwardes Sq W8. 071-937 1811. One large bar with scrubbed wood tables and chairs. Sit amidst old clocks and plates, stuffed animals and frosted glass windows in front of an open fire. You may well spot the odd famous face. Extensive bar menu. **B** *to 22.30.* **££**

🍷 **Sherlock Holmes** **4 F4**
10 Northumberland St WC2. 071-930 2644. Perfect replica of Holmes' study at 221b Baker Street has been constructed for devotees of the cult. The whole pub is saturated with relics of the legendary fictitious detective. French and English cooking in the restaurant. **D** *to 21.15 Mon-Sat.* **££**

**Spotted Dog, The Old**
212 Upton Lane, Upton E7. 081-472 1794. Handsome inn dating back to the late 15thC and used by the city's merchants during the Great Plague. Original oak beams, plaster whitewash and prints. Restaurant. **D** *to 22.00.* **££**

◗ **Turk's Head** 6 G1
10 Motcomb St SW1. 071-235 2514. Bass Charrington pub with an open fire warming the fancy Victorian setting. Taped music.

**Watling, Ye Olde** 5 D2
29 Watling St EC4. 071-248 6252. Old oak-beamed tavern rebuilt by Wren after the Great Fire of 1666. Stands on one of the oldest roads in London.

**White Horse**
1-3 Parsons Green SW6. 071-736 2115. Beautiful old Victorian bar with huge windows and wooden floors. Four regional beer festivals each year plus an old ale festival in November. Also regular theme nights with theme beers and fine food cooked with beer. **B** *to 23.00, to 22.30 Sun.* **£-££**

◗ **Williamson's Tavern** 5 D2
1 Grovelands Court, off Bow Lane EC4. 071-248 6280. The original residence of the Lord Mayor of London before Mansion House was built. Now comprises a traditional bar, a library bar and a wine bar. *Closed Sat & Sun.* **B** *to 23.00.* **£**

◗ **Witness Box** 5 B3
36 Tudor St EC4. 071-353 6427. Built in 1974 in the cellar of a modern office block, though the two bars are decorated in authentic Edwardian style. Wine bar on ground floor.

## WINE BARS

Wine bars are a well-established (and usually more salubrious) alternative to pubs. From the vast selection in London, the following includes a few carefully chosen establishments with good wines and a relaxed atmosphere. Almost all offer wine by the glass but it usually works out cheaper to buy a bottle. Many will provide food – cheese, pâté, quiche and salads are all typical wine bar fare. Some also have their own restaurants.

**Actor's Retreat** 2 D4
326 St John St EC1. 071-837 0722. The actors here seem to have retreated to the photographs on the wall, but this comfortable and hospitable basement wine bar is still well worth a visit. Conveniently located a few minutes' walk from Sadler's Wells. *Open to 22.45. Closed Sun.* A.Ax.V.

**Andrew Edmunds** 4 D3
46 Lexington St W1. 071-437 5708. This charming wine bar/restaurant has a devoted clientele and tempting daily specials to complement a decent wine list. The daily changing menu includes delicious smoked salmon and inventive pasta dishes and salads. *Open to 22.45, to 22.30 Sun.* A.V. **B D** *to 22.30* **££**

◗ **The Archduke** 5 A4
Concert Hall Approach, South Bank SE1. 071-928 9370. Pleasant green and glass decor, underneath the arches of Waterloo Bridge. Excellent bar food with good salads, pâtés and cheeses and a restaurant upstairs specialising in sausages from all over the world. Very handy for a pre-Queen Elizabeth or Festival Hall drink or two. Good range of wines and live jazz *nightly.* A.Ax.Dc.V. **B D** *to 23.00.* **££**

**L'Artiste Musclé** **4 C4**
1 Shepherd Market W1. 071-493 6150. A cheap and cheerful French wine bar/bistro, particularly appealing in summer when you can sit outside and indulge in a spot of people watching. Well-prepared French menu and a fine selection of cheeses. *Open to 23.00.* A.V. **B D** *to 23.30.* **£**

🍷 **Bar des Amis** **4 F2**
11-14 Hanover Place, off Long Acre WC2. 071-379 3444. Extremely lively and popular wine bar below the Café des Amis brasserie and Salon restaurant. Daily specials include vegetarian dishes and delicious savoury crêpes. The wine list includes over 20 wines from the New World, plus monthly specials. *Closed Sun.* A.Ax.V. **B** *to 23.30.* **££**

🍷 **Basil's** **3 G6**
Basil Street Hotel, 8 Basil St SW3. 071-581 3311. The entrance to this wine bar is by way of an imposing iron staircase, which leads to a vaulted cellar with arches, a bar along one side and café-style seating. French and north African cuisine, plus live music every *Wed & Fri. Closed Sat & Sun.* A.Ax.Dc.V. **B D** *to 22.00.* **£**

**Le Beaujolais** **4 E3**
25 Litchfield St WC2. 071-836 2955. Lively, mixed clientele in this popular and intimate French wine bar. The wine list includes their own-label house red and white plus, of course, Beaujolais. Authentic French cooking. *Closed Sun.* A.V. **B D** *to 22.00.* **£**

🍷 **Betjeman's** **5 C1**
44 Cloth Fair, Smithfield EC1. 071-796 4981. Housed in the Jacobean home of former Poet Laureate John Betjeman, this excellent wine bar boasts a range of bar snacks, a full restaurant menu and a wine list extensive enough to stimulate any muse! The Betjeman Society hold meetings here. *Closed Sat & Sun.* A.V. **B D** *to 22.00.* **££-£££**

🍷 **Bill Bentley's** **3 F6**
31 Beauchamp Place SW3. 071-589 5080. Below a superb fish restaurant, the wine bar here is cosy and old-fashioned with a relaxed atmosphere. There's an oyster bar serving delicious and well-presented snacks including fish cakes and potted shrimps, and a patio garden for summer drinking. *Closed Sun.* A.Ax.V. **B** *to 22.30.* **£**

**Bleeding Heart** **5 B1**
Bleeding Heart Yard, off Greville St EC1. 071-242 8238. This rather unpleasant address features in Dickens' *Little Dorritt* and the established, wood-panelled wine bar/restaurant is home to a fine collection of the author's first editions. Mainly French regional cuisine with shellfish straight from nearby Billingsgate market. The house wines include a Dickens claret, which can be sipped to the tune of live piano music – but beware the ghost of murdered Lady Elizabeth Hatton, who returns from time to time to scrub her bloodstains from the cobbles! *Closed Sat & Sun.* A.Ax.Dc.V. **B D** *to 22.30.* **££**

🍷 **Brahms & Liszt** **4 F3**
19 Russell St WC2. 071-240 3661. Conveniently located, just off the Covent Garden piazza, this is an extremely popular and lively wine bar with live music downstairs – though it's more likely to be soul, rock or contemporary jazz than Brahms or Liszt! Downstairs *open to 01.00, to 22.30 Sun.* A.Ax.Dc.V.

🍷 **Cork & Bottle** **4 E3**
44-46 Cranbourn St WC2. 071-734 7807. Invariably crowded, this

*The Crusting Pipe, Covent Garden*

spacious basement wine bar near Leicester Square has an excellent selection of wines and bar snacks. If you're a wine ignoramus, read the walls – they're covered with prints and posters about wines and champagnes. A.Ax.Dc.V. **B** *to 23.00.* **£**

### ● The Crusting Pipe　　　　　　　　　　　4 F3
27 The Market, Covent Garden WC2. 071-836 1415. Part of the Davy's chain, located underneath the piazza; the outside tables are a particularly good vantage point for watching the goings-on of London's most famous market. Good food, including grills and bar snacks, and reasonably priced wines. A.Ax.Dc.V. **B** *to 23.00.* **£-££**

### Daniel's　　　　　　　　　　　　　　　4 D3
68 Regent St W1. 071-437 9090. At the back of the Cafe Royal, this pleasant, relaxed wine bar has a resident pianist, conventional bar snacks and a varied wine list. *Closed Sat & Sun.* A.Ax.Dc.V. **B** *to 22.30.* **£**

### Dean's Wine Bar　　　　　　　　　　　4 E2
26-29 Dean St W1. 071-437 4809. A wide range of international wines and an excellent menu, produced by the famous Leoni's Quo Vadis restaurant next door. *Open to 22.30. Closed Sat & Sun.* A.Ax.Dc.V. **B** *to 21.00.* **£**

### Dover Street Wine Bar　　　　　　　　4 D4
8-9 Dover St W1. 071-629 9813. Basement wine bar with wooden panelling and atmospheric candlelight. Live jazz, funk or soul bands *every night. Open to 03.00. Closed Sun.* A.Ax.Dc.V. **D** *to 01.30.* **£**

### Downs
Arch 166, Bohemia Place, Hackney E8. 081-986 4325. Reasonably priced east London wine bar housed in a converted railway arch. Candlelit tables make for an intimate atmosphere and the char-grilled dishes are particularly popular. A.Ax.Dc.V. **B D** *to 22.45.* **£**

### ● Ebury Wine Bar　　　　　　　　　　　7 A2
139 Ebury St SW1. 071-730 5447. Wine bar/restaurant serving nouvelle cuisine and 70 different wines. The mural of book shelves on the wall is well worth a read! A.Ax.Dc.V. **B** *to 22.30.* **£**

### ● Gate Street Wine Bar　　　　　　　　4 G2
10 Gate St WC2. 071-404 0358. Opening out onto a secluded backstreet, this wine bar/restaurant offers a welcome retreat from the bustle of High Holborn. There's a good selection of French and New World wines and excellent, predominantly English cuisine. *Closed Sat & Sun.* A.Ax.Dc.V. **B** *to 23.00.* **£**

### 🍷 Gordon's Wine Bar                                  4 F4
47 Villiers St WC2. 071-930 1408. This famous 300-year-old wine cellar has escaped demolition on more than one occasion, much to the relief of its regular punters. The ancient stone walls and ceilings often drip with water but somehow this just adds to the charm of the place. Excellent selection of wines, ports and sherries plus wholesome buffet food. *Closed Sat & Sun.* No credit cards. **B** to 21.00. **£**

### Hollands
6 Portland Rd, Notting Hill W11. 071-229 3130. Filipino wine bar well known for its well-prepared Filipino and international cuisine (don't miss their seafood hot pot and exotic fruit crumble) and extensive wine list. Their roof-top conservatory is particularly pleasant on clear summer evenings. A.V. **B D** to 23.00. **££**

### 🍷 Jimmie's Wine Bar                                  3 C5
18 Kensington Church St W8. 071-937 9988. Wooden floors, natural brick and wooden booths make for a cosy atmosphere in this wine bar, notable for its clarets and home-made food. Jimmie's also hosts live bands; their rhythm and blues night on *Thursdays* is particularly popular. *Closed Sun.* A.V. **B D** to 22.30. **£**

### 🍷 Julie's Bar
137 Portland Rd, Notting Hill W11. 071-727 7985. Trendy west London wine bar, crammed full of plush Moroccan furniture and potted palms. Choose from around 50 wines, including organic champagne. Tempting bar menu changes daily. *Open to 24.00, to 22.30 Sun.* A.V. **B** to 22.30. **££**

### Kettners Champagne Bar                             4 E2
29 Romilly St W1. 071-437 6437. Attached to the sumptuous Kettner's restaurant, this snazzy bar boasts over 60 varieties of champagnes available by the glass, bottle or even magnum for those who want to really splash out. *Open to 24.00.* A.Ax.Dc.V. **B** to 23.00. **££**

### 🍷 Morgan's                                          4 D2
4-6 Ganton St W1. 071-734 7581. Smart but friendly Soho bar covering two floors. The basement alcoves offer a more intimate alternative to the main bar above, which is full of office workers during the week. A fair selection of wines and beers and standard wine bar fare, plus Thai specialities. *Closed Sat & Sun.* A.Ax.Dc.V. **B** to 22.30. **££**

### Palookaville                                         4 F3
13a James St WC2. 071-240 5857. A basement wine bar/restaurant famous for its nightly live jazz. Hollywood stars stare out from the walls and the menu is typically French. *Open to 01.30. Closed Sun.* A.Ax.Dc.V. **B** to 00.30. **D** to 00.15. **£**

### Pitcher & Piano
Pleasant and airy wine bars, the Pitchers have well-chosen wine lists and a changing menu including their trademark: picker baskets – oriental savoury packets with various dips. A.Ax.V. **B** *(check branch for times).* **£**
8 Balham Hill, Clapham SW12. 081-673 1107.
🍷 214-216 Fulham Rd SW10. 071-352 9234.                 6 C4
🍷 871-873 Fulham Rd, Parsons Green SW6. 071-736 3910.

### 🍷 Shampers                                          4 D3
4 Kingly St W1. 071-437 1692. Despite its name, wine is Shampers' most impressive feature, with over 160 different varieties – although

the 20 different champagnes are certainly not to be sneezed at! Popular with a business clientele. Brasserie downstairs. *Closed Sat & Sun*. A.V. **B** *to 22.30*. **£**

● **Smith's**                                                                 **4 F2**
33 Shelton St WC2. 071-379 0310. Below Smith's Art Galleries, this comfortable cellar wine bar is a great place to wile away an evening chatting with friends. The staff are friendly and the menu offers light snacks, plus dishes from the excellent restaurant attached. Don't miss their fish soup. *Closed Sun*. A.Ax.Dc.V. **B D** *to 23.00*. **£-££**

● **Wine Press**                                                              **1 D5**
White House Hotel, Albany St NW1. 071-387 1200. Housed in the beamed cellar of a 1930s hotel, serving a wide range of French, German and Spanish wines. *Closed Sat & Sun*. A.Ax.Dc.V. **B** *to 20.30*. **£**

**Wolsey's**                                                                  **4 D1**
52 Wells St W1. 071-636 5121. Reasonably priced and popular bar, tastefully decorated with still-life paintings. Bar snacks downstairs, fish restaurant upstairs. *Closed Sat & Sun*. A.Ax.Dc.V. **B** *to 23.00*. **£**

# SPORT, HEALTH, FITNESS & LEISURE

There's more to nightlife in London than eating, drinking and clubbing. There are facilities for all types of sport whether you want to join in or just watch. Catch one of the big games at Wembley. Or how about a work-out in the gym, a swim or a dance class to get you into shape and make new friends? If that sounds too exhausting pamper yourself with a spa bath or sauna, or relax with a massage or yoga. Spend the evening at a bridge club or round a board game. Try one of these leisure activities for a taste of London's alternative nightlife.

## SPORT

Most sports are represented in London for the participant as well as the spectator. The following is a list of the capital's sporting venues and organisations. For indoor sports such as badminton, basketball, table tennis and volleyball see *Sports & Fitness Centres* under *Health & Fitness*.

### AMERICAN FOOTBALL

American football is now immensely popular in Britain. As well as national league division games, American league sides have exhibition games at Wembley Stadium. If you want to play or watch the great gridiron game, contact the:

**British American Football Association**                                     **3 B4**
92 Palace Gardens Terrace W8. 071-727 7760.

## BOXING

Whether you approve of it or not, there's no denying the excitement generated by a boxing match. Except during the summer, boxing events – both amateur and professional – are held regularly throughout the year. These range from regional, national or world title fights to the increasingly popular exhibition-type dinner/boxing nights. For detailed listings of both professional and amateur events, consult *Boxing News*.

**Dinner/Boxing Matches**: These take place throughout the year (*except Jul & Aug*) at hotels such as the Grosvenor House and the London Hilton and are organised by the:
**National Sporting Club**. 071-437 0144.

**Professional matches**: Venues remain the same for the major events. Other professional bouts take place at town halls and municipal swimming baths in Bermondsey, Lewisham, Shoreditch, Walworth, West Ham and Wimbledon. National fights at:
**Royal Albert Hall**                                    **3 E5**
Kensington Gore SW7. 071-589 8212. Matches *throughout the year.*
**Wembley Complex**
Wembley, Middx. 081-900 1234. Matches *throughout the year*.

**Amateur matches**: Tend to be held in clubs around London on varying dates. Closed season *May-Oct*. Amateur dinner/boxing matches are also organised at the big hotels. Information on amateur events from:
**London Amateur Boxing Association**
58 Comber Grove, Camberwell SE5. 071-252 7008.

## FOOTBALL

During the professional football season *(Aug-May)* there are regular weekday evening matches for London clubs, as well as international matches at Wembley Stadium. *Check Time Out for days and times.*

## GO-KARTING

**Playscape**
The Old Bus Garage, Triangle Place, via Nelson's Row, Clapham SW4. 081-986 7116. Zooming around the track here is an exhilarating experience. A kart gives a greater sensation of speed than even the highest performance cars and is a safe way to have a great deal of fun. There's another track at Hester Rd, Battersea SW11. Telephone as above. *Open Mon-Sun to 22.00.*

## GREYHOUND RACING

Going to the dogs can now mean a leisurely meal while watching the track through the restaurant's glass wall.
**Catford**
Catford Bridge SE6. Restaurant 081-690 2261. Compact and colourful. Small restaurant. *Open Mon, Thur & Sat at 19.00. Racing starts 19.30.*
**Walthamstow**
Chingford Rd E4. Restaurant 081-531 4255. Watch the track from the glass-fronted restaurant. *Open Tue, Thur & Sat at 18.30.*

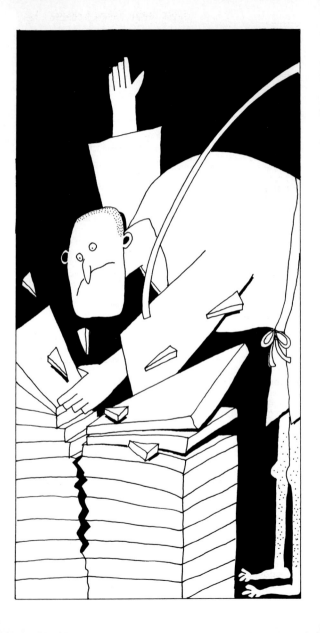

**Wembley Stadium**
Empire Way, Wembley, Middx. 081-902 8833. Large glass-fronted restaurant overlooking the track. *Open Mon, Wed & Fri at 19.30.*
**Wimbledon**
Plough Lane SW17. 081-946 5361. Popular south London track. Restaurant. *Open Tue, Thur, Fri & Sat at 19.00. First race 19.30.*

## MARTIAL ARTS

Whether it's a question of self-defence, keeping in trim or sheer trendiness, martial arts are a popular evening pastime. These are the main organisations to contact:

**Amateur Karate Association**                                    **1 G4**
80 Judd St WC1. 071-837 4406.
**British Judo Council**
1a Horn Lane, Acton W3. 081-992 9454.
**Martial Arts Commission**
15 Deptford Broadway, Deptford SE8. 081-691 3433.
**London Judo Society**                                           **7 E6**
89 Lansdowne Way SW8. 071-622 0529.

## SKATING

British successes in ice skating have increased its popularity. Ice rinks are a great place to spend an evening with music and refreshments laid on and plenty of helping hands for beginners. Nearly all rinks have changing rooms and skates for hire.

**Broadgate Ice Rink**                                            **5 F1**
Eldon St EC2. 071-588 6565. *Open Tue-Thur to 20.00, Nov-Apr.*
**Lea Valley Ice Centre**
Lea Bridge Rd, Leyton E10. 081-533 3151. *Open Tue-Sat 20.00-22.30. Ice hockey at 19.00 Sun.*
**Queens Ice Skating Club**                                       **3 C3**
17 Queensway W2. 071-229 0172. *Open Mon-Sun 19.30-22.00 (to 22.30 Sat).*
**Sobell Centre Ice Rink**
Hornsey Rd, Holloway N7. 071-609 2166. *Open Mon-Fri to 23.00, to 22.00 Sat & Sun.*
**Streatham Ice Rink**
386 Streatham High Rd, Streatham SW16. 081-769 7771. *Open Mon-Sun 19.30-22.30 (to 23.00 Sat).*

## SKIING

Artificial skiing in London may not provide you with an alpine setting, but it is great practice and can be great fun. Most ski centres run courses for beginners and have recreational open practice sessions. You can hire all the necessary equipment but remember to wear long sleeves, long trousers and mittens to protect yourself from burns and scrapes should you fall over!

**Hillingdon Ski Centre**
Park Road, Uxbridge, Middx. (0895) 255183. *Open Sun-Fri to 22.00, Oct-Mar, Tue & Thur to 22.00, Apr-Sep.*

**Mountaintop Ski Centre**
Beckton Alps, Alpine Way, East Ham E6. 071-511 0351. *Open Mon-Sun to 23.00 all year round.*

## SPEEDWAY

Very popular, noisy, dirty but exciting. The season is *Mar-Oct*.
**Wimbledon Stadium**
Plough Lane SW17. 081-946 5361. *Phone to check days and  times.*

## SQUASH

Squash is one of the most popular participant sports in the UK. Squash clubs are generally sociable places – most operate in-house leagues and many have bar facilities for much-needed refreshments after the game.
**Broadway Squash Centre**
Chalkhill Rd, Shortlands, Hammersmith W6. 081-741 4640.
**Ealing Squash Courts**
Haven Green, Ealing W5. 081-997 3449.
**London South Bank Squash & Fitness Club**          7 E5
124/130 Wandsworth Rd SW8. 071-622 6866.
**New Grampians Squash Club**
Shepherd's Bush Rd, Hammersmith W6. 071-603 4255. For a complete list of private and municipal squash clubs plus coaching schemes and tournament dates contact:
**The Squash Rackets Association**
The Salons, Warple Way, Acton W3. 081-746 1616.

## STOCK CAR RACING

**Wimbledon Stadium**
Plough Lane SW17. 081-946 5361. *Phone to check days and times.*

## SWIMMING

Magnificent Olympic-size pool at Crystal Palace National Sports Centre, Ledrington Rd SE19. 081-778 0131. *Open to public only when no training in session – phone for details.* Most public indoor pools close early on *Sat.* The following closing times refer to weekdays.
Caledonian Rd N1. 071-837 0852. *Open Mon & Tue*          **2 B2**
*to 19.30, to 20.30 Wed-Fri.* Women-only Fri evening.
Elephant & Castle SE1. 071-582 5505. *Open Mon,*          **5 D6**
*Tue & Thur to 21.30.* Women-only Mon. Adults-only Tue & Thur.
Marshall St W1. 071-798 2007. *Open to 21.00 Tue-Fri.*          **4 D2**
Porchester Rd W2. 071-792 2919. *Open to 20.00.*          **3 C2**
Seymour Place W1. 071-723 8019. *Open to 20.00.*          **1 B6**
Swiss Cottage NW3. 071-413 6490. *Open Mon*          **1 A1**
*& Tue to 19.30, to 21.00 Wed, to 21.30 Thur.*

## TENNIS

There are over 2000 public outdoor tennis courts in central London and 325 clubs to join. Many parks also have courts but competition is fierce and you must book. The best places to head for are Battersea Park SW11 (**6 G5**); Bishop's Park (Fulham SW6), floodlit courts and very good facilities; Clissold Park (Finsbury Park N4); Highbury Fields (Islington N1); King George's Park (Wandsworth SW18); Lincoln's Inn Fields WC2 (**4 G2**); Regent's Park NW1 (**1 B3**). For a complete list of clubs and public courts contact the London Development Officer, The Lawn Tennis Association Trust, The Queen's Club, Palliser Rd, West Kensington W14. 071-385 4233.

### INDOOR TENNIS CENTRES
**Carlton Tennis Club**     **3 B1**
Alfred Rd, off Harrow Rd W2. 071-286 1985. There are three indoor courts at this prestigious club with a gymnasium, sauna, jacuzzi and pro shop. Coaching programmes for all levels. *Open Mon-Sun to 23.00.* Private club, but daily membership available.
**Islington Indoor Tennis Centre**
Market Rd, Islington N7. 071-700 1370. This centre has three indoor courts, plus three floodlit courts. Private/group tuition if required. Fitness studio. *Open Mon-Sun to 22.00.* No membership requirement.

### TEN PIN BOWLING

Not as palatial or as popular as its American parent, but still fun.
**Airport Bowl**
Bath Rd, Harlington, Middx. 081-759 1396. *Open Mon-Sun to 01.00.*
**Bexleyheath Super Bowl**
Broadway, Bexleyheath, Kent. 081-303 3325. *Open Mon-Sun to 22.30.*
**Lewisham Bowling Centre**
Belmont Hill, Lewisham SE13. 081-318 9691. *Open Mon-Sun to 24.00.*
**Streatham Mega Bowl**
142 Streatham Hill, Streatham SW2. 081-678 6007. *Open Mon-Thur & Sun to 24.00, to 01.00 Fri & Sat.*
**Trocadero Lazer Bowl**     **4 E3**
Piccadilly Circus W1. 071-287 0041. *Open Mon-Sun to 01.00.*

### WATERSPORTS

London has excellent facilities for messing about on the water, from canoeing to water-skiing. There's a good network of clubs which can provide equipment and tuition for beginners. Try any of the lakes, reservoirs, ponds and canals, as well as the Thames and Docklands area.
**Cremorne Riverside Centre**     **6 D5**
Cremorne Gardens SW10. 081-568 0672. Try your hand at canoeing, sailing and yachting at this boating centre. *Open Wed & Thur 18.00-20.00, Mar-Oct.*
**Docklands Sailing Centre**
Kingbridge, Millwall Dock E14. 071-537 2626. A purpose-built centre with 35 acres (14.5ha) of water in the dock and slipway access to the river. They offer canoeing, dragon boating, sailing and windsurfing. Bar. *Open Mon-Sun till dusk, Mar-Oct. Phone for details of winter opening times.*
**Docklands Watersports Club**
King George V Dock, Woolwich Manor Way, North Woolwich E16.

071-511 5000. The only place where you can go wet-biking and jet-skiing in London. Not cheap! *Open Thur-Tue till dusk.*

**Peter Chilvers Windsurfing**
Gate 5, Royal Victoria Dock, Tidal Basin Rd, off Silverton Way, North Woolwich E16. 071-474 2500. Windsurfing takes place on the 83 acres (34.5ha) of enclosed water at the end of Victoria Dock. There's a roped-off area for beginners to practise in and a shingle beach from which to launch. Well-organised tuition for beginners and the more advanced. *Open Tue-Sun till dusk, Apr-Oct.*

**Princes Water-ski Club**
Clockhouse Lane, Bedfont, Middx. (0784) 256153. A well-run centre offering water-skiing. All equipment is provided. They have three slalom courses and two jumps. *Open Mon-Sun till dusk, May-Oct.* Also weight-training, aerobics and squash *open to 22.00.*

**Westminster Boating Base**                                    **7 D4**
Dinorvic Wharf, 135 Grosvenor Rd SW1. 071-821 7389. Just upstream from the Houses of Parliament, pontoons lead down to the Thames. They offer canoeing, power boating and sailing. Tuition available for sailing. Classes in aerobics and yoga. *Opening times vary according to the weather – phone for details. Closed Nov-Apr.*

---

### WRESTLING

Two types of wrestling exist in England – professional and amateur. The professional matches are great entertainment and take place throughout the year. Amateur wrestling is a very much more serious sport. For listings see daily and sporting press.

---

## HEALTH & FITNESS

There is a huge choice of fitness centres and health clubs in London reflecting the current vogue for keeping fit and staying healthy. The following list will help you find where to go whether you want to pump iron, learn flamenco, relax in a sauna or meditate.

## SPORTS & FITNESS CENTRES

Many local boroughs have well-equipped sports and fitness centres with wide-ranging facilities and they are generally much cheaper to join than private clubs. Some of the clubs below require a modest membership fee, others charge for each specific activity.

**Barbican Health & Fitness Centre**    **2 E6**
97 Aldersgate St EC1. 071-374 0091. Top class facilities for fitness training: exercise machines, aerobics floor, 25m pool, running track, sauna, solarium, jacuzzi, whirlpool. Restaurant and bar. **M**. *Open Mon-Fri to 22.30.*

**Britannia Leisure Centre**    **2 G2**
40 Hyde Rd N1. 071-729 4485. Large indoor centre. Squash, badminton, weight-training, table tennis, basketball, volleyball, martial arts, swimming pool with wave machine and waterfall, sauna, sunbed, jacuzzi. Tuition in most activities. *Open Mon-Fri to 22.00 (swimming pool to 20.45).*

**Brixton Recreation Centre**
Brixton Station Rd, Brixton SW2. 071-274 7774. Indoor sports centre. Squash, badminton, weight-training, swimming pool, bowls, sauna, solarium. Classes plus social and cultural activities. *Open Mon-Fri to 22.00, to 20.00 Sat & Sun.*

**Finsbury Leisure Centre**    **2 E4**
Norman St EC1. 071-253 2346. Indoor centre with facilities for football, netball, badminton, squash, weight-training, outdoor tennis, basketball, martial arts, roller skating. Also swimming pool and Turkish bath next door (071-253 4011). **M**. *Open Mon-Sun to 22.00.*

**Queen Mother Sports Centre**    **7 C2**
223 Vauxhall Bridge Rd SW1. 071-798 2125. Large indoor centre, with multi-gym, solarium and swimming pool. Facilities for badminton, weight-training, squash, table tennis, martial arts, aerobics, yoga and gymnastics. **M** only for squash. *Open Mon-Fri to 22.00 (swimming pool to 19.30 Mon-Thur, to 20.30 Fri).*

**Sobell Sports Centre**
Hornsey Rd, Holloway N7. 071-609 2166. Large indoor centre adaptable to most sports. Facilities for badminton, basketball, cricket, gymnastics, martial arts, netball, squash, table tennis, volleyball, weight-lifting and yoga. There is also an ice rink and a sauna. *Open Mon-Fri to 23.00, to 22.00 Sat & Sun (ice rink times vary).*

**YMCA**    **4 E2**
112 Great Russell St WC1. 071-637 8131. Indoor only. Badminton, basketball, gymnastics, trampolining, keep fit, aerobics, sub aqua, swimming, canoeing, table tennis, multi-gym and weight-training, volleyball and yoga. Creche. **M**. *Open Mon-Fri to 22.30, to 21.30 Sat & Sun.*

## HEALTH CLUBS, SAUNAS AND TURKISH BATHS

Most health clubs have saunas, solariums, sunbeds, gymnasiums and swimming pools and some of the larger ones have jacuzzis, dance studios, beauty salons, relaxation areas and massage facilities. See also *Sports & Fitness Centres.*

### Allington Court Gym                                      7 B1
Allington St SW1. 071-828 3647. Gymnasium, solarium, sauna, swimming pool, aerobics. *Open Mon-Fri to 21.15.* Men and women. **M**.

### Dave Prowse Fitness Centre                               5 D5
12 Marshalsea Rd SE1. 071-407 5650. Fully equipped gymnasium which specialises in weight-lifting. Also dance and jazzercise classes. Sauna, solarium and showers. *Open Mon-Fri to 21.00.*

### Earl's Court Gym                                         6 B3
254 Earl's Court Rd SW5. 071-370 1402. Weights, aerobics, solarium, sauna. *Open Mon-Fri to 22.00.*

### The Fitness Centre                                       5 D4
Crown House, 56-58 Southwark St SE1. 071-403 6078. Gymnasium, sauna, steam. Dance and aerobics classes. Beauty salon. Health bar. *Open Mon-Fri to 21.00.* **M**.

### Hogarth Club
1a Airedale Ave, Chiswick W4. 081-995 4600. One of the largest gyms in London. Swimming pool, sauna, steam baths, spa tubs. Squash courts, outdoor tennis courts. Very sociable. *Open Mon-Fri to 23.00, to 21.00 Sat & Sun.* **M**.

### Holland Park Sauna
156 Shepherd's Bush Centre, Shepherd's Bush W12. 081-743 3264. Hot pool, hydrotherapy, cold plunge, jet stream, two saunas, jacuzzi, sunbed, gymnasium, massage. *Open Mon-Sun to 23.00.* Men only.

### Holmes Place Health Club                                 6 C4
188a Fulham Rd SW10. 071-352 9452. Swimming pool, two gymnasiums, steam room, sauna, sunbeds. Exercise classes. *Open Mon-Fri to 23.00, to 21.00 Sat & Sun.* **M**.

### Metropolitan Club                                        4 D2
27-28 Kingly St W1. 071-734 5002. Gymnasium with videos to relieve the tedium of exercising. Swimming pool with whirlpool attached, steam room, sauna and sunbeds. Dance studio with full range of work-outs. *Open Mon-Fri to 22.00.* **M**.

### Porchester Leisure Centre                                3 C2
Porchester Rd W2. 071-792 2919. Public and inexpensive Turkish baths. Also two indoor pools, laundry, private baths and showers. *Open Mon-Sun to 22.00 (last ticket 20.00).* Mon, Wed & Sat men-only. Tue, Thur & Fri women-only. Sun mixed couples-only.

### Riverside Racket Centre
Dukes Meadows, Chiswick W4. 081-994 9496. Squash and tennis plus indoor pool, dance studio and gymnasium. Sauna, solarium, steam room, physiotherapist. *Open Mon-Fri to 24.00, to 23.00 Sat & Sun.* **M**.

### St James's Health and Sauna Club                         4 D4
Byron House, St James's St SW1. 071-930 5870. Gymnasium, sauna, plunge pool, solarium, massage, restaurant. *Open Mon-Fri to 22.00, to 21.00 Sat & Sun.* Men-only.

### The Sanctuary                                            4 F3
11 Floral St WC2. 071-240 9635. Exotic health club with tropical plants and birds. Sauna, jacuzzi, sunbeds, swimming pool, relaxation area. Turkish steam rooms and all the beauty treatments imaginable. *Open Wed-Fri to 22.00.*

**Swiss Cottage Unisex Sauna**
2 New College Parade, Finchley Rd, Swiss Cottage NW3. 071-586 4422. Sauna, sunbed, massage. *Open 24 hrs.*

**West Ham Baths**
Romford Rd, West Ham E15. 081-519 5731. A traditional East End Turkish bath. Fully equipped with marble slabs, plunge pools, TV lounge and rest rooms where you can recover from the heat. *Open Mon-Fri to 21.00.* Check for details of women-only and men-only opening times.

**Westside Fitness Leisure Club**     **3 B6**
201-207 Kensington High St W8. 071-937 5386. Weight-training, sauna, fitness classes, karate, self-defence. Beauty clinic. *Open Mon-Fri to 22.00, to 20.00 Sat.*

---

### DANCE CENTRES

**Dance Attic**
212-214 Putney Bridge Rd, Putney SW15. 081-785 2055. A popular dance studio which holds classes in ballet, mambo, historical dance, contemporary, flamenco, jazz, lambada and tap. *Open Mon-Fri to 22.00.* Daily membership available.

**Dancercise Studios**
The Barge, Durban Lion Wharf, Old Isleworth, Middx. 081-948 0051. There are nine Dancercise studios around London with professional dancers and fully qualified instructors. Jazz of all kinds, Broadway ballet, contemporary, tap and disco classes, as well as work-out classes. Contact above address for list of studios and opening times.

**Danceworks**     **4 B2**
16 Balderton St W1. 071-629 6183. A wide range of classes are offered here including ballet, belly dancing, gypsy flamenco, jazz, salsa and tap. Cafe. *Open Mon-Fri to 22.00.* Daily membership available.

**The Fitness Centre**     **5 D4**
Crown House, 56-58 Southwark St SE1. 071-403 6078. Professional teachers take courses in aerobics, modern jazz, New York stretch, body conditioning, keep fit and self-defence. Dance-wear shop. *Open Mon-Sun to 22.00.*

**Pineapple Dance Studio**     **4 F2**
7 Langley St WC2. 071-836 4004. Qualified teachers for every type of dance imaginable including contemporary ballet, classical ballet, tap, rock, jazz, New York jazz, bodyshaping with weights, slim shape and stretch, keep fit and body conditioning, fast aerobics. Snack bar, dance shop. No need to book. *Open Mon-Fri to 20.30.*

---

### RELAXATION & THERAPY

**Community Health Foundation**     **2 G4**
188 Old St EC1. 071-251 4076. Oriental medicine based on the theories of the movement of energy between two poles, the yin and the yang. Shiatsu massage (like acupuncture it concentrates on energy points of the body), iridology (diagnosis of the body through the eye) and reflexology (massage of the feet). Also holistic massage and yoga. Macrobiotic cookery classes with a dietary counsellor. *Open Mon-Fri 09.00-17.30* for information. Classes and treatments *evenings and weekends.*

### The Isis Centre
5 Clonmell Rd, Tottenham N17. 081-808 6401. Treatments in acupuncture, homeopathy, holistic medicine, psychotherapy, massage, aromatherapy. Individual consultations. *Open Mon-Fri by appt.*

### Iyengar Yoga Institute
223a Randolph Ave, Maida Vale W9. 071-624 3080. Holds evening and weekend classes. Also has an information centre and can put you in touch with teachers all over the country.

### London Buddhist Centre
51 Roman Rd, Bethnal Green E2. 081-981 1225. Specialises in meditation and Buddhism, also holds classes in yoga, Alexander Technique, tai-chi, massage and yoga. Phone for details.

### Neal's Yard Therapy Rooms                                    4 F2
2 Neal's Yard WC2. 071-379 7662. Individual consultations (by appointment only) for acupuncture, Alexander Technique, aromatherapy, Bach flower remedies, biodynamic therapy, herbalism, homeopathy, applied kinesiology, massage and much more.

### Sivananda Yoga Centre
51 Felsham Rd, Putney SW15. 081-780 0160. Courses in meditation, yoga, vegetarian cookery; also arranges retreats.

## LEISURE

Head to one of London's amusement arcades for one-arm bandits, space invaders, pin-ball machines and racing cars. Or for something a little quieter, perhaps a game of bridge or chess.

### AMUSEMENT ARCADES

One-arm bandits, space invaders, pin-ball machines, racing cars, computer quizzes . . .

### Family Leisure                                               4 E2
99 Charing Cross Rd WC2. 071-734 3859. All the usual machines. *Open Mon-Sun to 24.00.*

### Family Leisure                                               4 E2
38 Old Compton St W1. 071-439 2178. A large busy arcade with all the old favourites. *Open Mon-Sun to 24.00.*

*Amusement arcades*

**Las Vegas**                                                    **4 E2**
89 Wardour St WC2. 071-439 0658. Right in the middle of Soho. What better place to gamble the evening away. *Open Mon-Sun to 23.45.*

## BILLIARDS & SNOOKER

Snooker is regaining its popularity, although it has come a little late to save some of the old, smoky, atmospheric halls that used to hide among the lurid Soho clubs. American pool, however, abounds in pubs all over London. Gentlemen's clubs still retain their splendid billiards rooms but you have to be a member or a friend of a member (and definitely male) to enter these inner sanctums. Most other clubs require a (small) membership fee and proof that you are over 18. All these listed below are *open every night* unless otherwise stated.

**New World Snooker Clubs**
A chain of London snooker clubs which will remain *open up to 24 hrs* if there are people still playing. Check the phone book for your nearest club.

**Centre Point Snooker Club**                                   **4 E2**
Centre Point, New Oxford St WC1. 071-240 6886. *Open to 06.00.*

**Kilburn Snooker Club**
50 Kilburn High Rd, Kilburn NW6. 071-328 6926. *Open 24 hrs.* **M.**

**London Leisure Snooker**
Bridge Rd, Edmonton N9. 081-807 8449. *Open to 01.00.*

**Ron Gross Snooker Centre**
289 Neasden Lane, Neasden NW10. 081-450 7369. *Open to 07.30.* **M.**

**Wandsworth Billiards & Snooker Centre**
63 Wandsworth High St, Wandsworth SW18. 081-874 1252. *Open 24 hrs.* **M.**

## BRIDGE

There are clubs throughout the whole of Greater London. Some have temporary membership for visitors.

**Green Street Bridge Club**                                    **4 B3**
3 Green St W1. 071-499 7658/493 2038. Strict **M.**

**Muswell Hill Bridge Club**
86 Muswell Hill Bdwy, Muswell Hill N10. 081-883 1927. *Open to 22.30. Closed Wed.* **M.**

**New Acol Bridge Academy**
86 West End Lane, West Hampstead NW6. 071-624 7407. Club and school. *Open Mon-Sun to 23.30.*

**St John's Wood Bridge Club**
Grove Hall Court, Hall Rd, St John's Wood NW8. 071-286 7465. *Open Mon-Sun to 01.00.*

**Young Chelsea Bridge Club**                                   **6 B2**
32 Barkston Gdns SW5. 071-373 1665. Duplicate bridge. Partnership arranged. *Open Mon-Fri.* Special events *Sat & Sun.* Phone for details.

## CHESS

If you're a keen chess player contact the following for your nearest league or union club:

**British Chess Foundation**
9a Grande Parade, St Leonards-on-Sea, Sussex. (0424) 442500.

# NIGHT SIGHTS

## SIGHTSEEING AFTER DARK

Many of London's historical buildings and monuments are lit up at night and look even more impressive than in daylight. Other places are sufficiently illuminated by street and shop lighting to be worth a visit. The evening is a romantic time to breathe in the atmosphere of London – the river, the villages, the people.

**Admiralty Arch**     **4 E4**
Entrance to The Mall SW1. Massive Edwardian triple arch by Sir Aston Webb, 1911. A memorial to Queen Victoria. Stroll along The Mall with St James's Park on one side, the elegant Regency Nash terraces on the other and, at the end, Buckingham Palace.

**Bankside**     **5 D3**
Southwark SE1. Thames-side walk with the finest views of St Paul's and the City across the river.

**Bridges**
Some of London's bridges look truly magical at night, bedecked with lights, which are reflected in the Thames flowing below.

**Albert Bridge**     **6 E4**
Built 1873. A masterpiece of ornate Victorian ironwork, at night it is elegantly decorated with hundreds of white lights.

*Albert Bridge from the Embankment*

*Tower Bridge*

### Chelsea Bridge 7 B4
Rebuilt as a suspension bridge in 1934. Original bridge dates back to 1858. Also prettily lit.

### Tower Bridge 5 G4
Victorian Gothic towers with hydraulic bascule bridge. 1894. Strikingly floodlit, and a good point from which to view the Tower of London and the City on the north bank, and Hay's Galleria and London Bridge City on the south bank.

### Waterloo Bridge 5 A3
Not especially interesting in itself. Concrete. 1940-45. But stunning views up the Thames to the Houses of Parliament, downstream towards the City, and across to the Charing Cross station development.

### Westminster Bridge 4 F5
Graceful cast-iron structure. Built 1862. Excellent close-up views of Big Ben and Parliament Square.

### Buckingham Palace 4 C5
St James's Park SW1. The permanent London home of the reigning sovereign. Originally built 1705; remodelled by Nash 1825; refaced 1913 by Sir Aston Webb.

### Canary Wharf Tower
West India Docks, Isle of Dogs E14. Tallest building in the United Kingdom at 800ft (244m) high; visible from miles around.

### Chelsea Harbour 6 C6
The glass dome and Belvedere tower (with a golden ball on its roof which slides up and down with the level of the river) mark this riverside development.

### Covent Garden Piazza 4 F3
WC2. Attractive and lively cobbled piazza providing street entertainment and plenty of places to eat and drink. Occasional big screen showings of live performances from the Royal Opera House in the piazza during Summer.

### Gerrard Street 4 E3
W1. The heart of Chinatown, a pedestrian walkway packed with restaurants, oriental stores and even Chinese telephone boxes.

### Hammersmith Mall
Upper & Lower Mall, Hammersmith W6. Boathouses and pretty riverside pubs.

*Harrods*

### Harrods                                                    3 G6
Knightsbridge SW7. The world-famous store is decorated with lights
all year round and makes a spectacular London sight.

### Houses of Parliament                                       4 F5
St Margaret St SW1. Victorian Gothic building 1840-68. Illuminated at
night are St Stephen's Tower, the Clock Tower and Victoria Tower. The
terraces overlooking the Thames are lit during summer recess only.

### Hyde Park Corner                                           4 B5
SW1. The impressive Wellington Arch is surmounted by the *Quadriga* –
a chariot pulled by four magnificent horses. Also, a statue of
Wellington – the Iron Duke – astride his favourite horse, 'Copenhagen'.

*Westminster from the South Bank*    *Lloyds of London*

**Lloyds Building**                                    **5 F2**
Leadenhall St EC3. A striking blue-lit silhouette which stands out
from the more general orange glow of London's financial centre.

**London Mosque**                                      **1 A4**
Hanover Gate NW1. A graceful building on the edge of Regent's
Park, it is the religious centre for London's Muslim population.

**Mansion House**                                      **5 E3**
Walbrook EC4. Opposite the Bank of England. Official residence of
the Lord Mayor. Palladian building by George Dance built in 1739.
Completed 1752.

**Marble Arch**                                        **4 A3**
W1. Designed in 1828 by John Nash to be the gateway to the forecourt of Buckingham Palace. Moved to its present position in 1851.

**National Maritime Museum**
Romney Rd, Greenwich SE10. The Queen's House, now part of the
museum, was built by Inigo Jones in 1619 for James I's Queen, Anne
of Denmark.

**Piccadilly Circus**                                  **4 E3**
The statue of Eros is surrounded by the constant flashing neon of
the world-famous advertisements, and by some magnificent illuminated buildings; the restored Criterion Theatre, London Pavilion, the
Trocadero and Tower Records.

**Peace Pagoda**                                       **6 F4**
Battersea Park SW11. Overlooking the Thames, this monument to
peace was built by Buddhist monks and nuns in 1984. Viewed from
the north bank by night it is particularly beautiful.

**Royal Hospital Chelsea**                             **7 A3**
Royal Hospital Rd SW3. The clock tower and portico are illuminated
at night.

**Royal Hospital Greenwich**
Greenwich SE10. Now the Royal Naval College, the site of the

*Piccadilly Circus*

former royal palace of the Tudor monarchs. Fine group of classical buildings by John Webb 1664, Wren 1694 and Vanbrugh 1728. Illuminated at night when functions held.

**St James's Park**                                                     4 E5
SW1. The oldest royal park, acquired in 1532 by Henry VIII. Duck Island with its bird sanctuary, the bridge and the fountain and island near Buckingham Palace are floodlit at night.

**St Katharine's Dock**                                                 5 G4
St Katharine's Way EC3. A yacht haven tucked under the shadow of Tower Bridge. A hotel, shops, restaurants and a pub overlook the pleasure craft and Thames sailing barges moored here.

**St Paul's Cathedral**                                                 5 D2
Ludgate Hill EC4. Wren's greatest work, built 1675-1710 replacing the previous church destroyed by the Great Fire.

**St Paul's Covent Garden**                                            4 F3
Covent Garden WC2. Fine 'ecclesiastical barn' by Inigo Jones. Rebuilt after the fire of 1795.

**Shaftesbury Avenue**                                                  4 E3
The heart of London's theatreland, this bustling Victorian avenue is illuminated by colourful signs advertising lavish productions.

**Soho**                                                                4 E2
W1. London's notorious red-light area. Not quite as sinful as it once was but still lots of flashing neon and peep shows. Well worth a visit, but perhaps not alone.

**Somerset House**                                                      4 G3
Strand WC2. On the site of a 16thC palace. Dates from 1776. Used to house the Register of Births, Deaths and Marriages in England and Wales. Now holds the Registry of Divorce, Wills and Probate, the Inland Revenue and the Courtauld Institute Galleries.

**South Bank Arts Centre**                                             5 A4
A starkly modern complex built on the south bank of the Thames with a superb view of old London across the river. Started in 1951 with the Festival Hall, the complex now comprises three concert halls, the Royal National Theatre with its flashing information board, two cinemas, the Museum of the Moving Image and the Hayward Gallery surmounted by a colourful neon kinetic sculpture. From the Embankment (near Cleopatra's Needle) walk across Hungerford Footbridge to the complex.

**Tate Gallery**                                                        7 E2
Millbank SW1. An imposing classical building which should be included on a floodlit walk along the Thames.

**Telecom Tower**                                                       1 E6
A prominent feature of the London skyline visible from miles around.

**Tower of London**                                                     5 G3
Tower Hill EC3. A keep, a prison and still a fortress. Spectacular when lit at night and best viewed from the river or Tower Bridge. As a contrast, look across to the new glowing glass structure of London Bridge City and the imposing archway of Hay's Galleria.

**Trafalgar Square**                                                    4 F4
WC2. Laid out in 1829; Nelson's column dates from 1840. The column, fountains and the National Gallery overlooking the square assume a picture-postcard beauty at night.

*The National Gallery overlooking Trafalgar Square*

### Victoria Embankment 4 G3

EC4. WC2. SW1. Romantic, breathtaking – the river at night displays its full splendour. A longish riverside walk would lead past the ships permanently moored on the Thames, King's College and Somerset House with views across the water to the South Bank Arts Centre, past Cleopatra's Needle and the last leg leading to Westminster Bridge and Parliament Square.

### Westminster Abbey 4 F6

Broad Sanctuary SW1. Original church built for Edward the Confessor 1065. Rebuilding began in 1245 and additional work continued during 1376-1506 with final completion of the towers (left unfinished) in 1734.

### Westminster Cathedral 7 C1

Ashley Place SW1. Wonderfully inspired Byzantine-style church dating from 1903. The most important Roman Catholic church in England.

### Whitehall 4 F4

SW1. Wide thoroughfare used for ceremonial and State processions. The Cenotaph and several notable statues divide the lanes of traffic. Lined with Government offices, some of which are illuminated at night.

**Banqueting House** 1619-25. 17thC Palladian style by Inigo Jones.

**Dover House** 1755-58 by Paine. One of the most elegant buildings in Whitehall.

**Gwydyr House** 1772. Handsome building, originally a private dwelling, now home to the Welsh Office.

**Horse Guards** Stone-faced building from 1750-60.

**Old Admiralty Building** 1722-26. Fine Robert Adam columnar screen 1760.

**Old Scotland yard** An asymmetrical building dating from 1888.

**Old War Office** Victorian baroque 1898-1907.

## TRIPS AND TOURS

A sociable way to spend the evening is to take a sightseeing tour around the city at night; you can view London from the top of a double-decker bus or if you want to be a little more adventurous splash out on a river cruise. Whether you prefer to travel by road or river, the trips and tours listed below provide an enjoyable way to discover London by night.

---

### GUIDED TOURS

**London Transport**
071-222 1234. A guided bus tour of London and the river by night
*Mon-Sun, Easter to December*. Pick-up points and times are:

| | |
|---|---:|
| Victoria Bus Station SW1 at *19.00 & 21.00*. | **7 C2** |
| Marble Arch (Park Lane bus stop) W1 at *19.05 & 21.05*. | **4 A3** |
| Elizabeth Hotel, Lancaster Gate W2 at *19.10 & 21.10*. | **3 E3** |
| Paddington Station (Praed St) W2 at *19.15 & 21.15*. | **3 E2** |
| Oxford Circus (Regent St) W1 at *19.20 & 21.20*. | **4 D2** |
| Piccadilly Circus (Haymarket) W1 at *19.25 & 21.25*. | **4 E3** |

Book at **London Transport Travel Information Centres** at Victoria
Station and Oxford Circus Underground Station (see *Useful
Information*). Booking advisable.

---

### RIVER CRUISES

**River Boat Information Service** 071-730 4812. *24 hr* telephone
information service (*recorded after 18.00 and at weekends*) for
everything to do with the river, including details of cruises.

**Catamaran Cruises**                                    **5 A4**
Charing Cross Pier WC2. 071-839 3572. Disco cruises from Westminster
Pier to Tower Bridge and Greenwich. Booking essential. Phone for details.

## NOTORIOUS NIGHTS

For a completely different night out, discover the more sinister aspects
of London. If you would rather be chilled than thrilled, you can visit the
haunts of the infamous – robbers, traitors, highwaymen, ghosts and
killers – as well as sites where less than savoury happenings took place.

---

### EARLY EVENING

To whet the appetite, walk round the city's streets and alleyways,
stopping at places of gruesome historical interest. Here are a few
places with a notorious past:

**Amen Court**                                           **5 C2**
Off Warwick Lane EC4. Once the graveyard of prisoners executed at
Newgate. Also haunted by the ghost of a female baby strangler.

**Birdcage Walk**                                        **4 D5**
St James's Park SW1. Said to be haunted by the decapitated wife of
a sergeant in the Coldstream guards. The lady was stabbed to death
because of suspected infidelity. Her body was found in the lake in
1816 and her head discovered elsewhere.

**Gloucester Road**                                      **6 C1**
South Kensington SW7. In a basement flat, John Haigh drank the
blood of his victims before disposing of their remains in an acid bath.
He was hanged in 1949.

**Lincoln's Inn Fields**                                 **4 G2**
Off High Holborn WC2. Anthony Babington, a prominent 16thC
Catholic, was hanged and quartered here for conspiring to kill Queen
Elizabeth I, supposedly by black magic. Some say his ghost still remains.

**Tavistock Square**                                      **1 F5**
Off Woburn Place WC1. In the late 17thC, two brothers duelled over a woman whom they both wanted to marry. The issue was resolved when the unhappy pair killed each other while the lady looked on.

**Whitechapel**
E1. The East End area chiefly associated with London's most infamous murderer, 'Jack the Ripper'. The savagery of the killings caused a national outcry in the late 19thC and today the ghost of the fourth victim, Catherine Eddowes, continues to haunt Mitre Square, still known as Ripper's Corner.

---

## MIDDLE EVENING

By this time you should be ready for some liquid refreshment to steady the nerves.

**Blind Beggar**
337 Whitechapel Rd, Whitechapel E1. 071-247 6195. Famous East End pub where gangster Ronnie Kray shot George Cornell in 1966.

**The Flask**
West Hill, Highgate N6. 081-340 3969. Dick Turpin is said to have once hidden in the cellars here.

**Jack Straw's Castle**
North End Way, Hampstead NW3. 071-435 8885. Jack Straw was one of the leaders of the peasants' uprising in 1381 and was hanged from a gibbet outside the tavern. There is also a restaurant with wonderful views over Hampstead Heath and London.

**London Dungeon**                                        **5 E4**
34 Tooley St SE1. 071-403 0606. Spooky scenes of torture, disease, punishment and evil practices in dark, dank vaults. Encaged live rats add to the atmosphere. The Dungeon can be hired for large private parties. Food, drink and disco. *Bookable every night 19.30-24.00.*

**Magdala Tavern**
2a South Hill Park, Hampstead NW3. 071-435 2503. Ruth Ellis, the last woman to be hanged in Britain, shot her lover in the doorway in 1955.

**Red Lion**                                              **4 D4**
23 Crown Passage SW1. 071-930 8067. It is said that a nearby secret passage from St James's Palace was used by Henry VIII to escape for an evening's revelry. Anne Boleyn discovered him returning one night and the ensuing argument is supposed to have set her on the road to the executioner. This secret passage is also the reputed site of the last duel fought in England.

**Spaniards Inn**
Spaniards Rd, Hampstead NW3. 081-455 3276. Renowned 16thC inn where highwayman Dick Turpin stayed when he was riding and robbing with Tom King. His pistols are on display along with a musket ball he fired while waylaying the Royal Mail coach.

**Town of Ramsgate**
62 Wapping High St, Wapping E1. 071-488 2685. Name derives from the Ramsgate fishermen who landed their catch at Wapping Old Stairs. Execution Dock stretches from the pub to St John's Wharf and is where pirates and smugglers were hanged. In the cellars of the pub are dungeons where convicts were chained awaiting deportation to Australia.

### LATE EVENING

Perhaps not the best time to stake out sites with a murky past. But to complete an eerie evening, a visit to the floodlit Tower of London – scene of countless crimes, royal treachery, torture and death, and to this day supposedly haunted by some of its vanished inmates – will evoke a grim fascination. Or, by consulting our *Late and all night cinemas* listing, you could pass the darkest hours by watching a horror movie. Alternatively, you may find the magical, mysterious or bizarre at the following:

**The Hippodrome**                                          **4 E3**
Hippodrome Corner WC2. 071-437 4311. Lavish nightclub. Black and silver decor complemented by an amazing laser system. *Open Mon-Sat to 03.30.*

**Xenon**                                                   **4 D3**
196 Piccadilly W1. 071-734 9344. Light and water shows, mime, magic, jugglers and dance troupe entertainment. Lots to enthrall and entrance you here. *Open Mon-Thur to 03.00, to 06.00 Fri & Sat.*

## NIGHT WALKS

Bearing in mind that there's safety in numbers, there are organisations that take parties on walks, some with scary themes.

**City Walks**
071-700 6931. Re-trace the footsteps of 'Jack the Ripper', be spooked by 'Ghosts, Rogues and Old Newgate' or sup a few quiet pints on the 'Fleet Street Pub Walk'. Start from various underground stations. Tours *most evenings*. Phone for details.

**Londoners Pub Walk**
081-883 2656. Historical pub walks. Discover 'The Lambeth Walk' and 'The Shakespeare Walk', or follow 'In the steps of Dr Johnson'. From Temple underground station. *Fri 19.30.*

**London Walks**
071-624 3978. Visit several pubs of historical interest. Themes include 'Jack the Ripper Haunts', 'Dickens' London' and the 'Ghost Walk'. Start from various underground stations. Tours at *19.30 most evenings*. Phone for details.

## NIGHT EVENTS

**SPRING AND SUMMER**
**Funfairs**
Traditionally go on late into the night when their lights and music are at their headiest. Bank holiday fairs held at Blackheath, Hampstead Heath and Wormwood Scrubs (*Easter, spring Bank hol, summer Bank hol*). Other fairs are held at Clapham Common (*mid-Apr*), Crystal Palace (*early May & Aug*), Tooting Common (*early May*), and Victoria Park (*early May*). There are often several smaller ones to be found around the outskirts of London during the summer.

**The Proms**                                                    **3 E5**
The Henry Wood Promenade Concerts, Royal Albert Hall, Kensington Gore SW7. 071-589 8212. A series of classical music concerts which the whole of London wants to attend on the first night – and the whole world on the last! On these two nights singing, banner waving and foot stomping abound. Tickets for last night by ballot only. *Late Jul to Sat nearest 15 Sep.*

## AUTUMN AND WINTER
### Guy Fawkes Night
Anniversary of the discovery of the 1605 Gunpowder Plot. 'Guys' are still burned on bonfires accompanied by firework displays to commemorate the ringleader Guy Fawkes. Many public as well as private displays. *5 Nov.*
### Christmas Decorations
Regent St and Oxford St W1. Could be lasers, sequins or traditional scenes in lights stretching along these two main shopping streets. Also see the decorations on the outside of the big stores like Harrods, Knightsbridge; Liberty, Regent Street; Selfridges, Oxford Street. Large illuminated Christmas tree in Trafalgar Square, traditionally a gift from Norway. Erected around *10 Dec-12th night.*
### Carol Singing                                                **4 E4**
Trafalgar Sq WC2. Around the Christmas tree. Taped music, but also some live bands like the Salvation Army. *Every evening from about 14 Dec.*
### New Year's Eve
Trafalgar Sq WC2. Singing of 'Auld Lang Syne' by massed crowds. Much revelry and dancing around the fountains. St Paul's Cathedral EC4 (outside). Watchnight Service of traditionally-dressed Scots. *22.00-24.00.*
### Chinese New Year                                             **4 E3**
Around Gerrard St, Soho W1. Huge and colourful Chinese dragons, firecrackers and festivities through the streets in the centre of London's Chinese community. *Jan or Feb.*

# LATE AND ALL-NIGHT LONDON

## LATE-NIGHT SHOPS & SERVICES

Late-night shops are generally gathered together in particular areas of London. The best areas to try are Queensway and Westbourne Grove W2, Earl's Court Road W8, Fulham Road SW7, Leicester Square WC2, Piccadilly Circus W1 and Covent Garden WC2. Some areas have shops which are open late on a particular day of the week (eg Oxford Street W1 on *Thur*, Kensington High St W8 on *Wed*). Most of the shops in the areas mentioned above close around *20.00.* Some of the following close a little later.

---

### SHOPPING CENTRES

**Brent Cross Shopping Centre**
Brent Cross NW4. 081-202 8095. Major shopping complex housing 82 stores and shops, many of them well-known West End chains. Huge car parking facility. *Open Mon-Fri to 20.00.*

**Covent Garden Piazza** 4 F3
Covent Garden WC2. 071-836 9137. Original central market building skilfully renovated and converted into a stylish shopping centre. Colonnades and roofed halls containing galleries, restaurants, general, speciality and food shops. Market stands selling bric-a-brac, antiques, arts and crafts. *Open Mon-Sat to 20.00.*

**London Pavilion/Trocadero** 4 E3
7 Coventry St W1. A large indoor shopping complex. *Open Mon-Sun to 22.00.*

**Victoria Place Shopping Centre** 7 B2
115 Buckingham Palace Rd SW1. 071-931 8811. Large shopping centre alongside Victoria Station. *Open Mon-Sun to 20.00.*

### BOOKS

**Dillons The Bookstore** 4 F4
Grand Building, Trafalgar Sq WC2. 071-839 4411. Extensive range of specialist academic books, plus a wide selection of general titles. *Open Mon-Sun to 22.00.*

**Pan Bookshop** 6 B5
158 Fulham Rd SW10. 071-373 4997. A wide range of paperback books. *Open Mon-Fri to 21.30, to 22.00 Sat, to 21.30 Sun.*

**Waterstone's** 3 C5
193 Kensington High St W8. 071-937 8432. A vast range of paperbacks and hardbacks. *Open Mon-Fri to 21.00.*

### CHEMISTS

**Bliss** 4 A3
5 Marble Arch W1. 071-723 6116. Invaluable centrally-located chemist. *Open Mon-Sun to 24.00.* Also at 50-56 Willesden Lane, Kilburn NW6. 071-624 8000. *Open Mon-Sun to 24.00.*

**Boots** 3 C3
75 Queensway W2. 071-229 9266. *Open Mon-Sat to 22.00.*

### FILM PROCESSING

**Joe's Basement** 4 E2
113 Wardour St W1. 071-434 9313. A professional photographic laboratory *open 24 hrs.* Colour transparency film back in 2 hrs, black and white in 6 hrs; colour print film in 24 hrs.

### FLOWERS

**Angela Saunders** 4 B4
London Hilton Hotel, Park Lane W1. 071-493 8000. A flower shop where you can buy a bouquet or a single orchid. *Open Mon-Sat to 22.00.*

## FOOD

**Cullens**      **6 C4**
182 Fulham Rd SW10. 071-352 7056. Pricey supermarket with a decent deli and a good range of fresh vegetables. *Open Mon-Sun to 23.00.*

**Europa Foods**
A chain of late-night supermarkets selling fresh fruit and vegetables, groceries, wines and spirits. *Open Mon-Sun to 23.00.*

| | |
|---|---|
| 12 Craven Rd W2. 071-723 6965. | **3 E2** |
| 174-176 Fulham Rd SW10. 071-370 2394. | **6 D3** |
| 167-169 Shaftesbury Ave WC2. 071-240 0082. | **6 B5** |
| 178 Wardour St W1. 071-734 4845. | **4 D2** |
| cnr Whitehall/Northumberland Ave SW1. 071-930 5996. | **4 F4** |

(this branch is *open 24 hrs*).

**Goldrings of Holborn**      **2 D6**
2a Farringdon Rd EC1. 071-253 5488. Bakery and sandwich shop, ideal if you want a very early breakfast. *Open Mon-Fri 04.00-17.00.*

**Harts**      **6 D2**
50-52 Old Brompton Rd SW7. 071-581 1526. Well-stocked grocery with a good range of specially imported foreign products. *Open 24hrs.*

**Midnight Shop**      **3 F6**
223 Brompton Rd SW3. 071-589 7788. All kinds of cooked (hot and cold), preserved and fresh food; small household items. *Open Mon-Sun to 24.00.*

**Perry's Bakery**      **6 A2**
151 Earl's Court Rd SW5. 071-370 4825. Well-known and loved locally, Perry's is an appealing bakery and pâtisserie with a small seating area. *Open Mon-Sun to 24.00.*

**Portlands of Charing Cross**      **4 E3**
75-77 Charing Cross Rd WC2. 071-734 5715. Sells food, wine and spirits. Also has a delicatessen offering all-night sandwiches. *Open 24 hrs.*

**7 Eleven**
Serves snacks and hot drinks as well as frozen foods and alcohol. *Open 24 hrs.*

| | |
|---|---|
| 384 Edgware Rd, Paddington W2. 071-723 2123. | |
| 119 Gloucester Rd SW7. 071-373 1440. | **6 C1** |
| 134 King St, Hammersmith W6. 081-846 9154. | |

*Portlands of Charing Cross*

*Tower Records, Piccadilly Circus*

---
### GIFTS
---

**Covent Garden General Store**                                       **4 F2**
105-111 Long Acre WC2. 071-240 0331. A big bright shop full of
bamboo, basketwork, china, leather and lots of interesting ideas for
presents. *Open Mon-Wed to 23.00, to 24.00 Thur-Sat, to 22.00 Sun.*
**Gift Centre**                                                       **4 F1**
140 Southampton Row WC1. 071-837 4084. A wide selection of
gift ideas for all pockets and tastes. *Open Sun-Thur to 22.00.*

---
### MUSIC & VIDEO
---

**Tower Records**                                                     **4 D3**
1 Piccadilly W1. 071-439 2500. An immense record store on four
floors, offering the full spectrum of sounds. Exceptionally large selection
of compact discs, videos and US imports too. *Open Mon-Sat to 24.00.*
**Virgin Megastore**                                                  **4 E2**
14-30 Oxford St W1. 071-631 1234. Massive store with a huge
selection of CDs and videos. *Open Mon-Sat to 20.00.*

## LATE-NIGHT EATING & DRINKING
### RESTAURANTS AND BARS

If you're feeling hungry after a night at the theatre or you're in need
of refreshment after an energetic night's dancing, the following
restaurants and bars are all *open until at least 02.00.* Some will still
be serving at daybreak! In most late bars you should expect to pay
higher prices than during normal hours and some will charge for
entry after a certain time.

**Bar Italia**                                                        **4 E2**
22 Frith St W1. 071-437 4520. The most authentic Italian café in
Soho, full of Italians and Soho trendies. The decor and the atmosphere

*Bar Italia*

have changed little since the 1950s and it's always lively and vibrant. Serves snacks – parma ham sandwiches, pizza, panettone. Unlicensed, but this does not seem to detract from its popularity! *Open very late (to at least 04.00), 24 hrs Sat & Sun.* No credit cards. **£**

**Bar Madrid**　　　　　　　　　　　　　　　　**4 D2**

4 Winsley St W1. 071-436 4649. Large, lively and fairly authentic tapas bar. Paellas, Tex-Mex dishes and 20 varieties of tacos. **Corky's Wine Bar** above serves alcohol until *03.00. Open to 03.00. Closed Sun.* Late charge. A.Ax.V. **£**

**Bar Sol Ona**　　　　　　　　　　　　　　　　**4 E2**

17 Old Compton St W1. 071-287 9932. Basement bar with lots of nooks and crannies in which to linger over your drinks, nibble tapas, and attempt to make yourself heard over the flamenco music. Paellas, pollo con ajillo, or calamares. Attracts a friendly, party-minded clientele. *Open to 02.00. Closed Sun.* A.Ax.V. **£**

**Blushes Café**　　　　　　　　　　　　　　　　**6 F3**

52 King's Rd SW3. 071-589 6640. A French-style café/brasserie with a menu offering French, Italian and Mexican dishes as well as traditional English breakfast. There's live music *at weekends. Open to 24.00, to 04.00 Thur-Sat.* A.Ax.Dc.V. **£**

**Calamitees**

104 Heath St, Hampstead NW3. 071-435 2396. American-style restaurant serving hamburgers and pizzas to the bright young things of Hampstead who have managed to stay bright until the small hours. *Open to 02.30, to 04.30 Fri & Sat.* A.V. **££**

**Cuba Libre**　　　　　　　　　　　　　　　　**2 D2**

72 Upper St N1. 071-354 9998. This bar/restaurant, decorated in Cuban style, has live music *most evenings.* Start with aperitivos 'Cuba Libre', a mixture including dips and fried plantain. Follow with pollo con aguacate (steamed chicken fillets with a Parmesan cream sauce, avocados and coriander). And finish off with bitter-sweet crème caramel with dried fruit and a sweet sauce. *Open to 02.00 Tue-Sat, to 24.00 Sun & Mon.* A.Ax.V. **££**

**Dover Street Restaurant & Wine Bar**　　　　　**4 D4**

8-9 Dover St W1. 071-491 7509. Traditional French cuisine, live music and partying into the small hours. The wine list is mainly French, with some Italian additions. *Open to 03.00 (food served until 01.30). Closed Sun.* A.Ax.Dc.V. **££**

**Harry's Bar** 4 D3

19 Kingly St W1. 071-434 0309. Do people go to Harry's because they have stayed out late, or do they stay out late because they are going to Harry's? After sampling the late-night cooked breakfast you'll realise this is a serious question. A nightclubbers' institution. *Open to 06.30*. No credit cards. **£**

**Hodja Nasreddin**

53 Newington Green Rd, Islington N1. 071-226 7757. A family-run Turkish restaurant with a homely atmosphere. The boreks (cheese samosas) are excellent and the feta cheese salad is massive. *Open to 02.00*. A.Ax.Dc.V. **£**

*Harry's – a nightclubbers' institution*

**Istanbul Iskembecisi**

4 Stoke Newington Rd, Stoke Newington N16. 071-254 7291. This tastefully decorated Turkish restaurant has a mellow and relaxed atmosphere with its starry ceiling and muted lighting. The menu, however, is for the strong-stomached – boiled brain, roast head of sheep and lamb's tongue. You can of course choose a more conventional shish kebab or moussaka. *Open to 05.00.* No credit cards. **£**

**Lido**                                                                                         **4 E3**

41 Gerrard St W1. 071-437 4437. Lots of people tell stories about how they found a wonderful Chinese restaurant that was still open at dawn. The chances are the restaurant in question is Lido, a busy and relatively friendly establishment on three floors. *Open to 04.00.* A.Ax.Dc.V. **££**

**Los Locos**

Good, cheap Tex-Mex food in a large authentic Mexican restaurant which attracts lively, good-time gringos from all over town. At Russell Street branch, disco from *23.30 every night.* Both branches *open to 03.00. Closed Sun.* A.Ax.Dc.V. **££**

24-26 Russell St WC2. 071-379 0220.                                              **4 G2**

14 Soho St W1. 071-287 0005.                                                       **4 E2**

**Marquee Café**                                                                         **4 E2**

20 Greek St W1. 071-287 3346. This café is owned by the Marquee Club which is situated directly behind. Decorated with musical instruments and graffiti, the café is popular with clubbers who can enjoy a meal after an energetic night's dancing, or for those who like to listen to music while eating; live bands play *every night.* Burgers, barbecued dishes, or bangers and mash. *Open to 03.00.* A.Ax.Dc.V. **£-££**

**Mayflower**                                                                            **4 E3**

68-70 Shaftesbury Ave W1. 071-734 9207. Good Cantonese restaurant with some Pekingese dishes and some exciting specials. Stewed salt fish with chicken and beancurd or stuffed fish stomach with prawn meat and crab meat sauce. Very popular with tourists and after-theatre-goers. *Open to 04.00.* A.Ax.Dc.V. **££**

**New Diamond**                                                                       **4 E3**

23 Lisle St WC2. 071-437 2517. Elegant and courteous atmosphere. A pale green and grey establishment with widely spaced tables. Seafood a speciality. *Open to 02.30.* A.Dc.V. **££**

**Paradise Cottage**

477 Bethnal Green Rd, Bethnal Green E2. 071-729 6119. A restaurant where East End and Middle Eastern culture meet. Prints of old Istanbul adorn the walls. Try crisp borek (flat baked pastry filled with soft cheese and parsley). *Open to 03.30.* A.V. **££**

**Ranoush Juice Bar**                                                               **3 G2**

43 Edgware Rd W2. 071-723 5929. Very relaxing place to come and enjoy a drink or a snack while listening to Arab music or watching the goldfish in the pool. Large selection of freshly squeezed juices including carrot, melon and tamarind, and snacks including felafel, bean dishes and sharwama sandwiches. *Open to 02.00.* No credit cards. **£**

**Up All Night**                                                                        **6 C4**

325 Fulham Rd SW10. 071-352 1996. Steaks, burgers and spaghetti served by smiling staff who seem much happier and livelier than they should be, given the time. *Open to 06.00. Closed Sun.* A.Ax.V. **£**

**Yung's**                                                4 E3
23 Wardour St W1. 071-437 4986. This small, comfortable Chinese restaurant on three floors is a must for the fish dishes. Shark's fin and chicken soup, and fried noodles and prawns are recommended. All-round good value and gracious service. *(Reserve) open to 04.30.* A.Ax.Dc.V. **£-££**

**Yus**
7 Hammersmith Rd, West Kensington W14. 071-603 3980/9148. More international than authentic, this Persian restaurant offers courteous service and excellent cuisine. For starters, try the mustkhair (thick strained yoghurt with cucumber), followed by kebabi-barg (strips of lamb with rice and grilled tomatoes). Finish with tea and zulbia. *(Reserve) open to 24.00, to 06.00 Fri & Sat.* A.Ax.Dc.V. **££**

---

## TAKEAWAY FOOD

**American Fried Chicken**                                 4 E3
19 Wardour St W1. No phone. Just what the name says. *Open to 04.00. Closed Sun.* No credit cards. **£**

**Beigel Bake**                                           5 G1
159 Brick Lane E1. 071-729 0616. Traditional Jewish bakery serving up fresh bagels all night. Try the salmon and cream cheese. *Open to 06.00.* No credit cards. **£**

**Burger King**                                           4 E3
17-21 Leicester Sq WC2. 071-930 0158. Member of the well-known chain, serving burgers which can taste remarkably good when you're hungry at that time of night. *Open to 04.30, to 02.00 Sun.* No credit cards. **£**

**Fish & Chips**                                          4 E3
Cranbourn St WC2. No phone. Dishes up surprisingly presentable versions of the great British dish. *Open 24 hrs.* No credit cards. **£**

**Mr Pumpernink**                                         4 E3
cnr Piccadilly Circus/Shaftesbury Ave W1. No phone. Pizzas by the slice, hot dogs, sandwiches, soft drinks and doughnuts. *Open Mon-Sun to 24.00.* No credit cards. **£**

**Ridley Hot Bagel Bakery**
13-15 Ridley Rd, Dalston E8. 071-241 1047. For a generation now, this bagel bakery has satisfied the hungry appetites of many a party-goer. Serving delicious fresh, hot bagels with fillings such as egg mayonnaise, chopped liver, chopped herring, cream cheese and smoked salmon. *Open 24 hrs.* No credit cards. **£**

**Shawarma Orient**                                       4 E3
13 Shaftesbury Ave W1. 071-437 1256. A kebab house with a take-away service. *Open Mon-Thur to 02.30, to 04.00 Fri & Sat.* No credit cards. **£**

---

# LATE AND ALL-NIGHT CINEMAS

A lot of cinemas have late shows on *Fri & Sat*. Chain cinemas in the West End usually show films from the week's programme. In the repertory cinemas you'll find older or cult films, and all-nighters.

**Camden Parkway**                                        1 D2
Parkway NW1. 071-267 7034. Late show *Fri & Sat (phone for details).*

**Gate Cinema**     **3 B4**
87 Notting Hill Gate W11. 071-727 4043. Frequent good value double bills. *Fri & Sat 23.15.*

**Greenwich Cinema**
108 Greenwich High Rd, Greenwich SE10. 081-853 0053. Shows recent oldies for those who missed them the first time round. *Fri & Sat (phone for details).*

**Lumière**     **4 F3**
42 St Martin's Lane WC2. 071-836 0691. Late show *Fri & Sat 23.15.*

**MGM Baker Street**     **1 B6**
Station Approach, Marylebone Rd NW1. 071-935 9772. Late show *Fri & Sat (phone for details).*

**MGM Haymarket**     **4 E3**
63-65 Haymarket SW1. 071-839 1527. Late show *Fri & Sat 23.00.*

**MGM Oxford Street**     **4 E2**
18 Oxford St W1. 071-636 0310. Late show *Fri & Sat 23.10.*

**MGM Piccadilly**     **4 E3**
215-217 Piccadilly W1. 071-437 3561. Late show *Fri & Sat 23.00.*

**MGM Trocadero**     **4 E3**
Trocadero, Piccadilly Circus W1. 071-434 0031. Late show *Fri & Sat 23.45.*

**Odeon Kensington High Street**     **3 B6**
Kensington High St W8. (0426) 914666. Late show *Fri & Sat (phone for details).*

**Odeon Leicester Square**     **4 E3**
Leicester Sq WC2. (0426) 915683. Late show *Fri & Sat (phone for details).*

**Odeon Marble Arch**     **3 G2**
10 Edgware Rd W2. (0426) 914501. Late show *Fri & Sat (phone for details).*

**Rio Cinema Dalston**
107 Kingsland High St E8. 071-254 6677. General release. *Sat at 23.15.*

**Ritzy Cinema Club**
Brixton Rd, Brixton SW2. 071-737 2121. Double and triple bills, plus frequent theme all-nighters. *Sat at 23.15.*

**Scala**     **1 G4**
275-277 Pentonville Rd N1. 071-278 8052. All-night cult and off-beat films. *Sat (phone for details).*

**Screen on Baker Street**     **1 B5**
96 Baker St W1. 071-935 2772. Late-night showings of different films. *Sat at 23.15.*

**Screen on the Green**     **2 D2**
83 Upper St N1. 071-226 3520. Late-night showings of different films. *Fri & Sat at 23.00.*

**Screen on the Hill**
203 Haverstock Hill, Belsize Park NW3. 071-435 3366. Late-night showings. *Sat (phone for details).*

## ALL-NIGHT RADIO

For those who like to listen into the small hours or for insomniacs, there is a choice of radio stations. BBC Radio 1 and 2 are on air *24 hours a day.* Radio 1 (98.8 FM) offers bright and breezy music; if it's easy listening you're after tune in to Radio 2 (89.1 FM). BBC World Service (198 kHz LW and 648 kHz MW) continues all through the night with news, drama, talks and features. Capital Radio offers *24 hr* pop music, news and features on Capital Gold (1548 kHz MW) and Capital FM (95.8 FM). LBC also has a *24 hr* programme with news and information on LBC Newstalk (97.3 FM) and conversation and phone-ins on London Talkback Radio (1152 kHz MW). Kiss 100 FM has *24 hrs* of dance and national news (100 FM), Melody Radio (104.9 FM) gives you *24 hrs* of easy listening and news, and Jazz FM (102.2 FM) will keep you company through the night with smooth jazz, blues and soul.

## ALL-NIGHT TV

If you're a late-night viewer, ITV run through the night with a mixture of films, news, sport and features until TV-am comes on screen at breakfast-time.

---

# WITH THE DAWN

Having made it through the night and assuming you are in condition to cope with the new day, London still has plenty to offer. The presses have been rolling since the night before, and early editions of the daily papers are available from soon after midnight. As the city reawakens, the first signs of life appear around early morning markets. A number of pubs affiliated with the markets have special licence extensions that enable them to serve drinks at this hour. You will have to persuade the landlord that you are associated with the market in a bonafide capacity to enjoy the privilege. Basic coffee and sandwich stalls can also be found close to the markets. But if you are looking for a more substantial breakfast, there are two possibilities. Either go directly to a bakery to buy hot, fresh bread or pastries, or else wait around *till 07.30* for cafés and restaurants serving breakfast to open. The tradition of the English breakfast still survives in a few of the established hotels. Be warned though, this tradition is not cheap. If a night of revelry has not sapped all your stamina, a bit of physical exercise such as a dip in one of the open-air pools should finish you off.

## FIRST WITH THE NEWS

### Breakfast TV
For those who feel bright-eyed and bushy-tailed in the morning, BBC programmes run from *06.30-09.05 Mon-Fri*, ITV from *06.00-09.00 Mon-Fri* and Channel 4 from *07.00-09.00 Mon-Fri*.
### Newswires
Up-to-the-minute news information print-outs, a condensation of

the Press Association's source teleprinters. Machines usually operate *07.30-24.00* but longer during elections. Teleprinters can be found at some of the larger hotels.

**Early papers**
Early editions of the national dailies appear on Fleet Street newsstands *soon after midnight*. Or else try W.H. Smith at station bookstalls *from 07.00*. Independent street vendors tend to *open earlier*.

# MARKETS

The variety of goods sold in London's street markets is staggering, and all – so the stall owners would have you believe – at bargain prices. The best advice is to get there as early as possible; the only rule for bargain hunters is first come first served.

**Brick Lane**                                                5 G1
Brick Lane E1. Where you'll find anything and everything that people have thrown out. Browse through piles of (mostly) old junk. *Open from 05.30 Sun*.

**Cutler Street Silver Market**                               5 F2
Off Houndsditch E1. Predominantly a dealers' market specialising in jewellery, particularly silver. Some coins and medals. *Open from 06.00 Sun*.

**Farringdon Road Book Market**                              2 C6
Farringdon Road EC1. Several stalls selling old, rare and second-hand books, manuscripts and newspapers. Weather permitting. *Open from 06.00 Mon-Fri*.

**New Caledonian**                                            5 F6
Tower Bridge Rd SE1. Predominantly a dealers' market. Wide range of antiques, including furniture, ceramics and silver. *Open from 05.00 (officially 07.00) Fri*.

**Petticoat Lane**                                            5 F1
Middlesex St E1. Huge, bustling market radiating into many streets. Nearly everything imaginable on sale, lots of tat. *Open from 07.00 Sun*.

**Portobello Road**                                           3 A2
Notting Hill Gate W11. Half the market is dedicated to antiques and the other half, at the flyover end, to a glorious mixture of junk and bizarre clothes. Not many bargains to be had any more. In the middle is the local food market. *Open from 07.00 Mon-Sat. Closed Thur*. Antiques *Sat only*.

## WHOLESALE MARKETS

Officially these markets sell in bulk only, but interesting to look around anyway.

**Billingsgate**
West India Docks E14. This 13½-acre site for the famous fish market follows the design and layout of the original. The traders hope to carry on the traditions and language of Billingsgate as it was in the City. Porters wear leather helmets, enabling them to carry fish on their heads. *Open from 06.00 Mon-Sat*.

**New Covent Garden**                                         7 D4
Nine Elms Lane SW8. Some of its traditional charm and vitality was lost

in the move from Covent Garden. As London's foremost fruit, vegetable and flower market it is still worth a visit. *Open from 04.00 Mon-Sat.*

**Smithfield**                                                           **2 D6**
Charterhouse St EC1. One of the world's largest meat markets, covering 10 acres. Architecturally very interesting. *Open from 06.00 Mon-Fri.*

**Spitalfields**                                                         **5 G1**
Commercial St E1. Five acres of covered fruit and vegetable market. Extensive underground chambers: one of the main centres for ripening bananas. *Open from 05.00 Mon-Sat.*

# BREAKFAST

'Hot bread' and pastries can be obtained (unofficially) as early as *06.00* from bread shops with bakeries on the premises. If you can wait till *08.00* various Continental-style patisseries and cafés will have opened serving fresh croissants and coffee. The more adventurous can try the stalls around the various antique and wholesale markets. The very hungry in search of sausage-eggs-bacon with all the trimmings should try the cafés around the markets and main-line stations, or else splash out at one of the more traditional hotels.

## BAKERIES

Remember that it pays to be charming if trying to secure your bread before official opening time. Most bakeries are closed *Sun*.

**Grodzinski**
223 Golders Green Rd NW11. 081-458 3654. *Open from 06.30 Mon-Fri & Sun.*
53 Goodge St W1. 071-636 0561. *Open from 07.00 Mon-Fri.*      **4 E1**
22 Leather Lane EC1. 071-405 9492. *Open from 07.00 Mon-Fri.*   **2 C6**

**Holborn Bakery**                                                       **2 B5**
50 Lamb's Conduit St WC1. 071-405 4542. *Open from 08.00 Mon-Fri, 08.30 Sat.*

**John Forest**                                                          **6 D4**
401 King's Rd SW10. 071-352 5848. *Open from 04.00 Mon-Sat.*

**Justin de Blank**                                                      **6 E2**
46 Walton St SW3. 071-589 4734. *Open from 07.30 Mon-Sat.*

## PATISSERIES, BRASSERIES AND CAFES

From the list below choose a continental breakfast, a light cooked breakfast or something a little more adventurous. *All are open before 09.00.*

**La Brasserie**                                                         **6 E2**
272 Brompton Rd SW3. 071-584 1668. A French-style café and brasserie for continental breakfast. *Open from 08.00 Mon-Sat, 10.00 Sun.*

**Brasserie St Martin**                                                  **1 F6**
Marlborough Crest Hotel, 10 Bloomsbury St WC1. 071-636 5601. Large, pompous breakfasts for the business crowd. Continental buffet, traditional English, seasonal specialities. *Open from 07.00 Mon-Sat, 07.30 Sun.*

**Chandos Sandwich Bar**                                                 **4 F3**
60 Chandos Place WC2. 071-836 0060. Fresh sandwiches, light snacks or a full breakfast. *Open from 06.30 Mon-Sat.*

**Charlotte Restaurant**
221 West End Lane, West Hampstead NW6. 071-794 6476. Relaxing, charming room in a quiet guest house. Very reasonable. Traditional English or continental breakfast. *Open from 07.30 Mon-Sat.*

**Farmer Brown** 4 F3
4 New Row WC2. 071-240 0230. Looks like an Italian delicatessen. Marvellous selection of sandwich fillings. Full breakfast. *Open from 07.30 Mon-Fri, 08.00 Sat.*

**Fleur de Lys** 6 C1
13a Gloucester Rd SW7. 071-589 4045. Delicious pâtisserie with everything baked on the premises. *Open from 08.00 Mon-Sat.*

**Harrods** 3 G6
Knightsbridge SW1. 071-730 1234. Full waitress service in the West Side Express offering a mixed English and American menu. *Open from 07.45 Mon-Sat.* You can also help yourself to an impressive choice of English and continental breakfasts in the Georgian restaurant. *Open from 09.00 Mon-Sat.*

**La Pâtisserie** 4 D3
10 Conduit St W1. 071-499 8110. *Open from 07.00 Mon-Fri, 08.00 Sat.*

**Maison Bouquillon** 3 C3
41 Moscow Rd W2. 071-229 2107. Very French pâtisserie. Marvellous coffee and croissants. *Open from 08.30 Mon-Sun.*

**Maison Pêchon Pâtisserie Française** 3 C2
127 Queensway W2. 071-229 0746. Strangely, this very French pâtisserie serves typically English bacon and egg breakfasts! *Open from 07.00 Mon-Sat, 08.30 Sun.*

**Pâtisserie Valerie** 4 E2
44 Old Compton St W1. 071-437 3466. In the heart of Soho. Fresh croissants, hot coffee or chocolate. *Open from 08.00 Mon-Sat, 10.00 Sun.*

**Sartori Coffee Shop** 3 F1
84 Edgware Rd W2. 071-262 5218. *Open from 07.15 Mon-Fri, 07.30 Sat.*

---

### HOTELS

The following hotels are a short selection of those which will serve breakfast to non-residents *from around 07.00-07.30 (08.00 Sun).* You can normally choose from a wide range of traditional breakfast foods including eggs, bacon, kippers and kidneys.

**Athenaeum Hotel** 4 C4
116 Piccadilly W1. 071-499 3464.

**Brown's Hotel** 4 C3
Dover St W1. 071-493 6020.

**Churchill Hotel** 4 B2
Portman Sq W1. 071-486 5800.

**Gloucester Hotel** 6 C2
Harrington Gdns SW7. 071-373 6030.

**Great Eastern Hotel** 5 F1
Liverpool St EC2. 071-283 4363.

**Grosvenor House Hotel** 4 B3
Park Lane W1. 071-499 6363.

**Holiday Inn** 4 B2
134 George St W1. 071-723 1277.

| | |
|---|---|
| **Hotel Russell** | **2 A6** |
| Russell Sq WC1. 071-837 6470. | |
| **Hyde Park Hotel** | **4 B5** |
| Knightsbridge SW1. 071-235 2000. | |
| **Inn on the Park** | **4 B4** |
| Hamilton Place W1. 071-499 0888. | |
| **London Marriott Hotel** | **4 B3** |
| Grosvenor Sq W1. 071-493 1232. | |
| **May Fair Hotel** | **4 C4** |
| Berkeley St W1. 071-629 7777. | |
| **Royal Garden Hotel** | **3 A6** |
| Kensington High St W8. 071-937 8000. | |

## LAST THING YOU'D EXPECT

### SWIMMING IN THE PARKS

For a quick early morning dip try the following open-air ponds or baths. The ponds are chlorine-free, so it is advisable not to touch the rather slimy bottom, and to beware of fishing enthusiasts. Most of the following (except for the Serpentine) are outside the central London area.

**Eltham Park South Baths**
Eltham SE9. 081-850 4756. *Open from 07.15 Mon-Fri, 08.00 Sat, 09.00 Sun; summer only.*

**Highgate Ponds**
Highgate N6. 081-340 4044. *Open from 06.30 summer, 07.00 winter. Men only.*

**Kenwood Pond**
Highgate N6. 081-348 1033. *Open from 07.00 summer and winter. Women only.*

**Parliament Hill Lido**
Kentish Town NW5. 071-485 3873. *Open from 07.00 summer only.*

**Serpentine**                                                                  **3 F4**
Hyde Park W1. 071-724 3104. *Open from 09.30 summer only.*

# EMERGENCY INFORMATION AND SERVICES

### ACCIDENT

When in an accident with another vehicle you must stop and exchange names, addresses and insurance details with the other driver. Remember to take the licence plate number. There is no need to call the police to the scene unless a person is seriously injured, in which case **dial 999** immediately. In the case of a person being injured but able to walk away or where the other driver fails to stop, then this must be reported to the nearest police station within *24 hours*.

## CAR BREAKDOWN

**AA (Automobile Association)**
Freephone breakdown service 0800 887766. *24 hrs Mon-Sun*. You can call the AA out if your car breaks down, but you will have to join on the spot if you are not already a member. A.V.

**National Breakdown**
Freephone breakdown service 0800 400600. *24 hrs Mon-Sun*. Non-members will pay more for rescue/recovery than members. A.V.

**Olympic Breakdown Service**
071-286 8282. *24 hrs Mon-Sun*. An AA and RAC-approved recovery service covering the whole of London. A.Ax.V.

**RAC (Royal Automobile Club)**
Freephone breakdown service 0800 828282. *24 hrs Mon-Sun*. You will need to be a member of the RAC, or join when they arrive. A.Ax.V.

## CHEMISTS (LATE-NIGHT)

The local police station keeps a list of chemists and doctors available at all hours.

**Bliss Chemist**                                              **4 A3**
5 Marble Arch W1. 071-723 6116. *Open to 24.00 every day of the year*. Also at 50-56 Willesden Lane, Kilburn NW6. 071-624 8000. *Open Mon-Sun to 24.00*.

**Boots**                                                      **4 E3**
Piccadilly Circus W1. 071-734 6126. *Open Mon-Sat to 20.00*. Also at 75 Queensway W2 (**3 C3**). 071-229 9266. *Open Mon-Sat to 22.00*.

**Warman Freed**
45 Golders Green Rd, Golders Green NW11. 081-455 4351. *Open to 24.00 every day of the year*.

## HOSPITALS

In an emergency dial 999 and ask for an ambulance, or make your own way to one of the casualty departments listed below where you can be treated for injuries and sudden illness if you are unable to get to a doctor.

**Charing Cross Hospital**
Fulham Palace Rd, Hammersmith W6. 081-846 1234.

**Queen Mary's Hospital**
Roehampton Lane, Roehampton SW15. 081-789 6611.

**Royal Free Hospital**
Pond St, Hampstead NW3. 071-794 0500.

**Royal London Hospital (Whitechapel)**
Whitechapel Rd, Whitechapel E1. 071-377 7000.

**St Bartholomew's Hospital**                                  **5 C1**
West Smithfield EC1. 071-601 8888.

**St Thomas's Hospital**                                       **4 G6**
Lambeth Palace Rd SE1. 071-928 9292.

**University College Hospital**                                **1 E5**
Gower St WC1. 071-387 9300.

**Westminster Hospital**                                       **7 E2**
Dean Ryle St, Horseferry Rd SW1. 081-746 8000.

## LOCKED OUT

The police keep a list of local locksmiths or look in the *Yellow Pages* for a list of locksmiths with a *24-hr service*.

## LOST CAR KEYS

If you know the number of your car key (keep a note of it somewhere in your wallet) the AA or RAC can probably help members (see phone number under *Getting Around*) if a nearby garage or the police can't.

## LOST PROPERTY

Inform the police if you lose anything (for insurance purposes) and they will be able to help. Only dial **999** (emergency number) if violence has been involved.

**Airports**
Lost property is held by each individual airline. For property lost in the main airport buildings phone the British Airport Authority's Lost Property Office, Heathrow Airport, Middx. 081-759 4321.

**British Rail (trains)**
If you lose something on a train, contact the station where the train you were on terminates. They will be able to inform you whether your belongings have been recovered, and if so, where they have been taken.

**London Regional Transport (tubes and buses)**　　　　　**1 B5**
Lost Property Office, 200 Baker St W1 (next to Baker Street Station). For enquiries about lost property please call in person (or send another person with written authority) or apply by letter. No telephone enquiries. *Open Mon-Fri 09.30-14.00. Closed Bank hols.*

**Passports**
Report the loss to the police and to your embassy/high commission.

## PETROL

See *All-Night Garages* in *Getting Around* chapter for a list of *24-hr* petrol stations.

## POST

Most post offices close at *17.30 Mon-Fri & 12.00 Sat*. However, there is one late-opening office in London:

**Post Office**　　　　　**4 F3**
24-28 William IV St, Trafalgar Sq WC2. 071-930 9580. *Open Mon-Sat 08.00-20.00*

## RAPE

**London Rape Crisis Centre**
071-837 1600. A free and confidential service run by women for women who have been raped or sexually assaulted and need support, information or any other help.

**Survivors**
071-833 3737. National organisation for men who have been raped or sexually assaulted. *Open Tue & Thur 19.00-22.00.*

| ROBBED |
|---|

If a theft occurs from your hotel room contact the assistant manager immediately, who will take appropriate steps on your behalf. The quicker you make your report the faster the hotel staff can go into action. If you are robbed in the street, immediately report it to the nearest police station.

If you have lost an **Access** or **Visa** card issued by a bank in the UK, contact the emergency number of the issuing bank:

**Barclays**
(0604) 230230. *24 hrs.*

**Lloyds**
(0702) 362988. *24 hrs.*

**Midland**
081-450 3122. *24 hrs.*

**National Westminster**
(0532) 778899. *24 hrs.*

**Royal Bank of Scotland**
(0702) 362988. *24 hrs.*

**TSB**
(0273) 204471. *24 hrs.*

If you have lost a **MasterCard** or **Visa** card issued abroad, contact the following:

**MasterCard**
(0702) 362988. *24 hrs.*

**Visa**
(0604) 230230. *24 hrs.*

Contact the emergency numbers listed below if you have lost the following cards:

**American Express**
(0273) 696933. *24 hrs.*

**Diners Club**
(0252) 516261. *24 hrs.*

**Eurocheque card**
(0532) 778899. *24 hrs.*

**Bank cheque cards**
Telephone your own bank as soon as possible. Most foreign banks have a branch in London where you can report the loss.

**Building Society cards**
The following have a *24-hr* emergency number for lost or stolen cheque cards:
**Abbey National** (Head Office – will put you through to the relevant department) – 071-486 5555.
**Halifax** – (0422) 330200.      **Nationwide** – (0793) 510067.

| WHEELCLAMPED |
|---|

If you get wheelclamped, take the label attached to your vehicle, plus the fixed penalty notice, to one of the police car pounds listed below. You will have to pay a fine before the clamp is removed (A.Ax.Dc.V.). It can be some time before someone arrives to remove it, but you must return to and stay with your car. In an emergency telephone 071-252 2222. It is possible that if you were causing an obstruction your car will have been towed away to one of the following pounds. Fines for recovery of your vehicle are very high.

**Camden Town Car Pound**     **1 D2**
Oval Rd NW1. *Open Mon-Sat 08.00-24.00.*

**Hyde Park Car Pound**     **4 A3**
NCP Park Lane Car Park, Marble Arch W1. *Open 24 hrs.*

**Mount Pleasant Car Pound** 2 B5
cnr Calthorpe St & Farringdon Rd EC1. *Open 08.00-24.00.*
**Warwick Road Car Pound**
245 Warwick Rd, West Kensington W14. *Open Mon-Sat 08.00-24.00.*

## WOMEN'S AID

071-251 6537. An emergency service *open 24 hrs* that will refer you
to the nearest refuge and provide counselling, support and advice.

# INDEX

# NICHOLSON

# MAPS

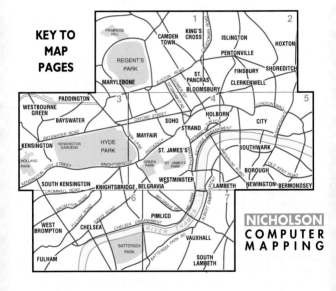

**KEY TO MAP PAGES**

NICHOLSON
COMPUTER
MAPPING

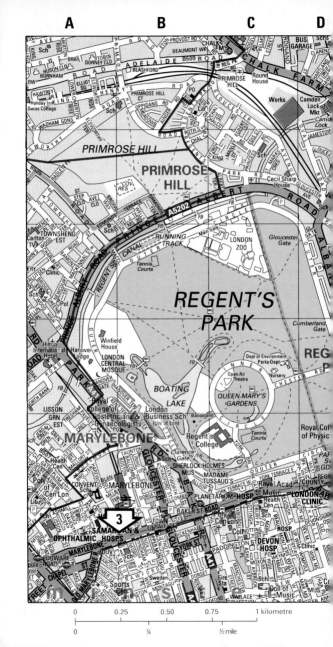

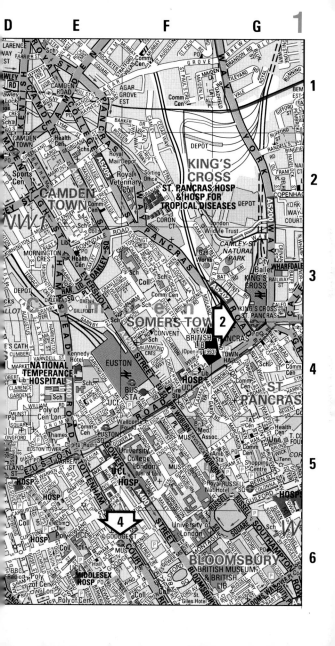

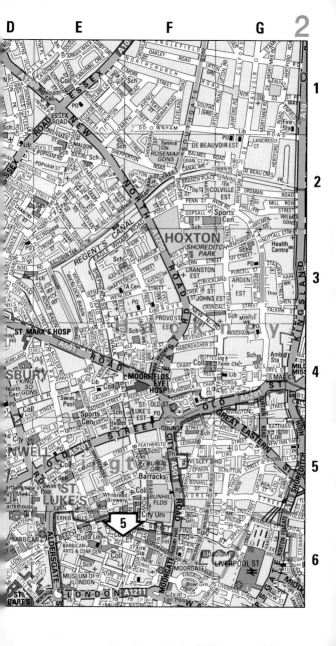

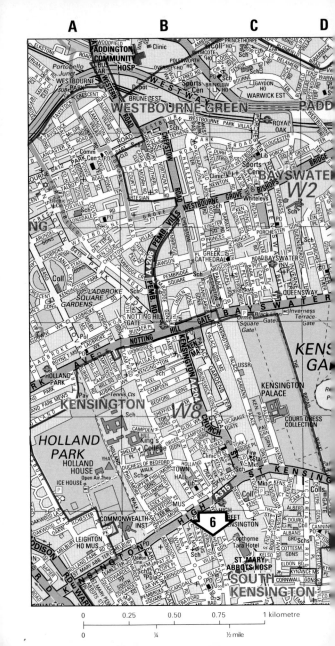

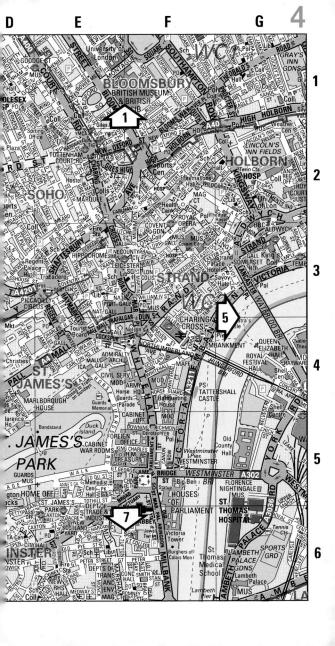

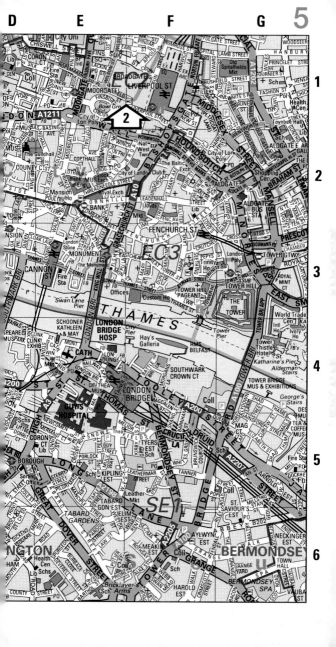

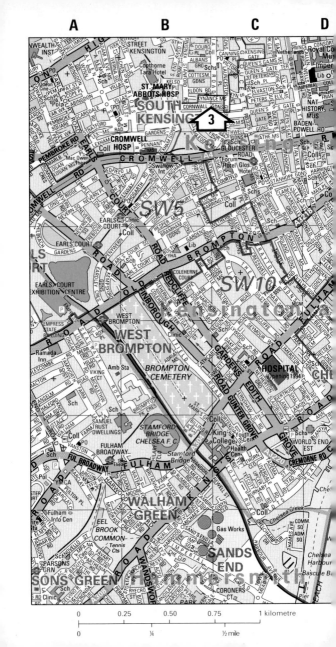

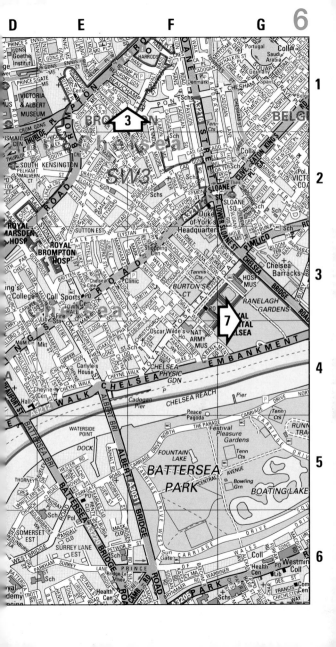

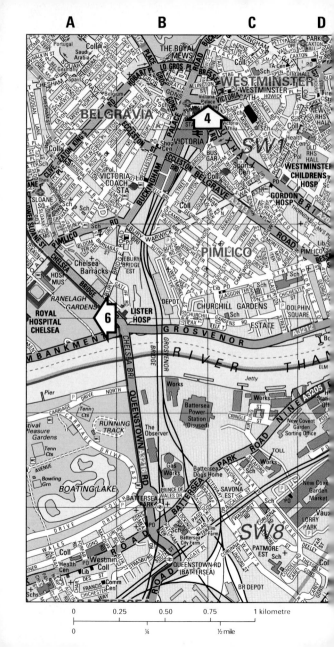

# WEST END THEATRES & CINEMAS

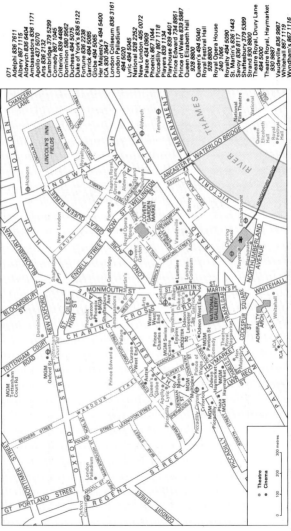

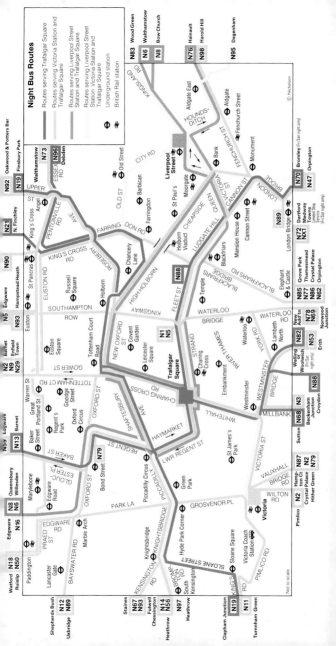

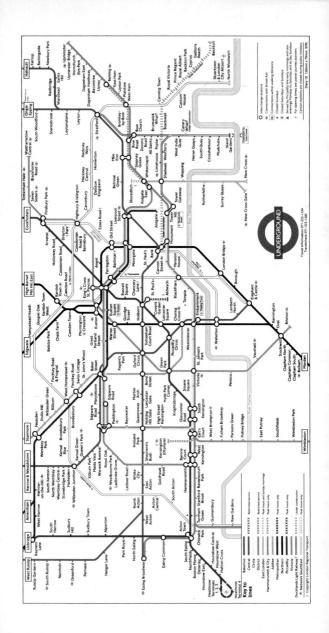